BEYOND SCIENCE FICTION!

Jim Wilhelmsen

iUniverse, Inc.
New York Bloomington

Beyond Science Fiction!

iUniverse books may be ordered through booksellers or by contacting:

iUniverse
1663 Liberty Drive
Bloomington, IN 47403
www.iuniverse.com
1-800-Authors (1-800-288-4677)

ISBN: 978-1-4401-0471-8 (pbk)
ISBN: 978-1-4401-0472-5 (ebk)

Printed in the United States of America

iUniverse rev. date: 12/05/08 (Current Date)

Additional copies can be purchased on line at
echoesofenoch.com

Personal correspondence, help and questions
should be e-mailed to the author at:
Awitness41@aol.com

Beyond Science Fiction!

A Comprehensive Biblical Study of UFOs and Aliens and Their Involvement in Human Affairs.
By **Jim Wilhelmsen**

With a special thanks to the editing assistance of:
Dale Waltman
Tanya Pace
Susie Waggoner
Mark Thompson of Blue Dragon Graphics for the Cover and Graphics
Without their help this book would not have made sense.

Special thanks to:

Dr. Mike Heiser for his technical assistance in some of the ancient language word usage.

To my children **Jason , Rebecca and David** for their inspiration and moral support through the many hours and years of research.

To my late Mother and Father **Irene and Bill** for their loving support in the beginning.

To my many **friends and web visitors** for your encouragement and friendship, whose input for the last seven years has greatly helped me in presenting this information in an organized manner.

To my patient wife **Debra** who unselfishly worked and filled in many gaps to allow me to work, study and complete this book.

To my Lord and Savior **Jesus Christ**, without your guidance none of this would have ever been.

Forward

Supernatural Beginnings:

For me this is a difficult situation to explain. Nevertheless I must in all honesty, explain how much of the content or at least the perspective for the content of this book was inspired to me. While God has blessed me with a clear enough mind to comprehend and have a desire to research, I cannot claim the content of this book to be contrived by my own intellect or imagination. It started with a very vivid dream..

January 1996, I abruptly woke up at 4:00 am. (I would realize that this was going to be a pattern to hear from the Lord) I quickly wrote down the dream before I forgot it.. It was one of those intense dreams where you still feel the emotions, sights, and even smells, as if you were really there. I have had intense dreams before, but they were about normal personal things that I knew the Lord was speaking to me about. This however was a little bit out of the ordinary.

The dream:

I was in some kind of underground complex. My entrance was behind some wall of electrical equipment. I could hear echoed voices speaking in this well lit cavern-like place, coming somewhere in front of the equipment, I headed toward the voices to see what was going on. I could smell an intense smell of ozone, as if there was a lot of electrical activity going on. When I turned the corner behind the wall, there it stood.

The center of attention within this area was an object that looked like a UFO. But something was very wrong. It kept switching it's form as if it was a hologram, like somebody changing a TV channel back and forth. The first image I saw looked like something alive. It was sort of pink with blue pulsating veins running through it. The overall shape was like a manta ray or the SR71 spy plane. When it changed it became a metallic nut and bolt type flying saucer like something right out of the 50's Sci-fi movies. When this image was metallic, I saw an opening and went inside. Everything was a fuzzy white and you could see no walls or floors. Close in front of me I could sense a wall. On the wall I saw writing that looked like Hebrew. As I stood there watching, I heard a woman's voice saying, "For over 50 years this mystery has gone unsolved. Technicians and the best minds in the country have tried to figure out the writing on the wall and the mystery of the craft. But no one seems to know for sure." Without even thinking I blurted out, The writing on the wall it is Hebrew! The only answer is going to come from the Bible! You have to know what the Bible says. All the answers for everything we will ever be faced with are in it!" Then I woke up and wrote it down. Phew! Was that a weird one!

Daniel and other prophets experienced very similar events.

"Then was the secret revealed unto Daniel in a night vision. Then Daniel blessed the God of heaven".
Dan 2:19(KJV)

Inspired of God?

To be "inspired of God" does not mean that this is an infallible oracle from God. It means that as a human filter, I have been prompted to witness a general concept and ideas to convey to you. But it is still filtered from an imperfect human source.

This kind of experience demands discernment by the Word of God creating a balance to the experience. Thus began my search and research of the scriptures for answers. This process has continued right up to the present day. I have had other dreams and visions since that first one. They have served as clues and pointers to help in approaching the Scriptures. Some of these were upsetting to my own personal preconceived ideas which were taught to me in college. However in spite of that, part of my Christian education stresses that anything we encounter whether natural or supernatural must be referenced with scripture and compatible to the written Word of God. With all diligence, obedience and faithfulness I have done my best to find the answers to this mystery and in this way be an obedient servant of the Lord. As a witness then I neither impose nor demand or defend this work but merely offer this witness to what I have experienced. With an open mind just file this in the wait and see category for future reference.

Patiently read this rather long forward and you will see a typical historical response to visionary things that are ahead of their time.

Will History repeat itself?

Let me say that I'm the first to admit that many of the topics introduced here will seem to be somewhat "on the lunatic fringe" from the mainstream. I'm far from the first person to impress upon others what might be around the corner. However, allow me to share with you one such story from my studies of military history.

Billy Mitchell was a decorated flying ace of the First World War. After the war, Billy dutifully stayed with the US Army Air Corp, rising to the rank of General. From this hard-earned position of influence, he tried to impress upon the US War Department the integral role that "air power" (an almost unheard of term at the time) would play in the future of warfare.

His unrelenting passion to make certain that America was strong and prepared for any wars yet to come, made him "a royal pain" to his peers. His eventual reward was to be court-marshaled with the loss of his rank, his command, and ultimately retiring in disgrace.

So what exactly was the crime that ruined his life? Quite simply, he was a visionary. Keenly aware of what was, he rightly discerned that which was inevitable. At a time when the naval battleship was the ultimate weapon of war, nobody imagined that a more effective assault weapon would be possible - much less needed - or especially, defended against. Nonetheless, Billy plainly saw what was on the horizon, and struggled for years to impress the War Department to rethink their soon-to-be outdated ways.

Finally, after years of harassment, the military powers-that-were offered him a chance to test his theories of air power. But contrary to his proposed strategies, they instead tightly defined the parameters he was to work within. You see, Billy was considered a "loose cannon," and he was finally being set up to fail. So in his very public display before U.S. and international military leaders, he was told to make a high level bombing run upon a specified target - an old captured German battleship, The Ostfriesland., Several times the high altitude bombing runs failed to sink or even hit the ship. Relieved, and confident in Billy's failure, the leaders felt secure that they had made their point.

In that moment, Billy Mitchell had an agonizing decision to make. Should he simply call it a day, and fly back to the base with his tail between his legs? Or would he dare break an order to challenge his complacent leadership's "dogma," and sacrifice his personal security for what he knew to be true — and for the sake of the nation he had sworn to protect?

On another pass Mitchell signaled the rest of his crew. They knew what to do. Peeling off in a straight dive at the target they unloaded their bombs, making direct hits, and sinking the ship in minutes. History records that the American leaders openly wept.

Later, from his obscure station near the U.S.- Mexican border, the demoted Captain Billy Mitchell wrote the War Department one final letter. After a trip to Japan, he felt that our next war would be started by Japan with carrier based airplanes against one of our island outposts - most likely Hawaii's Pearl Harbor, with a second attack at Wake Island. The most incredible thing was he wrote this letter in 1924!

The official response questioned his mental competence which led to Billy's decision to resign from military service. Twelve years later, in 1936, Billy Mitchell died as an outcast. Then on December 7, 1941 - like a prophecy fulfilled - Billy's worst nightmare became a reality.

In hindsight, a WWII bomber plane was named after Mitchell, and he was posthumously awarded a special Congressional medal in 1946. Mitchell was finally recognized for the hero he always was. Regretfully he never lived to see the fruit of his labors, or the day when others finally acknowledged the truth of his vision, and acted accordingly.

Before Mitchell, the biblical prophets were likewise visionaries with an unpopular message. They met similar or worse fates, from a people who did not want the truth, if it meant sacrificing their dogmas. They too, would not live to see their dreams and visions fulfilled, but nonetheless they willingly faced scorn, ridicule, and the censure of authorities to impart their message, rather than relent. They too were heroes.

One person came and claimed to be "The Way, The Truth, and The Life." He too was met with unbelief by a people who would not accept challenges to their comfortable dogmas. He also had a choice to make the night before he met his destiny. He was quoted as saying, "Nevertheless not my will, but your will be done." The next day Jesus willingly gave his life on a Roman cross for a world that didn't want the truth. He was the greatest of heroes, and the inspiration for this book.

What about you? Are you willing to consider a message that has the potential to disrupt your comfortable, secure belief system? One that just might be true, but certainly unpopular? Can you set aside preconceived ideas or prejudices just long enough to even imagine a different perspective? Or like the military leaders presiding over Mitchell, will you impose limits upon your reality to prevent the message from even being possible?

Bible Scholar and Professor Michael S. Heiser makes this intellect-provoking statement, with his book *The Facade* (Superior Books, 2001):

"Most people don't really want the truth. They're just looking for answers that confirm their prejudices."

So what about you? To be forthright, here's what you are in for if you continue reading this book : a history of man made UFO's, a hollow earth, parallel dimensions, time travel, cloning, Nazis and the New Age movement, secret societies and a global conspiracy that includes all of the above. Even more amazing is a 21st century insight of a sound biblical model which make this all possible... predictable and inevitable! I certainly do not expect anyone to quickly or blindly accept any of this, without sufficient documentation, as well as textual analysis consistent with orthodox biblical interpretation. It took me many years to digest and sort out some of these revelations. But I now stand ready to present them against the winds of false doctrine and attacks on God's Word that are prevalent today."

There will be slight problems for two distinct sets of people reading through this book. For people outside the Christian faith or nervous about Bible quotes, there is a lot of scripture given, with an emphasis on the mechanics of the original languages. This is necessary to show what the scriptures are truly saying, beyond what is generally taught in Sunday schools. This being a book from a Biblical perspective, rather than offer my own human ideas, I often simply quote the scriptures, and allow them to speak for themselves. The fact that you are reading this shows that you are not too nervous about these things. That is a good thing. However, this is not a typical "religious" book. It is a book based upon serious research from an ordained minister trained in the specifics of Biblical interpretation, but one who is also personally involved with UFO research as a religious researcher and member of Mutual UFO Network (MUFON).

For the person professing a faith in the Bible, and perhaps trained to some degree in the Scriptures, you may be surprised to learn here that many things are not just "an illusion" or trick of the devil. There are real, tangible entities which many people today call "aliens." There are also real nut and bolt objects called "Flying Saucers." The controversy to be discussed here is, Who they really are and where do they actually come from.

For the record, I do hold to the truths all Bible believing Christians hold dearly to. The loving unchanging nature and character of God and His simple plan of salvation in Jesus Christ are my anchors, and the material presented here will not conflict with these beliefs, but rather enforce them (albeit without "majoring" on them for the bulk of this presentation). Certain interpretations of other passages will be called into question at times though, so a re-examination of the Scriptures from the original languages will prove necessary, even for the Christian reader. Many prophetic scriptures have been made into inflexible doctrines that while familiar to many, are in reality mere speculation without true scriptural support. This means you must be flexible enough to set aside your preconceived ideas if indeed proven false by this work, and be willing to view some in another way. If some non-essential (to salvation) doctrines are indeed idols, or sacred cows, to you, then perhaps you'll be uncomfortable at times while reading this, but no challenges to popular ideas will be made without sufficient scriptural basis, and no violence will be rendered to the historical Christian faith. I of course remain ever open to correction, so long as the whole counsel of scripture is the corrective rod, rather than man-made traditions and dogmas which cannot be supported by honest Bible scholarship.

For all readers, you picked up this book because this topic, from this perspective, captures your interest. If nothing else, I promise to take you on a journey that is intriguing, fascinating, and truly BEYOND SCIENCE FICTION!

My desire for you is to remain open minded enough to read through and become exposed to another way of looking at some very real things. I am not asking you to believe everything that is written here. At best, just file away the content in the "wait and see" category of your mind. If I am right, someday you might have a scriptural foundation for many unexplained events that are soon to happen.

Sincerely In His Service, Jim Wilhelmsen

Table of Contents

Beyond Science Fiction!

This book contains a lot information describing a story that includes many interlinking aspects. The only way to provide the reader with a logical flow was to break the story into two parts.

The first section we will discuss Flying Saucers as defined by the Bible. We will discover just what the clouds of heaven really are, how they function and where they travel. We will understand a prophesied plan to imitate and replace the clouds of heaven with a lying sign and wonder. We will discover the development of a technology obtained through the occult which produced a man made Flying Saucer. We will discover who, where and why this technology is and continues to be used. We will see how the Flying Saucer helps to usher in what some perceive as a "New Age of Promise" while others perceive this as the "End of Time". By the end of this section you will know why there is a cover up. We will learn the part Globalists and Secret Societies play in this plot against humanity and God. We will learn the Antichrist's role and connection to Globalism, the New Age movement and the use of "Aliens" which concludes in a Global Conspiracy of the big lie.

In the second section we will discuss Aliens from a Biblical perspective. We will learn what they are, who is who in the different types and what they are doing. We will understand just what abductions and cattle mutilations are all about. We will discover what their agenda is and how this dovetails into the Flying Saucer deception. We will come to understand an alliance of both human agents and non-human entities. We will see a two part invasion of planet Earth. One invasion is clandestine spanning time and space, the other is the final battle of Earth know as Armageddon.

In the Bibliography section, full documentation of sources right down to page numbers are provided. I will also include a discussion about any theological controversy or disputes along with additional footnoted information and documentation. A reference section with some key scriptures which explain how I broke them down from the original languages is included on my web page for further research.

Without leaving the reader in despair you learn the hope, promises and assurance that a loving God is still in control and has a plan for you.

Section One: Flying Saucers

Introduction

The Common Christian Attitude: So Who Cares?

To the Christian this has never been much of a concern or a matter to ponder or debate. Once touched by God's love, most believers are content to accept the idea of a fluffy chunk of water vapor as being the clouds of heaven. Daily living and Biblical principles needed to develop a transforming personal relationship with Christ, become the main concern. For oneself, this should be the foremost concern. But what about the ability to give an answer for the hope that is within to others? When asked, "What are the clouds of Heaven?" the official Christians response to most are; " fluffy chunks of water vapor", or "I dunno, I never really thought about it." A person of faith can accept this concept, no matter how illogical it may seem. However, to someone standing outside of faith to a personal God, this can sound pretty simplistic and lame.

Spaceships of the Gods?

An idea to be reckoned with is that these clouds of heaven are spacecraft from other worlds. As strange as this might sound to many Christians, it is well presented by the UFO community and becoming widely accepted. It is explained that ancient people, being ignorant of mechanical technology had misidentified the vehicles and occupants as angels and gods. Books written with this idea, two by "Christian" ministers, are very convincing. Without any other information, it would seem the only logical conclusion for an open-minded person of today. The danger of this conclusion is that there is no personal God, only aliens in spacecraft. The lack of an intelligent response from the church only adds to the credibility of this idea. Within this void, can the Bible provide us with a better answer? Or are we left with a fluffy chunk of water vapor to defend the faith?

Rules of Engagement (Bible interpretation)

The problems with Biblical presentations of this subject are improper use of scripture to prove a point. There is much more to understanding the Bible than just surface reading and pulling things out that you want or like. We are separated by several thousand years from an ancient culture that used now dead or evolved languages which are foreign to us. Because of this it is necessary to get into a deeper study to find truth.

Minister or lay person, certain rules apply when determining what is being said in the Bible. Any serious student when approaching the Bible (from an Evangelical/Fundamental background) learns several things about interpretation. It is not from one's own personal skill, intellect, or perception to interpret the Bible. God in His mercy has not left that kind of confusion on our heads. We are told that the Bible will always interpret itself by itself.

> **"Knowing this first, that no prophecy of the scripture is of any private interpretation."**
>
> **2 Pet 1:2,0**

In this I mean that you cannot take a scripture out of its context, cafeteria style and make it say what you want it to say. You must study the context it came in, who is speaking to whom and under what condition. You may need to know the culture, expressions and historical background. A word study is important to see the pattern of consistency in word use. To completely understand a subject or event, a topical study examining all passages related is necessary. This is also necessary in determining a symbolic, literal or figurative meaning. Prophetic utterances and other encrypted styles have a consistent pattern of application that must be understood and also sited.

It is a myth that evangelical Christians only follow a literal interpretation because they are simple- minded, led by blind faith. Serious study requires time and effort to let this process speak on it's own without preconceptions. The Western mind is reflective of the Hellenistic perception of thought in that something is either figurative or literal. The Hebrew mind however follows four distinct types or levels of Bible interpretations. It can be layered much like an onion skin. Sometimes these can overlap on the same scripture text giving much more information that what a surface reading can produce. That is why there are Biblical Institutions to study on this level. Computer programs and reference materials have made this process easy for the average, serious student to achieve, after becoming familiar with the basic principles. But the above practices must be applied to get an accurate understanding.

To circumvent this process as someone professing to be a Biblical scholar of sorts, becomes blatant willful ignorance on their part and produces only deceptive doctrines. Others quoting scripture with assumed authority disregarding this interpretive process, as sincere as they may be, will only produce the same deceptive results. The UFO community and others who treat the scriptures lightly, as easy reading have abused these principles for far too long. The lack of being challenged by ordained of God Church leaders, only adds to the "credibility" of their false claims. So, using the proper system of interpretation lets see just what the Bible does have to say about the clouds of heaven.

Chapter One

What are the Clouds of Heaven?

Part One

Biblical Clouds of Heaven

Clouds of heaven are described in many passages as being the form from which God's presence radiated a Shekinah glory. This cloud was God's abode in the Old Testament. The cloud was over the Ark of the Covenant and appeared over the temples signifying God's presence within. It appeared to Moses on Mount Sinai and was before the children of Israel day and night leading them through the wilderness.

There were also clouds of heaven associated with angelic visitations. These were objects that anyone left or entered Earth from. Elijah's ascension on a fiery chariot, Jacob's ladder with angels climbing down, even Jesus' ascension and promised return in the same manner was described as clouds. Num. 9:15, Num. 14:14, 2 Chron. 5:13, Isa. 19:1, Isa. 25:5, Ps. 104:3, Dan. 7:13, Mat. 24:30, 1 Thess. 4:17, Acts 1:9. In all of these texts the description and characteristics clearly show much more than a fluffy chunk of water vapory-cumulonimbus cloud.

Even theologians agree that this is more than a description of a fluffy chunk of water vapor. They have given this "cloud" a name called a Theophany. This is a rather fancy name to define the supernatural form of God's appearance. Basically it means they have no idea what it is, so they have given it this name tag to define it as more than a mere cloud.

Ezekiel's wheels describe uncharacteristic details of something more than just a cloud. Within the UFO community this is the most often used text to prove nut and bolt UFOs were in fact the clouds of heaven. Much of Ezekiel's experience included symbolic imagery describing cycles of events and periods of time. However, the initial account with a cloud of heaven was a literal event. Because of this symbolism the whole experience is seen as just a vision by many. Visions that are symbolic and are not intended to be a literal story will never include names of people or specific geographical locations. When we do find names in context, it is telling us that this is a literal event.

While I agree with UFO researchers who make the point that this is an actual event, you must see the transition to a vision not to be taken literally. And you cannot exclude the end of the story that returns to a literal event and defines just what Ezekiel saw. His conclusion in context is this,

> **"This is the living creature that I saw under the God of Israel, by the river Chabir; and I knew that they were the Cherubim."**
>
> **Ezek.10:20**

What Ezekiel saw, he identified as a living creature. Was he just a primitive, misidentifying technology as something alive? By his certainty this was something he was already familiar with. He identified this living creature as "Cherubim", an order of angelic being. I believe Ezekiel, under the inspiration of the Holy Spirit, was impressed to include this important fact. This would require a further topical study of the clouds of heaven. If this is some kind of Biblical fact there would have to be other scriptures that confirm this idea.

More Clouds: A living Vehicle of God

In these next few scriptures you will see a pattern of word usage that is self-explanatory even on the surface!

> **"The Lord rides upon a swift cloud..."**
>
> **Isa 19:1**

> **"...and he (God) rides upon a cherub, and did fly, he did fly upon the wings of the wind."**
>
> **Ps 18:10**

> **"...and he rode upon a cherub, and did fly: and   was seen upon the wings of the wind."**
>
> **2 Sam 22:11**

You can see that between these three scriptures we have the interchangeable use of clouds and Cherub. Being one in the same they are what the Lord "rides upon." All Christian commentaries that I have ever come across declare that this riding is in a figurative sense. In their minds, this vehicle is not a means of transportation, but the physical action of accomplishing God's will through angels. That argument would have some ground to stand on, except that we have another scripture that clarifies just what kind of vehicle He is using.

> **"Who makes the clouds his chariot: who walks upon the wings of the wind"**
>
> **Ps 104:3**

In no uncertain terms the clouds are something to be ridden upon. In the Hebrew, *chariot* means, **"to be ridden upon."** There is no other variation for this word. This is to be taken literally and not figuratively.

In these few scriptures we have discovered what the Bible really states the "clouds" of heaven really are: an order of an angel used as a protective vehicle for God. Amazing as it may sound we are also told in the Bible how they operate!

Part Two

How do they Fly?

Wings of the Wind: Anti-Gravity Flight?

A possible method of flight is alluded to by the continual mention of the "wings of the wind." The most popular imagery of this text is of the wind catching something like an eagle's wing into upward flight. However, we have a vivid description of the winds of heaven in the Ethiopic text of the Book of Enoch, called Enoch 1. I must cautiously warn that this book was not included in the canon as one of the books of the Bible. Written in several styles, complete authorship is uncertain. This was probably the only reason it failed to measure up to the standard to be included as canonical literature. The Apostle Jude quoted in his Epistle, from the beginning of Enoch 1. (Jude14-16) This text was known in the time of Jesus and accepted as authentic by the Jews. This at least gives it historical credibility. Much in the same manner many Pastors use Antiquities of the Jews by Falvius Josephus to enhance a historical background to the scriptures; I use the Book of Enoch 1 in the same manner. With that said, if this is a connection to the Biblical mention of the wings of the wind, an amazing discovery can be understood!

> *"I also beheld the four winds, which bear up the earth, and the firmament of heaven. And I beheld the four winds occupying the height of heaven. Arising in the midst of heaven and of earth, and constituting the pillars of heaven. I saw the winds, which turn the sky, which cause the orb of the sun and of all the stars to set; and over the earth I saw the winds, which support the clouds. I SAW THE PATH OF THE ANGELS."*
>
> *Enoch 18:1-7*

The winds Enoch is describing are not just meteorological results of weather patterns. He is talking about the power of gravity! The force of gravity which holds everything in place and directs movement! This universal movement then, being caused by light and controlled by gravity creates our sense of time! He continues to include that this same force supports the clouds, and the path of the angels. This is the applied power of gravity in some manner (anti-gravity?) that creates the "pathway of the angels." This is an amazing and important definition for the "wings of the wind". In support of this use is the physical evidence that coincides with this idea.

Interesting observations about all UFO sightings are the electro-magnetic disturbances experienced during a sighting. These same disturbances are experienced with ghost apparitions and demonic encounters. The common denominator in all of this may be a biological function. This biological function then is somehow related to electro-magnetic fields.

BUFORIA, a British counterpart of America's Project Bluebook concluded in its findings that UFO's had more in common with occult activity than it did with any extra-terrestrial origin. Their findings were based in part on these electro-magnetic disturbances. I should also include that many people who have encountered UFOs, Ghosts or demonic activity, have smelled the ionized air, which is associated with electrical and magnetic currents and the smell of sulfur, associated with everything demonic and subterranean. The Biblical name for this is brimstone!

Good and Bad Ones

In Satan's fall, some of the angelic orders joined with him in this rebellion against God. It would stand to reason that some of this Cherub/cloud order followed as well. Ancient Ugaritic texts refer to the god Baal as "a rider of the clouds" This is not to equate

Baal with God but rather to compare a similar observation and understanding. This could explain why Satan is also described as the "prince and power of the air" (Eph2:2).

Part Three

Where do they Travel?

The Bible Teaches Different Dimensions

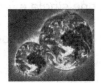

Heaven and Earth are Two Different Dimensions: A Biblical Concept of Time and Space

The Bible explicitly teaches that "Heaven," the dwelling place of God exists outside of our dimension. As Jesus stood before Pilate at his trial, he was asked if he were in fact a king and if he was where was his kingdom?

> **"Jesus answered, My kingdom is not of this world:..."**

This was a baited question to trap Jesus into a confession of usurping the authorities of Rome and the Jews. His startling reply explains much more than what is on the surface. Many within the UFO community have used his reply to improperly prove Jesus was an extraterrestrial. The Greek word for "world" means much more than just this globe called earth. The word used is **Kosmos**. Our English word Cosmos is derived from this. It literally means the entire ordered arrangement of this entire material universe! In this sense, it defines this complete dimension. Jesus' reply was that His kingdom was not of this dimension!

The Bible also explicitly teaches that "Heaven" the dwelling place of God exists outside of our sense of time. The conclusive evidence of this is found in, Ecclesiastes 3:15

> **"That which is has already been, and what is to be has already been; and God requires an account of what is past."**

In no uncertain terms, "Heaven" is truly outside of linear time. If God requires an account of everything that is past, from His dimensional perspective, everything is already history! It is why the prophecies in the Bible are 100% accurate and true. They are the recorded and completed history of mankind from the beginning to the end of time.

To illustrate these two realities, imagine standing on a street corner watching a parade go by. One by one you see the various floats and bands go by until the end. Your reality is only what you see now and what you remember passing by. Someone high above in a helicopter would be able to see the entire parade as one single event. From there He could lower himself into any part of the parade he desired. In a very real sense, this is how the Angels and God travel. It is not space and distance that is being traveled, but time as the separating factor from one dimension into the other.

Linear Time: A Condition From The "Fall" of Man

In no uncertain terms the Bible defines time as a created illusion as a part of the "fall" of man. It was never intended for man to live in a linear existence. Man was to be eternal and live with God in eternity.

> **"And the LORD God said, Behold, the man is become as one of us, to know good and evil: and now, lest he put forth his hand, and take also of the TREE of life, and eat, and live for ever: Therefore the LORD God sent him forth from the garden of Eden,..."**
> **Gen 3:22-23**

In Genesis 2:9, the Hebrew word for tree has more of an emphasis on the wood from the tree, and not the actual tree itself. It also has a meaning of function to close or seal. In this sense the tree is more of a door or portal. The word for tree also has much in common with the Hebrew word for generations. It is how and why we get the idea of a "family tree." This could indicate a progression of life in either dimension. From this perspective, the two trees of Genesis, the tree of the knowledge of good and evil and the tree of life could represent dimensional portals. Entrance would depend upon a decision of faith in God or of self-reliance in man.

The fruit, which the Bible never said was an apple, is the catalyst that transforms man, time and space into a mortal, linear existence. This was never the intention of God but the result of a wrong decision by man. Man was then sent away from the eternal dimension for his own safety, so that he would not be in this second rate physical existence forever. The final result is a parallel dimension bringing about the death of all things. This offshoot dimension became a means of quarantine from the rest of a healthy eternal dimension. I hope you are now able to see from these few scriptures the dimensional difference between Heaven and earth.

The Bible Declares Inter-Dimensional Travel

The next amazing verse of scripture taken from the context in 2 Sam about clouds is a connecting link to everything I have mentioned. The surface meaning does not seem to make any sense at all. The Bible translators certainly did not mistranslate. In their time none of the above concepts of space and time were even thought of. They used proper variables for the understanding they had which was the best they could do in their time. I will show you several versions of this scripture, then my own rendering using other proper variables. I base this upon the original languages and a 21st century perception. It is truly amazing!

> **"And he made darkness pavilions round about him, dark waters, and thick clouds of the skies."**
> **2Sam 22:12 (KJV)**

> **"He made darkness his canopy around him, the dark rain clouds of the sky."**
> **2 Sam 22:12 (NIV)**

> **"He appointed obscurity as a temporary dwelling for his enclosure as a binding together of transition, a covering of a cloud."**
> **(The unofficial Jim W.version) 2Sam 22:12 UJWV)**

I hope the above rendering will become clear as I show you how this comes together. It is God who decided to reveal himself as a "shekinah glory" from a temporary enclosure. This cloud is used while in transition as a binding. What is this binding? It is the bridging together of the two dimensions! In this sense it is like a portal or opening for His presence to "slip into" without being a part of this dimension. Man could not enter God's presence before Christ. God the Father could not be in the presence of sin. This cloud explains this transitional problem. This cloud then is like a protective bubble or wrap around enclosure.

Recent speculations by "fringe scientists" claim that traveling by warping or bending of space could be possible. The preceding verse says the Lord, "bowed the heavens" to travel in this cloud. This text of scripture could be revealing this very kind of travel as a fact. The word for bowed means to bend! What is being bent here is space! The theoretical idea is that time would also be a factor. Biblically then, God is traveling from his realm being outside of time into the fallen linear dimension bound by time. This is simply the way God chooses to travel! This gives a whole new meaning to the phrase, "the anointed Cherub that covers" It also gives us a clue to what kind of travel is taking place. The travel is a dimensional one of time!

This Biblical response to the false claims of aliens in spacecraft as being "God", offers a better challenge than chunks of water vapor. As I hope I have shown, it is Biblical and it is TRUE!

Part Four

Does This Take Away From God's Supremacy?

This does not take away God's sovereignty. It only explains it. Much the same way a virgin birth can now be understood by artificial insemination. It does not take away from the fact that God Himself became a man from His eternal dimension to undo the paradox created in the Garden, becoming the Savior of all mankind at Calvary. Explained or not it still happened.

The only thing that might be taken away is the unknown mystical magical perception that a small child may have for his parents. As this child becomes an adult, he gains a mature understanding of his parents and the magic disappears. A trusting child would only be drawn into a deeper appreciation and love for his parents while a doubting or vain child would perhaps begin to think of him or her self as equal or even superior and therefore reject and rebel against his parents. The parents' love has not changed only the children's understanding and perception of his parents.

This is not to lower God to human parents but rather, to compare our reaction to understanding earthly parents to our Heavenly Father. In the same manner, as a society beginning to understand more about the Cosmos which might explain some of the Physics of God, how will we react toward God? Disbelieve in his very existence? Will we rebel and think we can "be like God", or as a trusting child, will we grow deeper in our appreciation and love. Regardless of our view, His love has not changed toward us.

Unconditional Prophecy: A Need to Know Basis

God told the Prophet Daniel that many things he saw as visions would be concealed until near the end- time. Knowledge and travel would increase. (Daniel 12:4) This was the key element as to how the visions would become known. Science and technology has advanced to a point of grasping god-like qualities such as cloning and space/time travel. Our knowledge of the things of God needs to be known, to put into proper perspective these new concepts. In this time, a fresh look at the scriptures from this technological view would be vital. In this manner we are equipped from being deceived by a master plan from the enemy. This plan could go undetected for what it really is without understanding these important revelations about the clouds of heaven and space/time.

1. They are an order of angelic being used as a literal vehicle.

2. Their biological process includes a form of electro-magnetic anti-gravity travel.

3. Their travel is inter-dimensional with time being a separating factor and the dimension being traveled.

A plan from the Enemy.

We have now covered the full definition of the clouds of heaven. We understand what they are, how they function and where they travel. It is very important to see these simple truths for what they actually are. The enemy of God and man has a plan. Prophesied in the Bible, there will come a time when the great deceiver and imitator will offer to his chosen human agents, Signs and lying wonders as a part of a great deception. This deception will be part of a catalyst to create a one world government and religion called "The New Age"! The nut and bolt man made UFOs just may be the object referred to as the sign and the lying wonder the message of the "New Age" movement as we shall see next!

Chapter Two
Signs and Lying Wonders:

Part One

A Specific Plan to Replace and Imitate

The Apostle Paul mentions in 2 Thessalonians 2:7, a "Mystery of Iniquity" which is a plan carried out all through the history of mankind. Satan himself mentions this plan in the famous five "I wills" of Isaiah 14. This is a specific five-point plan that copies and overlays everything God would do, in the same but opposite fashion.

Two of the five points to this plan is in Verse 14,

> **"I will ascend above the heights of the clouds; I will be like the Most High"**

Another possible rendering of this text can read,

> **"I will elevate myself upon the backs of the clouds, I will resemble the Most High"**

Even a comment in Vine's notes on Strong's numbers makes the statement that:

> ***"The Bible's metaphorical use of the "backs" of the clouds and the waves of the sea gives problems to translators: "I will ascend above the heights [bam-ah] of the clouds; I will be like the most High"***
> ***Isa. 14:14..."***

The difficulty is that word mechanics proclaim that this should be taken literally. However, from their perspective it does not seem to make sense. From the perspective I have shown you, it is just what should be expected and consistent everywhere else in word application!

Understanding just what the clouds really are from prior scriptures adds a whole new dimension to this verse! Defined by the Bible itself, we can now see more than the image of Satan simply rising into the sky to take on God. This is a plan to explain away faith with technology. The clouds of heaven become a nut and bolt flying saucer. In this ruse, the very existence and presence of God is replaced with Satan's own elect the Antichrist. As the Antichrist appears to the world in association with the flying saucer under the created scenario of "Aliens" as our real creator and protector, the fame, the glory and even worship is transferred or rather robbed away from the God of all creation to Satan indirectly by mans own vanity through science and technology.

Part Two

An Object Bearing a Philosophy

Consider this next scripture in context; it describes events surrounding the appearance of the Antichrist at the end times.

> **"Even him, whose coming is after the working of Satan with all power and signs and lying wonders,"**
> **2 Thhess 2:9**

Signs and lying wonders as commented by one of the top Ancient Greek scholars of today, Spiros Zodhiates Th.D., states that,

> *" these two words do not refer to different classes of miracles, but to different qualities of the same miracle. Teras (wonders) is a miracle regarded as startling, imposing...frequently used elsewhere for STRANGE APPEARANCES IN THE HEAVENS. Semeion (sign) a "miracle with an ETHICAL END and purpose. They are valuable not so much for what they are as for what they indicate."*

With this understanding we can expect strange appearances from the skies bearing an ethical or moral message. One that is contrary to the God of the Bible and points to the coming Antichrist!. I do not know of any other two fold event that could sound more like the sightings and reported messages of UFOs and the messages of the occupant "Aliens"!

Part Three

Technology not Magic

The Powers of Heaven Are Shaken

> **"... and the dragon gave him his power, and his seat, and great authority."**
> **Rev 13:2**

Modern man has made science his unquestionable religion. The subtlest form of power today would be that of technology. But it is a technology obtained through occult beliefs. Now let's take this out of conjecture and see if there are any scriptures that would indicate this.

Jesus himself told us that in the last days prior to his return there would be certain events happening. One of them is the idea of the powers of heaven being shaken.

> **"Men's hearts failing them for fear, and for looking after those things which are coming on the earth: for the powers of heaven shall be shaken."**
> **Luke 21:26**

Traditionally, this has been understood to be the mention of some "heavenly earthquake". This misconception is probably based on misunderstanding the significance of the word *"shaken"*. In its most general use it means to agitate. However it also has a meaning according to Thayer's as being **"cast down from one's (happy and secure) state"**. This understanding opens up a whole new dimension to the text. To add to this controversy, the word for *"powers"* means **"miraculous power"**. The miraculous powers of heaven are being displaced, lowered from heaven to earth! This displacement is from a secure place to one of instability in the hands of mortal man.

An actual earthquake, in context is both illogical and isolated from all other events. When viewing this instead, as a displacement of knowledge, it fits like a puzzle piece with the rest of the story.

This rearrangement of heaven's security and constant is mentioned in another place in the Bible

"At that time his voice shook the earth, but now he has promised, "Once more I will shake not only the earth but also the heavens."
Hebrews 12:26 (NIV)

The writer of Hebrews reminds the reader about the importance of listening to God. In context he goes on to say that this time the Lord would not only shake the earth but heaven also. This "shaking up" would be in a very physical way. It would be a rearrangement of the very heavens.

A result perhaps of an intrusion and disruption of the space-time continuum! By Satan imparting to man a physics of the eternal realm not meant for him in his fallen state, abuse would be the only outcome. It may be why in the very end of all things, a "new heaven and new earth" are seen by John in the Revelation given by Jesus.

"And I saw a new heaven and a new earth: for the first heaven and the first earth were passed away;"
Rev 21:1

Science and Technology from the Occult

This form of knowledge would be considered "secret" knowledge, which is the definition for the Occult. Something the Antichrist exclusively would understand and use.

"And in the latter time of their kingdom, when the transgressors are come to the full, a king of fierce countenance, and understanding dark sentences, shall stand up."
Dan 8:23 (KJV)

Understanding dark sentences can mean the ability to apply and use secret knowledge. This I believe is the forbidden physics to produce a technological lying sign and wonder!

This secret knowledge would also be considered "Ancient knowledge" when it will come to fruition in the last days. This knowledge does not just appear but rather reappears from another time in our past.

Technology Will Come From " Ancient Knowledge"

"Is there anything of which it might be said, "See this is new" It has already been before in ancient times".

Ecclesiastes 1:10

Prior to the Great Flood, fallen angels are said to have scattered the secrets of heaven to mankind. This was in addition to a hybridization of the human race, which also happened at this time.

"These are the angels who have descended from heaven to earth, and have revealed secrets to the sons of men, and have seduced the sons of men to the commission of sin...A commandment has gone forth from the Lord against those who dwell on the earth, that their end may be; for they know every secret of the angels."

Enoch 63:1 and 64:6

A forbidden knowledge of Physics will be given to Satan's human agents for the purpose of deceiving the whole world. The creation of a nut and bolt UFO becomes the lying sign and wonders that helps to usher in the New World Order. Understanding just what the clouds of Heaven really are, how they function and where they go enables us to see that when a mechanized imitation is created the same abilities are also given to mortal man. In order to see the series of historical events leading to man made UFOs we have to look at the time just before the flood. A time not well understood today. This was a time of Giants, fallen angels, men of renown, distorted animal life and the disruption of the human genetic line. This mysterious time of the unexplained is where we begin the amazing story of man-made UFOs.

Chapter Three
The History of Man - Made UFOs

Part One

The Great Flood

To understand the complete story of the creation of man made UFOs, we have to look in the Bible and examine two major events, The world before the Great Flood and the Tower of Babel. By a careful examination of both stories in light of recent knowledge and technology of the 21st century, a slightly different yet more complete story unfolds. This perspective offers a more logical flow, which leads to answers about the many mysteries of today.

As it was in the Days of Noah...

"Now it came to pass when men began to multiply on the face of the earth, and daughters were born to them, that the sons of God saw the daughters of men, that they were beautiful; and they took wives for themselves of all whom they chose... There were giants on the earth in those days, and also afterward, when the sons of God came in to the daughters of men and they bore children to them. Those were the mighty men who were of old, men of renown."

Gen 6:1-4 (NKJ)

Within this text in Genesis 6th Chapter, we are told that the "sons of god" (fallen angels) inter-bred with the human race. Their objective was to undermine the first prophecy in the Bible. This prophecy stated that from the seed of a woman would come one who would crush the head of the serpent. This was the foretelling of Jesus, the Son of God and God the Son, who would become incarnate through the human lineage to redeem mankind. (Gen 3:15)

By contaminating the human bloodline these "sons of god" tried to stop God's plan. They were only eight people away from success. For the sake of continuity we will assume this as fact. There are many debates over this text of scripture. In the appendix I will present the debate and give supportive evidence of facts that will resolve the controversy. I would suggest reading *Alien Encounters by Chuck Missler* and *The Omega Conspiracy by IDE Thomas*. Both of these books cover the Genesis 6 account extensively.

The Fallen Angels that interbred with the human race before the flood were further mentioned in the Book of Enoch.

> **"These are the angels who have descended from heaven to earth, and have revealed secrets to the sons of men, and have seduced the sons of men to the commission of sin...A commandment has gone forth from the Lord against those who dwell on the earth., that their end may be; for they know every secret of the angels."**
>
> **Enoch 63:1 and 64:6,**

It would stand to reason, that if fallen angels came down and dwelt among humans, they would certainly want to have their cake and eat it, too. Fallen Angels are not too concerned about rule breaking. They would provide themselves with the conveniences of their home while here on earth. This could mean that the pre-flood society was technologically more advanced than what we assume. Skeptics might cry out, "Where is the proof of an advanced civilization!" The proof when found is not understood because the Old World is not understood.

A Highly Advanced Pre-Flood World?

It is true we have never found a highly developed mechanized society in fossil records or ancient ruins. There is a very simple reason for this.

First, this advanced civilization was not based on petroleum, the internal combustion engine and machinery, as we know of it today. Neither could it have been a petroleum based technological society.

I am reminded of a lecture/debate I attended in 1975 at the University of Michigan featuring Dr. Duane T. Gish. He stated that fossils needed very specific conditions to be produced. Yet, we have an abundant amount of them worldwide. These findings indicate that if these conditions are random local and multiple events over time, mathematically then the earth had to be hundreds of billions of years old, which it is not.

The only other alternative situation would have been a single global catastrophe. Such a single event could have created the ideal conditions to produce the fossil evidence that we do find worldwide. The Bible records this one time event as the great flood. With confidence the claim can be made that the vast amount of fossils we find, corresponds to what the Bible declares. There is a layer of silt covering the entire earth that would indicate a flood of world proportions.

From the Mt St. Helen's explosion we discovered that the fossilization process once thought to take thousands of years took only a decade to produce. Also discovered was the illusion of evolutionary layers of life. As the silt covered all living organisms, larger animals would bloat and float to the top strata or layers that would form. Trees and plants would stay in the middle with small life forms settled on the bottom, giving the illusion of a progression of life at different levels. In actual truth everything was buried at the same time!

If you could believe the Bible's account of the flood, gas and oil are the end result and final resting-place of all life before the flood. In that sense there were no vast oil fields or huge pockets of natural gasses to be used before the flood! We burn and use up the old civilization in our tanks. If you really think about it most all machinery is used to form things that will produce objects that move from one place to another based upon the internal combustion engine and the oil it runs on.

In this way, maybe you can visualize the reality of the pre-flood world. If you harness the use of gravity you don't need the machinery to form or produce parts to manufacture machines that move people and objects. What you might find is a rather simple society, with complicated structures and wonders that seem to defy normal constructional means (being based on anti-gravity methods). This sophisticated society could not have been based on engines and machinery but rather alternate forms of energy.

The old civilization used another means of power. It is known that crystals can store vast amounts of energy and electronically coded information. Light amplified through crystals can create sources of power, i.e. Laser. Harmonics is another emerging form of power with a physics that can be applied without identifiable machinery. When these crystalline objects are found, they are perceived as "religious" objects rather than pieces of technology. In this misidentification, an advanced civilization is not recognized for what it really is and can be easily suppressed. The evidence is not so much in finding machinery and technology defined by our standards, but rather the end resulting "wonders" that cannot be duplicated even by our own technology today. Here are just a very few examples of such items.

Ancient Sumeria

Amongst ruins in an ancient Sumerian city (1st settlement after the flood) was found what Archeologists claimed was a "fertility relic". This was a sculpture "model" that resembled a double helix coil of the Human DNA! Zecharia Sitchin deciphered Sumerian cuneiform tablets describing a twelve-planet solar system. It depicted Neptune as a blue green planet of frozen gasses. After publishing his findings, months later Voyger2 sent back information confirming his findings based upon these Ancient Sumerian tablets!

Giza Pyramids

It has long been assumed that a slave labor force built the Giza Pyramids. They allegedly used logs as rollers or mile long ramps made of packed dirt, which rose up to the heights of the pyramids which enabled them to place the two to ten ton blocks of solid granite in place.

In 1996 NBC aired a documentary titled: *The Mysterious Origins of Man*. Geologists Dr. Robert Schock, French Archeologists Mr Boval, Civil Engineer Mr. West and Researcher/ Journalists Graham Hancock author of *Fingerprints of the Gods* challenged this traditional view. Each in their field of expertise explained how illogical, impractical and impossible the traditional explanations really are!

The ramp would take as long to build in the allotted 20-year time span declared by Egyptologists as the pyramid itself. It would take more than the entire population of the world to build it in that time span. Having no hard wood trees natural to the area, it would take a system of logistics unheard of, even in modern times to import such a vast amount.

These pyramids are built to near perfection. From the very center of the top in relation to the area of the base, it is off center by less than 1/4 of an inch! This is including the thousands of years of settling. Man today with all of his technology and machinery cannot reproduce anything near this. Even if we could, why would we want to? It would be economically impractical! The four corners of the Large Giza pyramid is less than one degree off from pointing to the four true magnetic points of the compass! It is the most near perfect object built on this earth.

It is more incredible to attempt an explanation in natural terms, than it is to realize and explore alternative means. As technology has advanced enough to gain understanding of other methods, such as anti-gravity with supportive evidence to this, it is quickly debunked as impossible because this technology is understood only in a theoretical sense and not a functional part of our society as a known technology.

Based upon that, those in power refuse to accept that a technologically advanced society ever existed in our past. Egyptologists and other traditional scientists are a hierarchy unto themselves. They cling to ideas originated a hundred years ago, which was the best attempt anyone had to explain the unexplainable then. Our knowledge has increased to the point of considering alternative answers that make more sense than these outdated assumptions. However they are an established institution that will not be easily changed. Entire careers are based upon certain traditional ideas that if now incorrect, would appear to be disastrous. For them, it becomes a matter of survival.

Ruins of Tiahuanaco

In Tiahuanaco, Bolivia, there are ancient ruins which local legends claim were built and occupied by the Viracocha (white masters from the skies). Included in the ruins are conduit systems going throughout the buildings. Traditional Archeologists have explained these as possible aqueducts for distributing water. The problem is that these conduits run up along walls with 90-degree bends over ceilings. They have been said to look more like electrical conduits to house wire or cable not water.

The cities buildings and walls are constructed with huge blocks weighing tons. They are carved out with laser precision with seams so tight that they didn't even need mortar.

Legends recorded by Spanish explorers state that the Viracocha built the city in one night by placing the blocks together magically by the sound of a trumpet. An ancient Sufi text of magic from the mid-east describes the floating of objects with the use of a magic flute.

Could these be trace memories of a lost technology, perhaps a form of sonic technology recently tagged as harmonics? This type of fringe science does not require machinery, as we would identify it.

The structures point to a knowledge of Celestial Mechanics that are out of context for that time, or so assumed. And just what time is this in? Reliefs on the walls at Tiahuanaco depict mammals that were supposed to have been extinct long before mankind was even around!

Off the wall Egyptian Style

Zachariah Sitchin built a working electrical light bulb from inscriptions on an ancient Egyptian wall relief. Crude forms of batteries have also been found that when refilled produced a charge. Some identifiable technology is found, but again explained away.

Pirie Reis Map

The Pire Reis map has been scrutinized and determined to be authentic. This map was made in Constantinople in 1513 based on older maps. The dating has been tested to be true. The map showed the western coast of Africa, the eastern coast of South America and the northern coast of Antarctica.

In 1513 no one knew there was an Antarctica! It was not even discovered until 1818! The map also shows an ice-free coast of Queen Maud Land (Later named Neu-Schwabenland by the Nazi's). Geological evidence states that the Antarctic has not been ice-free for at least 4000 years BC, just about the time before the flood! So where did the map come from?

Professor Hapsgood had the map checked out by the U.S. Air Force in 1960. Comparing the Swedish British seismic mapping done in 1949 the Air Force agreed with the accuracy of the map. Recent satellite photos using an infrared method have also agreed with the accuracy of the map.

These few anomalies alone proclaim that we have a very different past than what is declared by conventional science. When the Great Flood came upon the earth, it destroyed the entire world along with most of these secrets. Well...at least the ability to apply the technology was lost. The theories probably were not. And we will see that the Tower of Babylon was made for that purpose.

Part two

Tower of Babylon: More Than a Tower.

In the time of the next great act of rebellion of God, about 560 years after the flood another event happened: The Tower of Babel. Even with such a long period of time, people were still living to a ripe old age of about 600 years. The Babel event would have been only one generation from the remembrance of the pre-flood era. Babel was not about trying to climb up to pull God down from heaven. It was not a space program as Zecharia Sitchin claims. It was about preserving what was remembered of the secrets of heaven, including how to travel it.

Genesis 10:8-10, 11:1-9

"And Cush begat Nimrod: he began to be a mighty one in the earth. He was a mighty hunter before the lord: Wherefore it was said, even as Nimrod the mighty hunter before the Lord. And the beginning of his kingdom was Babal, and Erech, and Accad, and Calneh in the land of Shinar...And the whole earth was of one language and of one speech. And it came to pass, as they journeyed from the east, that they found a plain in the land of Shinar; and they dwelt there. And they said to one another, go to; let us make brick for stone, and slime had they for mortar. And they said, Go to let us build us a city and a tower whose top may reach unto heaven; and let us make a name, lest we be scattered abroad upon the face of the earth. And the Lord came down to see the city and the tower, which the children of men built. Now nothing will be restrained from them, which they have imagined to do. Go to, let us go down and there confound the language of all the earth: and from thence did scatter them abroad upon the face of all the earth."

The Old Tradition is Challenged:

Shortly after mankind's preservation from the Great Flood, we are introduced to a fierce leader named Nimrod. The families of Japheth, Shem and Ham, (Noah's sons) were told to populate the earth. Instead, Nimrod bands the people together and unites them as one, migrating into the plain of Shinar. This was the Sumerian culture that gave rise to the Babylonian Empire, with strong influences to the Assyrian and Egyptian Empires.

The story of the Tower of Babel has been conveyed through the ages as a rather childish fairy tale. That is not to demean any one from the past or present. The full meaning could never have been understood until our cosmology and technology "caught up" to some of the descriptions contained within a few key words of this story. Traditionally this has always been the text to exemplify the thought of teamwork. I have heard some very good sermons, in the sense of unity and the accomplishments that can result.

Unity isn't the total picture to this story, neither is building a tower. We have to see past the tower to question why it was being built. The objective of this tower, as traditionally taught, was for the builders to climb into heaven. As this was an act of rebellion to God, why did they try to climb into heaven? As primitives did they think they could pull God down? Our understanding of this story has for centuries taken on this rather child like image.

In the past, there was no other evidence to conclude anything else. Back then; it would not have been an important issue. There was nothing else that challenged or threatened our faith by these thoughts. Most would accept this matter as one of the "mysteries of the Bible" and let it go.

That Was Then, This is Now!

In our present time it is very important to have a clear understanding of just what took place. Now we have very well thought out ideas being presented that challenge the very foundation of our faith in a personal God.

Author, Hebrew scholar and Ancient Historian, Zecharia Sitchin claims that the tower of Babel was man's attempt to imitate the "gods" and produce their own space program. Sitchin claims that the plural use of God is describing the Annaunki, Sumerian gods that came from heaven to assist mankind. The Elohim, Sitchin claims is another group of extra-terrestrials who created man to be a slave labor force to mine the planet. As absurd as this might sound to some, many colleagues do not take him lightly.

Within the UFO community he has become an icon for melding ancient myth with science. He denies the idea of a personal God and butchers the Bible to prove his point. Any Christian attending a Bible believing church has learned the plural use of God is simply acknowledging the triune nature of the one God. Many other Christian and Hebrew Scholars have pointed out a Jewish cultural tradition made up in their word use and language. The plural is used at times to emphasize an emotion as well as importance to a word use. This kind of use was only typical of the Hebrew culture.

Either case certainly does not indicate some amazing new truth. It only indicates gross negligence to already less known established truth. Sitchin has rewritten Genesis to make the creator of mankind nothing more than a bunch of self-centered Aliens.

Others like William Bramley, Author of *The God's of Eden,* Avon Books 1989, have taken his lead and further miss-represented the scriptures with very compelling arguments. For those of little or no faith in a personal God, it is very convincing. In light of these recent challenges, we need to get a fresh look at exactly what happened in the plains of Shinar around 5,000 years ago!

Lost but Not Forgotten: The Real Tower of Babel

You can see there is more to this story with just a simple look at the surface of this scripture; The first clue to the seriousness of this story is in God's response.

> **"...and this they begin to do: and now NOTHING will be restrained from them, which they have imagined to do."**
> **Gen 11:6**

This is a pretty awesome statement coming from God! He is saying that they will be able to do anything they imagine to do! Such a power would have to be more than the construction of a tower to climb into heaven. An act of such futility would only be laughed at. They would climb so high they would pass out from oxygen depletion, if they could even get that high.

Remember that these are not primitive simple people. They were only one generation away from parents who lived in a world filled with amazing accomplishments. It was their parents that shared a society with the fallen angels and their offspring of Human/ Angelic hybrids. These people developed more than a climbing program, or even Sitchin's space program. This was something that would enable them to do anything they imagined. It was said that they were given the secrets of heaven. There is only one idea that comes to my mind on this. Inter-dimensional travel for the nervous or Time Travel for the bold! Imagine if you thought you could arrange or re-arrange anything, the way you want it. This kind of power would give you the false belief that you could be all present, all knowing and all-powerful. The most incredible thing is when you take a deeper look at a few words used in this text. They confirm this very thought!

"This they begin to do." The Hebrew word *Chalal* is used here. It means to bore or pry open like a wedge in the sense of this being an act of polluting. There is no other way to look at this. They are actually trying to bore into or pry an opening into heaven, or the eternal realm outside of linear time!

As we have already let the Bible conclude for us, Heaven and earth represent eternal and linear time. They are separated from each other as a result of the fall or sin. But the actual physical separation is one of time - linear verses eternal. It stands to reason that the travel they are trying to accomplish here is inter-dimensional. The language here would confirm this. To pry or wedge is to open a portal into the eternal realm.

"Nothing will be restrained from them." The Hebrew word **"Batsar"** means secrets, mysteries or inaccessible things will no longer be restrained. This can only mean a breach in the space/ time continuum. *Zamam* is used for imagined and means to plot or devise in a negative sense. *"Tower"* has a figurative meaning as anything high or lofty. In all Bibles the words *"reached unto"* is italicized. This is because there are no original words to represent them. This was only an assumption by the translators. Equally acceptable in this context is the fact that instead of "reaching unto" it could be **"likened unto."** This understanding is one that lines up with another scripture speaking of the laws later given to Moses by God for mankind not to do.

"Thou shalt not make unto thee any graven image, or any likeness of any thing that is in heaven above, or that is in the earth beneath, or that is in the water under the earth:"

Exod 20:4 (KJV)

The tower of Babel was actually the pinnacle of occult knowledge. Occult simply means secret knowledge. The tower represents the attempt to reassemble and maintain this "secret" knowledge which we now can understand as the physics and technology used before the flood. They were not able to apply this for themselves but by their active participation in preserving what they knew, a future generation and person would restore and apply this technology. Further evidence of this is indicated by their contingency plan.

A Contingency Plan:

The Babel builders had a generalized knowledge of the future, from their knowledge of the stars. They probably did not know the particulars. That is why they developed the contingency plan. This plan is indicated by the phrase, ***"let us make a name"***. The etymology (cultural and historical use of words) of the Hebrew word "shem" for name, says volumes to us. According to *"Vine's notes on Strong's numbers"*, it is a memorial but it has the meaning also as something continual, with fame. Adding a slant that the root words give, it includes: "to set something in a conspicuous place, but to hint with a style of expression, marked by obscurity, a lofty or skyward sign". When you place this altogether you get an accurate picture of the meaning behind the mystery places all around the world!

The Giza Pyramids, Stonehenge, The Gateway to the sun, Easter Island, all of these places and many more, are these memorials spoken of in the Scriptures. They are the contingency plan.

Many "fringe" scientists and researchers, like Como, Hancock, West and Bouval have recently begun to understand and explain this skyward connection. They have pointed out a consistent pattern of a "sacred geometry" incorporated into the measurements and construction. There are also representations to the heavens representing a time before the Great Flood. Their anticipated scattering did happen and we see these resulting memorials scattered around the world today.

Judgment from God - Separation of Land and Confusion of Language:

One Language, One Continent

God's response to this dangerous act of rebellion is one that is not commonly understood. When God said He would scatter them abroad, He said in the Hebrew, that he would disperse and break in pieces in a miraculous way. We know the languages were suddenly changed at that time. However, did you realize that the continents were probably pulled apart from one big landmass? The people were not left with any choice but to scatter.

In Genesis 11:1, the statement is made,

> **"the whole earth was of one language and of one speech."**

Now this would appear to be a rather redundant statement at first glance. The Hebrew word **saphah** is translated in Gen11:1 as "language". This is the literal meaning, however in this narrative contextual use, a figurative meaning in the sense of a lip as a natural shoreline is constant elsewhere! (Shoreline Gen 22:7, a riverbank Gen41:3 and the edge of a material Exod 26:4).

This would mean that they are of one shoreline meaning only one huge continent! It survived one flood and now is about to be ripped apart! Could this be the memory of Atlantis? The lost continent never found because it actually consisted of all the continents together as one? This one scripture and word alone would not be enough evidence to make such a claim. We have another curious verse of scripture rather obscure, but mentioning this same event.

In Genesis 10:25 the lineage of Noah's three sons are given. From this lineage, 510 years after the flood and during the Babel account Peleg is born.

> **"And unto Eber were born two sons: the name of one was Peleg; for in his days was the EARTH DI-VIDED."**
>
> **Genesis 10:25**

The Hebrew word for **Peleg** means earthquake. The word for divided is **Palag** derived from the same root as **peleg**, which means to be ripped or torn apart. The earth had one common shoreline as one continent and suddenly it was ripped apart into the present arrangement.

How you might wonder could life survive such a catastrophe? Remember that the word for scattered abroad in Genesis 11:8 was in the sense of an act of something miraculous. The fossil records support this idea of a sudden displacement of landmasses.

In Siberia, mammoths have been found perfectly preserved, frozen with undigested tropical vegetation intact in their stomachs. This can only mean that these mammoths lived in a tropical environment and quickly froze to death by a sudden placement in an arctic climate. The hair of a wholly mammoth was hollow and actually served as a radiator keeping the animal cool in their natural tropical climate.

A Professor Hapsgood proposed a theory that the continents were actually "floating" on a thick molten mantel, something like a roller bearing. He believed that an imbalance of ice at the poles caused a shifting of the earth's crusts some 2,000 miles in the past approximately 12,000 years ago. This shifting would cause an instant displacement of landmasses. Einstein was one of the few scientists that encouraged Hapsgood's findings. Although this theory does not appear to concur with the Bible's account, it does at least allow that some modern scientists can accept the idea of a rapid displacement of landmasses with the survival of life.

As God divided peoples and places, it is only logical to realize He did it by their portion of understood occult knowledge. As the people broke off from building the tower, they formed into groups based on understanding each other by language. Then, a further act of physical removal from each other became the second part of the judgment.

These two acts insured that they no longer had one speech or a common border. In this action every newly developed culture and geographic location would hold their own piece of the puzzle. They would soon develop special places to maintain and practice their portion of understanding in worship form. In this they would hope for or already knew that at some specific time in the future everything would come back together again. By their active involvement they would have hopes of being a part of this future event. Secret societies and "Mystery schools" developed within would maintain this knowledge with levels of initiation to both preserve and protect its content. Their assurance would be that someday someone would gather together these pieces.

They will have the ability to extract the Physics and regain the applied knowledge to form new technology. This will be presented in a package as a promise to give mankind an "A New Age" of enlightenment. But always with the occult you will get more than you bargained for and never what you hoped for.

Part three

Time Travel in the Bible!

Whose Top May Reach Into Heaven?

As I have stated earlier, the builders of Babel were only trying to compile and contain the knowledge for future use. To illustrate, Let's say that I'm a Television engineer. I become stranded on an island, suddenly removed from all technology, I would know how to set up an operating television system, but I could not actually build one from scratch to aid in getting off the island. To extract the raw material and hand make all of the equipment would be an almost impossible act. All I could do is record the theoretical process of how it is done without actually being able to do it myself. In the same way, the memories of the pre-flood world could only be recorded not achieved.

It is indicated in the Babel story that their head (Satan) would try to reach into heaven at the right time and eternalize this dimension. When we go back to the verse **"Whose top may reach into heaven,"** it is reminiscent of the expressed desire of Lucifer, **"I will ascend into heaven"** Isaiah 14:13. The word for "*top*" also means **leader or head**. The Scripture in Ezekiel 28:13 describes something about Lucifer. **"Thy pipes were prepared in him"** The word for "*pipes*" means **bezel**. That is the upper facet to hold a gemstone. It could also be in that sense a capstone or the pinnacle of any building, i.e. the top or head. You only have to look at the reverse side of an American One-dollar bill to see who would like to be the Capstone. That is not God's eye on the capstone. It is the symbol of the Illuminati. The eye is that of the light bearer which the meaning of the name Lucifer is. With this in mind it gives a whole new meaning to the Scripture in Psalms 118:22 and Matt 21:42,

> **"The stone the builders rejected is become the head of the corner."**

The cornerstone is the one used to set lines and dimensions for the entire building. It is the first and foundational piece. That of course is prophetically speaking of Jesus. The builders rejected God and wanted to put their own god on top to reach heaven. These builders of Babel are bricklayers, which we call Masons today. Is it just a coincidence that we have a secret society called by that same name? This is an organization that boasts of an ancient origin.

Other symbols speak out the same desire of Satan. We have a popular occult symbol the Ouroboros, which is the serpent formed into a circle with his own tail in his mouth. This signifies the desire to create an eternal state for himself. He wants to be the Alpha and Omega of his own eternal realm.

 The Pentagram signifies the strategic five-point plan quoted in Isaiah 14 as to just how he will do this. To ascend into heaven, means to travel through the barrier between the eternal and linear dimension. Time is that barrier; the cloud of heaven is the vehicle. The understanding how, (the physics) was supposedly maintained in the tower of Babel. The contingency plan was to separately hold the pieces in the memorials. These are the mystery spots that we are all familiar with. One man will understand this mystery, he will be allowed by God for a short time to bring it all together again. But just for a short time...

Rebuilding the Tower in the Last Days:

The Antichrist Will Have the Key to Ancient Occult Knowledge:

There is a unique individual who will come. In his first of two appearances he will determine to do many things differently.

> **"And in the latter time of their kingdom, when the transgressors are come to the full, a king of fierce countenance, and understanding dark sentences, shall stand up.**
>
> **Daniel 8:23**

"**Understanding dark sentences,**" means not only to comprehend but also to be able to utilize a puzzle or secret knowledge. He will realize what the occult really is. Unlike any predecessor before, he will reassemble the scattered pieces of legends and myths from these mystery places back into a whole picture. In doing this he will extract the physics and redevelop the power used before the flood. It is said of God by Daniel,

> "**Blessed be the name of God for ever and ever: for wisdom and might are His: He changes the times and the seasons:..**"
>
> **Dan 2:20-21.**

He alters, changes or makes diverse the years and fixed appointed times. In context the original language does imply the changing of the seasons but it also includes a description of fixed or appointed times. This states that it is God who governs linear time and its arrangement. I think we can agree that this is not in reference to holidays. Yet these same Aramaic words are used in another text in reference with the Antichrist and have commonly been accepted as meaning holidays.

Here is the text in Dan 7:25.

> "**And he shall speak great words against the most High, and shall wear out the saints of the most High, and think to change times and laws: and they shall be given into his hand until a time and times and a dividing of time.**"

"**Speaking great words against God**" is elaborating in detail something against God. This would be like the elaborate lies of Aliens instead of God as our creator and provider. The "**wearing out of the saints**" is in the sense of a mental fatigue or harassment. Many of the New Age revelations of the "fringe sciences" are gradually being accepted by mainstream society. This is because many of them are truth sandwiched between a false premise and wrong conclusion. People who hold to traditional beliefs of a personal God are ridiculed. They become the image of ignorant, superstitious, non-inclusive and non-progressive people. They are accused of being fearful and jealous of the promising changes that this "New Age" offers.

"**He will think**" means he has a hopeful expectation to accomplish something. We are certainly not speaking about the mere changing of holidays and social laws through administrative action. If you are such a powerful leader, you can make laws and holidays easily to your desire, even in a democratic government. What is described here is much more serious than that. The same Aramaic word describing God's sovereignty of linear time is the same word used here for times. Exactly what the Antichrist hopes to change. The law he hopes to break is the improbable task of breaking the natural laws that govern time and space! He wants to alter appointed and fixed occasions of linear time by traveling through it, to have the power to control it! This is the power of heaven that is shaken, the wings of the wind, and the pathways of the angels as described by Enoch as gravity! This kind of travel is made possible by some means dealing with gravity!

Notice that it is God's power that becomes displaced. It is God who shakes the heavens as well as the earth this time. He allows this power to be used as part of His overall plan. Mankind's use of this technology given by Satan is not unrestrained. He allows this seemingly uncontrollable act to happen. He is giving their vain rebellious hearts just enough rope to hang themselves with. By their own actions they will be judged.

"Bending space" Gravity is the key

Gravity would be the one object of resistance to accelerated speed. Imagine a number line with zero being the speed of light. That point is at equilibrium with time itself. This would be the entry point to an eternal realm. A way to overcome gravity would be needed. Einstein's theory of relativity states that an object approaching near the speed of light would experience a slowing down of time in relation to the rest of the universe. In this sense the occupants of a vehicle would appear to jump into the future as they slowed back down to a stop from a near light speed travel. This ratio would increase nearer to the actual speed of light. The negative coefficient of this would be to travel beyond the speed of light. This would bring about the opposite results of reversing back into time. Fringe scientists who recognize "worm hole" and "black hole" theories declare that these speeds may not be necessary to travel backward, as a bending or looping of space may result in light speed entries into these phenomenons.

In any case, if these theories hold true, the necessary barrier to overcome would be gravity. An anti-gravity vehicle would be needed. The vehicle would need to create it's own electro-magnetic gravitational field. Enoch1:18 describe gravity and the pathways of the angels. In verse 2 it also mentions a "stone", as holding the Four Corners of the earth. This may give us a further clue to this method of travel. This could be the lodestone of occult alchemical myths. In conventional terms this would be a magnetic core creating an electro-magnetic gravitational field. This is what we find as the basis to penetrate this barrier.

An electro-magnetic anti-gravity system would create its own gravity separate from the rest of the cosmos. This would produce the effect of speed without any resistance. As a bar of soap would shoot out of your wet hands because you would not be able to hold or even touch it, so would a vehicle operating on this principle. Sudden accelerations or changes in direction would not affect occupants within the vehicle because they are within their own gravity field. They are separate from the surrounding gravity of the universe. In a sense they would be in-between time or dimensions while traveling at accelerated speeds.

There are several mentions in the Bible of looping and bending space. In context, one reveals the mechanics of how God rides upon the cherub, as mentioned before. The other in context tells us what evil the Antichrist and False prophet will achieve during the last days, in a period known as the Great Tribulation.

"He bowed the heavens" ...and came down

Wormholes alluded to in the Bible

Here is the same scripture in context, with my own rendering based on the original Hebrew variations in light of 21st technology.

> **"He bowed the heavens also, and came down: and darkness was under his feet".**
>
> **Ps 18:9(KJV)**

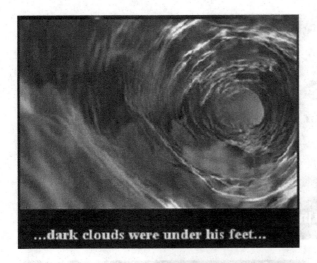

...dark clouds were under his feet...

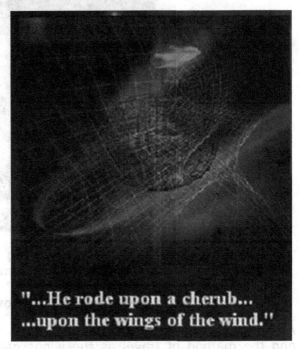

"...He rode upon a cherub...
...upon the wings of the wind."

9. He BENT the heavens to come down: the stream
   was below his feet as a path."

   (Cf/w Ezk 10:20)

10. And he rode upon a cherub, and did fly: yea, he
    did fly upon the wings of the wind.

..a binding together in transition...

A protective covering from heaven
Through the brightness before him were
coals of fire kindled. 2 Sam 22:13

11. He appointed a circular covering as a temporary dwelling for his enclosure as a binding together of transition, a covering of a cloud."
Ps 18:9-11 (My own rendering)

As we have already seen, this describes the cloud as the vehicle and the method of travel as the wings of the wind, which is gravity. To add to the whole process, we have the idea of "bending heaven," and a stream below him as in slip stream or wormhole! Alluded here as a Biblical fact! This is a concept that we are now only beginning to understand. Now we'll look at a couple of scriptures in which the imitator does the same thing!

An ultimate vanity and rebellion

A Heavenly Organic function transforms into a mechanical earthly imitation so man imitates God.

> "And out of one of them came forth a little horn, which waxed exceeding great, toward the south, and toward the east, and toward the pleasant land. And it waxed great, even to the host of heaven; and it cast down some of the host and of the stars to the ground, and stamped upon them. Yea, he magnified himself even to the prince of the host, and by him the daily sacrifice was taken away, and the place of his sanctuary was cast down. And an host was given him against the daily sacrifice by reason of transgression, and it cast down the truth to the ground; and it practiced, and prospered."
>
> **Dan 8:9-12**

Here is a text that could be so misidentified that it would appear to be something totally different. One of several keys is the italicized word "sacrifice". There is no word in the original language for sacrifice. It was added because of the assumption that the word for "daily" meant the sacrifice at the temple that was performed on a regular basis. You see the word for daily means, that which is done continual or continuum, a constant! In context it was interpreted as all being related to the Temple and its various servants and priests symbolized by the term stars. Proper symbolism used everywhere else means angels. This understanding would have been unimaginable to the Bible translators of 1648 or even 1900! To consider this as heavenly angels is to also imply that someone from a mortal linear plane has just breached the eternal one and taken prisoners!

Even today traditionally trained people are aghast to even consider such a thing. I believe the Bible says what it means and means what it says. To further exploit this possible understanding, the word for "magnify" used here several times in text, has a wide variety of meanings. It can mean to develop and mature in a growing, learning process. However, another meaning is to twist or festoon. To festoon means to wreath or form a loop! This double meaning may be more than an interesting coincidence! Only in our time, understanding space/time concepts, could any of this be understood from the original language. Just as God told Daniel that much of prophecy would be "shut up and sealed" until knowledge increased and people would travel to and fro, some revelations would be progressive with our understanding of the cosmos!

This text could be telling us that the little horn, (the Antichrist) will develop an ability to breach the space/time continuum. He will take heavenly truths from their secure places in the heavens and apply them here on earth. He is given an army to assist him. Notice too that God Himself gives this to him for a time, a dividing of times and times. He is not running ramped and loose with this. God is allowing man and Satan to go this far! It will ultimately serve to His desired will and Satan's total destruction. This text has always been cross-referenced with another event in Rev 12:3-4

> **"And there appeared another wonder in heaven; and behold a great red dragon, having seven heads and ten horns, and seven crowns upon his heads. And his tail drew the third part of the stars of heaven, and did cast them to the earth:"**
> **Rev 12:3-4**

This is the supposed description of a pre-Adamic battle between God's angels and Satan's rebellion. This is the Book of Revelation. It is describing future events not reflecting on past events. Nowhere else does this book, does it reflect back on the past. There is no indication that this is a description of any pre-Adamic anything! Even the original language does not bear this out. The "dragon" is not compelling this heavenly host to follow him. In the Greek, he has seized and captured them as prisoners!

This dragon is symbolically representing the entire rebellion. A part of this structure includes seven rulers, seven prior kingdoms and ten earthly helpers described as crowns, heads and horns. The tail does the drawing or catching. In Isaiah we may find a scripture that defines what the tail is. Used in symbolism the tail refers to a Prophet that speaks lies.

> **"The ancient and honorable, he is the head; and the prophet that teaches lies, he is the tail."**
> **Isa 9:15**

In Rev 13: 13-14, we are told of the False Prophet that brings fire down from heaven in the sight of men.

"And he does great wonders, so that he makes fire come down from heaven on the earth in the sight of men, And deceives them that dwell on the earth by the means of those miracles which he had power to do in the sight of men."

The purpose of this event is to deceive the entire world. The word for fire has a dual meaning of judgment! Again something heavenly is being brought down to the Earth to be trampled upon and abused by mankind. Perhaps a false judgment created by the breaching of the space/time continuum as we will discuss more later!

Part Four

Recent History Fulfills Prophecies!

We have now reviewed two Biblical stories in light of modern technology and knowledge. We have seen also in scripture what kind of signs and wonders would accompany the coming Antichrist. We have understood how he would obtain this secret knowledge and just what that knowledge is. In recent history then, we would look to see if anyone has followed these occult footsteps toward any assumed or alleged discoveries.

As the Antichrist proceeds to rebuild Babylon he is not reconstructing a city and a tower in the plains of Shinar again. This time he will collect from all over the world every piece of ancient artifacts, written legends and myths. By compiling all of this in one place he can have his scientists-priests extract the physics to apply in technology. New super weapons can be developed to rule and lead the world into a new world order.

If this is already history, then we are looking for a group of people, as a nation or movement that was occult based in their beliefs and policies. They would desire to dig into hell, and ascend into heaven. We would expect a space program of some type and radical departures from contemporary scientific research and development. They would have interest in obtaining "ancient knowledge" and some kind of belief in a Golden age of the gods" as the pre-flood condition. They would desire to bring back this world and view themselves as chosen to do so.

Their ability to actually pursue such an unorthodox agenda is financed by an elite few as we shall see next. To any history buff this should sound familiar because this has already happened over fifty years ago!

An Agenda Conspired by a Globalist Elite

Just before the flood the world was deceived on a global level by fallen angels. We are fast coming to another deception on a global scale as prophesied in the Bible. (Rev13:14) This is the gathering together of the entire peoples of the World as One government, One Religion and One Leader. (Rev 17:8-12) This will be conspired and controlled by ten powerful people who have the same goals and desires. They will give allegiance and their resources to the coming one, The Antichrist.

> **"The ten horns which you saw are ten kings who have received no kingdom as yet, but they receive authority for one hour as kings with the beast. These are of one mind, and they will give their power and authority to the beast".**
>
> **Rev 17:12-13**

This New World Order does not just happen. A carefully orchestrated and conspired deception will become necessary and successful. As a catalyst, UFO's and Aliens with man in the middle of an intergalactic struggle of good alien angels and bad alien demons, will force the world to rethink its world view and unite us as one. This unity will unfortunately leave a belief in a personal God behind. An earthbound technology will be suppressed and kept secret, so as to stage this whole scenario.

It stands to reason that such a conspiracy will not be known or believed until it has been able to accomplish its goals. Understanding this as a Biblical fact you perhaps can realize that there will never be any conclusive or tangible proof. Whatever proof will be given will not be believed by the majority of people. The best we can hope for are rumors and alleged events without proof. The lack of proof however can be off set by the suspicious attempts to cover- up any such people, events, or possible proofs. These suspicious actions of others, whether individuals or entire governments can be enough of a "smoking gun" to allow any skeptic to see that there is something more behind the many wild rumors and claims. The prophetic warnings in the Bible will be the only source that can sift through these claims and give you discernment to reveal any truth.

The Undisclosed Occult Agenda of Hitler and the Nazis: The Search For the Vril Power, Allies and a Hollow Earth

As we review our history, we would have to ask, has any one group or individual resembled these occult motivated actions? Are there even rumors of such things ever being accomplished? Are there any actions by others that would indicate a seriousness to such bizarre beliefs and actions? The answer to these questions would be yes. Now let's look at an unknown part of our own recent history.

This is a story of extreme unorthodox beliefs and practices that engulfed an entire Continent. This did not begin with a bunch of uneducated kooks or a radical outcast few. This was a movement that encompassed some of the richest, most influential people of Europe, as well as some of the most educated brilliant minds of the late 19th and early 20th century. A small, dedicated core of them overturned an entire world, that to this day has had lasting changes.

The Nazi Parties Unknown Other half: The Occult Hierarchy

When describing the rise of Nazism, conventional history only mentions the German Workers Party later named the National Socialists German Workers Party and their enforcement arm of power, the "Brown Shirts". This part of the movement grew from the lower and middle class beer hall crowd. The SS are included as the military elite and successors of the Brown Shirts, but their origin and backers are never mentioned. These groups were made the scapegoats for the atrocities at the war's end and they took the blame.

The real brains and spirit of the movement were never brought to trial and rarely mentioned in history. These were the intellectuals and the rich aristocratic elite. They were globalists with international connections who financed the Third Reich and were also members of occult secret society groups. Their occult beliefs provided the philosophy and motivation behind the Nazi movement. They were the invisible other half of the Nazi movement.

Two of the most prominent groups were the Thule and Vril societies. The Thule Society was the largest and most influential group of them all. They based their Occult beliefs on a book,

"The Secret Doctrines" by Helena P. Blavatski the founder of Theosophy. The Thule Society embraced Theosophy as their total ideals. They even copied the Theosophical symbol of the Swastika as their own. Theosophy was a mixture of Hinduism, Tao and Buddhists beliefs, including an origin from a hollow earth. The Aryan was seen as the chosen "master race" created by the ancient gods to rule mankind. Evolution of both man and earth were brought about by cycles of catastrophes and rebirth. Buddhists refer to this as the Dharma cycle. Contact and guidance by invisible forces was encouraged. Vegetarianism, Reincarnation and Karma melded into the Volkish beliefs of this Germanic order. Madame Blavatsky claimed an exclusive authority on the basis of her occult knowledge or gnosis. She also claimed her initiation into the doctrines came from two exalted mahatmas or masters called Morya and Hoot Hoomi. These dwelt in a remote and secret vastness of the Himalayas. She wrote the Secret Doctrine based on the Stanzas of Dzyan, which she claimed to have seen in a subterranean Himalayan monastery. The claim has been made that this text was of a pre-flood origin, describing a very different world than that of today. Much of this part of her life is in dispute and claims of plagiarism and of being a charlatan have followed until today. This is just the character one would be expect from the person who would be the counter part of Moses as the anti-Moses. She solidified the ancient occult and eastern mystic religions into one clear thought and agenda. It really doesn't matter if she made it all up, the end result is still the same; this one book has done much to influence the course of human history.

The other society was based on a Science Fiction Book written in 1871, *"The Coming Race"* by Sir Edward Bulwer-Lytton. He was known worldwide for his book, *"The last days of Pompeii"*. He was a member of the neo-pagan English social order the "Golden Dawn", a higher ranking Freemason and a Rosicrucian.

His book told the story of an encounter with an advanced subterranean civilization. The Vril-Ya was the name of a mystical power utilized by this inner earth society. These were described as large Caucasian people with the strength to control a strap on device of wings that enabled them to fly. (Could this be a possible allusion to angels?) The Vril power was developed through their minds and transferred into a crystalline staff that each member carried. They viewed mankind on the level of pets and had a life span lasting for centuries. They would someday rise from the earth to reclaim the surface. If this sounds familiar to you,

Disney pictures produced an animated movie adapted from the same source called "*Atlantis*". Occultists never received this book as fiction but rather truth veiled in the guise of fiction. The final result was that the Nazis believed and acted upon these strange ideas as their agenda.

In today's terms it would be as absurd as the Masons and the official Star Trek fan club merging to form a powerful political organization. The strangest thing is the fact that it actually happened. Their occult inspired beliefs inspired them to quest for these "truths" and apparently they found some.

There were two reasons why this other side of Nazism was never made public. At the end of the war, Winston Churchill was concerned that if these specific occult beliefs were released to the public, the Nazis could get off with a plea of insanity at the Nuremberg trials. Now, so many decades after the fact, people have forgotten and are too removed from those times to really care. The information is easily available to anyone interested and now is only a side note of history. The other reason is the fact that the very same international elite involved, own the media that is used to proclaim these events and create their version of history.

The SS AHNENERBE: Turning Myths into Realties of Technology

Heinrich Himmler had a special division of the Schutzstaffel, which in English are the Storm Troopers commonly known as the SS. This was another occult lodge The Order of the Black Sun. Within this organization was a section called The Occult Bureau, a part of the Ancestral Heritage Society known as the Ahnenerbe, sort of a Nazi Academy of Sciences for the SS. The Ahnenerbe can be described as a Humanities think tank with guns. They had an unlimited budget. They could work on any project, to pursue any theory, using any resources available. This included using humans without fear of accountability. In other words, they had a license to kill. But they had to produce results. Failure to do so could mean loss of their position and profession, imprisonment, and even their own life.

A founding member of the Thule Society, Guido Von List, influenced much of the Ahnenerbe's perceptions. He was a self- styled Aristocrat and Occult scholar. He coined the term "Wotanism" for his studies of Nordic mythology and ruins. He assigned mystical and ceremonial values behind the Runic language.

Today many in the New Age movement follow this system. Nazi doctrine progressed with Karl Hausehofer's geo-political ideas of "Lieberstorm" or "living space". The official claim was made that in whatever land where ruins or the Swastika was found; Germany had a legal right to reclaim that territory. The Swastika use was so wide spread that it was assumed the Aryan had global dominance during a pre-flood/ Golden age era. Therefore, world dominance was justified, in their reasoning. This concept also inspired the Eugenics program of mercy killings of the disabled and retarded, ending in the Final solution.

The Ahnenerbe spanned the globe accumulating every artifact, written myths and legends from all over the entire world. The activities included everything from archeological digs to looting museums in occupied lands. They visited all of these "mystery spots" to compile information for their scientists/ priests. Of special interest were any cultures using the runic languages or the Swastika. The Nazis believed this language and icon to be evidence of an ancient Aryan presence.

The SS Ahnenerbe made a trip to Iceland and studied the ancient ruins and the Nordic Edda with a fine-tooth comb. The purpose was to discover the entrance to "Thule"(Mythical Aryan capital of the inner earth). This led them to an expedition to Tibet led by Dr. Ernst Schafer in 1934-36 and again in 1936-39. The Buddhist Monks received the Nazis with great joy. They saw the Nazis as a prophetic fulfillment of the ones possessing the Shamballa power to complete the Dharma or cycle of the fifth root race, The Aryan. The monks accommodated them in every way. They gave the Nazi expedition a 108 volume sacred text and allowed entrance into the cavernous systems sealed off from the rest of civilization for ages. This produced scientific studies in earth magnetism, and other geophysical experiments, as well as ethnological studies. In their zeal to help fulfill the Nazi destiny over 200 monks were made SS officers and assigned to Himmler's staff as advisors at the Wewelsburg Castle. This was Himmler's occult center and think tank.

This was acceptable to Nazi ideology as they viewed the Hindu Indians and Tibetan Asians to be "spiritual Aryans". They believed that both groups were a connecting link to their own Aryan bloodline and descendants of the subterranean supermen. Their religions of Hinduism and Buddhism were a reflection of the religion of the Subterranean culture.

Of special interest to Hitler was an Aztec legend of Quetzalcoatl. As he departed the ancient Aztecs, it is recorded that Quetzalcoatl told them he was going back home to Tulla or Tullan. This was a place, according to their belief, that was once **" a country of the sun"**, but now, **"where ice reigned and the sun had disappeared"**.

In 1938 Nazi newspapers and propaganda literature announced that one of the high Lamas knew the opening to Agharti, the inner Earth realm according to Author/Researcher *Alec Maclellan*. In his book *The Lost World of Agharti* Souvenier Press 1982. This Lama was only known as the man with the green cloves.

In the same year, the expedition and partitioning of an area of the Antarctic was claimed by the Nazi's and renamed Neu-Schwabenland. Throughout the war submarines continued bringing equipment, supplies and men to this area. German submarines that were captured in southern areas, possibly in route to the Antarctic, were reported to have as many as 50 people in them. A full crew consisted of 8-10 people in a normal situation. Researchers *Renato Vesco and David Hatcher-Childress* in their book, *Man Made UFO's,* Adventures Unlimited Press 1994, have speculated that an underground complex was built. From operation Redoubt, the tunneling and placement of a huge underground complex in the Swiss Alps, we know the technology was there. This appears to be the end of the globetrotting trail that the SS Ahnenerbe completed on their Occult mission. For further understandings, I would suggest two excellent books on the Occult beliefs of the Nazi's; *Unholy Alliance by Peter Levenda,* Avon Books 1995 very insightful and *The Occult Roots of Nazism by Nicholas Goodrick-Clarke,* New York University Press 1992.

As strange as some of these beliefs were, as they ventured outside the ordinary, there is evidence they actually might have discovered a thing or two in their bizarre quest.

Mercury; an Example of Technology Extracted from a Myth

One such example of extracting science from myth would be Mercury, the legendary hero, the symbol and the element. Mercury in Roman and Hermes in Greek mythology was the swift messenger of the gods, as well as the god of commerce and travel. The symbol of Hermes staff shows a disk on either end of a central shaft, with two inter-twined serpents, with wings of flight above their heads. The intertwining could indicate the vortex principles understood by Victor Schauberger. The dual disks on the shaft representing the electro-magnetic energy generated from the mercury through a vortex implosion as symbolized by the intertwining serpents. The final result produced rapid flight, as represented by the wings. Although you might think this strange, this is the very methodology used which led to new technology the Nazis are claimed to have obtained by this unorthodox view of mythology.

The Nazis may have constructed Mercury plasma gyros. This system used an electrified mercury vapor. Further evidence of an unusual use of mercury was discovered in April of 1944. The ill-fated submarine U-859 left Germany and was sunk off the straits of Malacca in Indonesia. This sub had a cargo of 33 tons of mercury! This was strange cargo in such a huge amount and being treated as an important military cargo! In 1944 mercury was used for thermometers and switches, with no known military purpose. Some sort of unconventional use can only explain this strange cargo. It has been speculated by *Childress and Vesco* in their book *Man Made UFO's* that the ship was headed for a base in the Antarctic, as one of many that headed in that region all during the late 30s and 40s.

Another curious note was the death of Jack Parsons. He was the American Rocket scientist who invented solid rocket fuel. He died in a fire while working with mercury. And yes, he was involved with occult societies that had Nazi connections during the war. There does seem to be more to Mercury than just switches, thermometers and mythology! This is only one small example of how the Nazis approached legends and myths and attempted to extract a physics from them

Part Five

The Reality of Nazi UFOs

Traces of the Unorthodox

While Allied pilots were seeing "Foo fighters" in the sky above, below, the German people were experiencing the same electro-magnetic effects that many in the US would begin to experience in the 50's during UFO sightings. Automobile engines would die, radios would receive only static near several locations of Top Secret bases. These bases included a series of towers that at times produced these effects. This power of the Vril, searched for by several controlling secret societies within the Reich, may have been in research and development at these bases. The similar patterns are too consistent to dismiss as coincidence.

Unorthodox Scientist: Viktor Schauberger

One of the key scientists working for the Nazis that did not disappear at wars end, was Viktor Schauberger. From his observations of nature and water he developed a natural means of energy and power. Schauberger produced electrical power from a unique suction turbine by implosion principles, and later was pressured into developing a propulsion system using the same principles applied to air. Schauberger developed a low-pressure zone on the atomic level with a prototype, which whirled air or water radically and axially at a falling temperature. Schauberger referred to the resulting force as, "diamagnetic levitation power."

It has been said that all throughout the war effort he doggedly worked on ordered projects. It was only at the end of the war that he actually achieved a working prototype of a flying saucer. Schauberger was given a team of scientists to help him with his work.

After their research headquarters were bombed, they were all transferred to Leon Stein. There they perfected the "flying disc", powered by Schauberger's turbine. Schauberger's prototype was developed into a vehicle that could speed 1,200 mph in three minutes and fly in any direction at Mach 3! However, he had not perfected the ability to control its flight, as all the discs eventually crashed. This is now eerily reminiscent of current reports of "alien spacecraft" crashes. Other more recent UFO observations include the "slicing" through of clouds leaving a void pathway where the saucer flew through. Over oceans and lakes UFOs have been observed to suck up water. Refueling perhaps? Could this be evidence of a Schauberger technology?

At the end of the war, American Military officers seized everything in the laboratory and seeing Schauberger as a Nazi collaborator put him into protective custody for six months. The Munich publication, *Da Neue Zeitalter*, wrote in 1956 that, "Viktor Schauberger was the inventor and discoverer of the new motive power, implosion, which, with the use of only air and water, generated light, heat and motion".

The publication noted that the first unmanned flying disc was tested in 1945 near Prague, that it could hover motionless in the air, and could fly as fast backwards as forwards. This flying disc was reported to have a diameter of 50 meters. Schauberger was called to America. He was persuaded to provide a team of scientists, military and government officials with a record of everything he knew, and to sign some contracts. But eventually he became worried that some of his projects seemed to have been left sitting on the shelf and that no further research was being done. He then discovered that in actual fact he had signed the rights to his work away.

It has been said that he and his son worked for the US government on top-secret projects. His technology was incorporated in the High Frequency Active Auroral Research Program known as the H.A.A.R.P. program located in Alaska.

Other Projects, Scientists and Engineers:

Within Nazi Germany many others were also working on disk-type aircraft, and alternate propulsion methods. A significant problem was that many projects were working independent from one another.

The Vril Society had their own program, developing disk technology, and employed many other unconventional researchers, scientists, and engineers. The SS Order of the Black Sun also had its own program. Dr. Miethe, Rudolf Schriever, Dr. Habermohl, and Mr. Bellonzo being some of the more prominent developers of these crafts, worked for various factions and interests within the Reich. Some of these men were captured and made or allowed to continue their work for the Allies after the war in England, the United States, and Russia.

Some significant rumors with no real proof have also surfaced and might be worth mentioning. It is said that the Thule society as part of their occult practices as early as the 1920's obtained complete plans for a craft through a psychic reader. The Order of the Black Sun allegedly recovered a crashed craft found in the Black Forrest in 1932 and began their own programs back engineering even before the rise of the 3rd Reich.

Why Didn't the Nazi's win the War?

It is only logical to consider that if Nazi Germany developed such a vehicle, why didn't they win the war? The problem is one that really doesn't take a physicist to understand.

These craft are flying or slipping through the Earth's gravity by creating their own gravitational field separate from the Earth. With this understanding, you realize that you are not going to be able to send a projectile of any type through one field into another. Guns or Cannons mounted on this craft could do nothing to shoot an enemy down.

This would mean that this craft could not be used as an offensive weapon. Anyone who understands Hitler knows that if a weapon was not offensive it was not a top priority. The ME 262, was a Jet fighter that was copied by the US and Britain after the war. It was on the design boards as early as 1932. It was not seen as an offensive weapon and therefore delayed in development until much too late to be effective in the war. Had Hitler built an Air force with this weapon early on, there would not have been any great air war called the Battle of Britain, it would have been the slaughter of Britain. This was the thinking of Hitler and the reason other weapons were also delayed in development.

All the Nazis had at that time was a fast- moving, shiny craft that looked good but could do nothing to "shoot" an enemy plane or even ram another aircraft. The only thing possible is just what allied bomber pilots flying missions in 1945 had reported, "Foo Fighters." Shiny globes or disks were seen flying close to bombers having an effect on their electronics and navigational equipment. The technology was developed too late to effectively accomplish anything for the war effort.

The side effect of being able to travel so fast unhindered by resistance has been rumored to be a "looping" or bending of space/time and supposedly was accidentally achieved. However, these are only rumors and cannot be verified. Rumors are interesting enough in light of what the Bible alludes to. If I am right about the breaching of space and time, rumors are all we will ever know of. But rumors may be enough to indicate that this part of scripture is in the process of being fulfilled.

Part Five

Allied discoveries at the end of WWII

It is true we do not have an actual, fully functional Nazi UFO that we can produce as proof. What we do have is evidence that Nazi research and technology was headed in that direction indicated by what was actually recovered during allied occupation. Posted on my web site, are actual photos of captured aircraft, and drawings seized by the Allies after the war, at the Peenemunde launching site of V1 and 2 rockets, and the complex at Nordhausen.

Nordhausen was the huge underground research and development factory located deep within the Harts Mountains and the sister complex, Kahla in Thuringen.

The triangular "stealth" jet fighter and a smaller swept wing jet fighter were only months away from production. Cruise type missiles, a tow guided missile, even a TV guided missile were operational at the wars end! Awaiting its maiden voyage was the Amerika Bomber. This was a flying wing similar to our recent Stealth B1. Built and tested, it awaited the German Atomic bomb development. It was scheduled to fly over New York!

Even more eerie than that was the alleged documents and rough prints indicating an alternate source electro-magnetic, anti-gravity powered disk. Whatever the Allies gleaned from the fall of Nazi Germany, it was probably the leftovers. It may be that most of the actual projects were probably transferred safely to Neu-Schwabenland in the Antarctic. What is known is that Nazi technology was taking a radical turn toward circular and triangular aircraft with alternate propulsion sources.

Officials Make Comments:

In a very generalized manner, a couple of quotes allude to confirming some of the afore-mentioned findings. Great Britain's chief of the technical mission to Germany for Aircraft Production in 1945 said,

> *"I have seen enough of their designs and production plans to realize that if they (the Germans) had managed to prolong the war some months longer, we would have been confronted with a set of entirely new and deadly developments in air warfare."*

Captain Edward J. Ruppert, Chief of the U.S. Air force Project Bluebook stated in 1956,

> *"When World War II ended, the Germans had several radical types of aircraft and guided missiles under development. The majority were in the most preliminary stages, but they were the only known craft that could even approach the performance of objects reported to UFO observers......"*

The trail of this technology takes two different paths. We shall look at the more conventional one that is well documented first.

US Searches for Nazi Technology and Scientists: Operation Paperclip: The Trail to the West

As soon as the Nazi complexes were overrun by Allied forces and discovered the many unknown projects, the US went into action to procure the scientists, engineers, projects, papers and even the security agents involved. This we will see later was to our own undoing. Operation Paperclip allowed as many as several thousand Scientists, Engineers and Security officers and their families into the United States. Many were ardent Nazis with crimes overlooked for the price of new technology. Some of the justification for this compromise was the fear that Russia or other allies could claim this technology first. We will discuss Paperclip in detail later. For now it is important to see that we took this unorthodox development serious enough to act upon it. The US was not completely in the dark about alternate energy uses. We may have had our own failed attempts of using the unorthodox.

Probing Activity in the US

Even as the Germans were conducting their "alternate" energy source programs, we may have stumbled upon some of this technology by accident, with very bad results.

Nicola Tesla was a genius and held over one thousand patented inventions. It has been alleged that in his latter years, Tesla claimed he received information from "aliens". It has been said that he first had the understandings of electro-magnetic levitating devices in the early 1890's!

His last project was a government experiment using his famous Tesla Coils in project Rainbow. Rainbow was an attempt to make a ship invisible to radar by producing an electro-magnetic envelope around the ship. What happened we may never fully know.

Wild rumors and unproved claims indicate that the ship used, the USS Eldridge, disappeared from the harbor in Philadelphia in 1943. When it reappeared many crewman were burned with radioactive burns, disappeared or were imbedded into the very hull of the ship. A Science fiction movie was made according to these rumors called *The Philadelphia Experiment* produced by *John Carpenter* in 1984 distributed by Columbia Pictures.

It was also claimed that the ship actually slipped into a time warp and linked up with another experiment performed in 1984 at Montauk, New York by one of the remaining project's scientist, John Von Newman and former Nazi scientists. What we do know is that Tesla was involved with this top-secret project. He had become concerned with the dangers of the project and became confrontational, resulting in his dismissal. Shortly thereafter, Tesla died in his apartment of "natural means." Being elderly, it may have been so.

However, the fact that upon his death in 1943, the Department of Alien Acquisitions confiscated all of his inventions and locked them up in a United States Government vault without explanation. This was a highly suspicious act, as Tesla had become a citizen of the U.S. making this seizure illegal. Tesla's patents however are a matter of public record. Through the Freedom of Information Act, we know of his research and development in the areas of Electro-magnetic, Anti-gravity devices. His claim of receiving this knowledge from "Aliens" adds to a consistent pattern of occult connections to those developing this kind of technology.

Wilhelm Reich, another fringe scientist with occult connections was also a part of the Rainbow project. His understanding of what he called "Orgone" was a free energy source of electro-magnetic power, which like a grid over the earth could be "tapped into" and utilized. As a part of his somewhat eccentric beliefs, some of his ideas included Hindu Tantric sexual practices. This got him into trouble, and jail. These troubles seemed to appear only after the government obtained their needed understanding of his theories. In jail he committed "suicide". Upon his death, the U.S. government seized his lab, notes, experiments, and inventions.

The recent project, H.A.A.R.P. is a product of some of Reich's and Tesla's theories, along with the late Viktor Schauberger with his son allegedly assisting. Other than denial, there is no official position by the government about project Rainbow.

Government officials lately have offered a suggestion that the USS Eldridge was in the Philadelphia Harbor for a routine de-glossing process. This is the de-magnetizing of the ships metal hull making it harder for magnetic mines to lock on as a target. During WWII this was a rather routine and regular practice. This certainly would not require a "Project Rainbow" with a staff, including such top scientists like Tesla and Reich. These two combined on any project would tell you something out of the ordinary was taking place. The government's seizure of personal property, denial, or lame excuses when confronted, screams of a cover-up.

Most recently, Unsolved Mysteries featured the disappearance of a former rock band member of Iron Butterfly turned scientist. He graduated with honors and became a pioneer in communications for the government. It is claimed he created a mathematical formula to project radio waves faster than light speed. Before he disappeared, he phoned family and friends in what appeared to be a last good-bye. In less than a year from the airing of the show his body was found in his crumpled up van in the bottom of a ravine. His death was declared a "suicide".

This may be a coincidence or it may be a very familiar pattern. This pattern existed within the early history of UFO investigations. Dr. James E. McDonald and Morris K. Jessup are among others who made a connection to Nazis and/or dimensional time travel with UFOs and then "committed suicide". Their specific findings were never released to the public. There is a paper trail of many deaths related to what many believe is this suppressed technology.

I believe this trail for the U.S. was not so forthcoming in creating our own disk technology from gleaned leftovers. All we found was the "leftovers". Our entire space program however was the most visible result of Paperclip. On the more unorthodox discoveries, there is much controversy by skeptics and ardent believers of the E.T. origin.

The Nazi Saucer Scientist/Engineer Controversy

There has been a growing controversy over some of the claims made by authors/researchers on the subject of Nazi UFO's. A very well written paper attempting to debunk this whole topic has been made by Kevin McClure. It is well worth looking at to round out your quest for knowledge. Here is his web address: http://www.magonia.demon.co.uk/news/reviews/kevinindex.htm.

He sights some inconsistencies, embellished stories and the lack of tangible evidence to support his skepticism. Included in his information, is a full spectrum of other debunking subjects including alien abductions. He is in a sense a typical debunker of the supernatural but a clear thinker and presents his argument very well. However in spite of his claims, many which I believe are valid, he leaves out some other very relative and important information. Even if all the claims were true as he states, there still remains enough substantial evidence that something more in the way of circular craft and alternate energy sources were in fact being experimented on by the Nazis. This then still asks the question, " where did they go"?

SS General Hans Kammaler was the highest military official overseeing the entire alternate propulsion and aircraft research and development including the Saucer, Missile, Jet and Atomic programs. At war's end a clearly fake death was created but he was never sought after. Even Simon Wiesenthal's organization of Nazi hunters did not search for him. He just disappeared like many other personnel connected to this research.

Author *Henry Stevens* in his book, *Hitler's Flying Saucers published* by Adventures Unlimited Co 2003, sites the paper trail of these scientists and engineers. These were real people who had published real papers and books claiming their unorthodox theories and projects in various German and Austrian Universities. Nazi documents of military assignments to specific locations and work project teams combined with others, further confirm this kind of development. Stevens provides convincing documentation to also support these claims. With the additional evidence of captured circular craft powered by conventional means at the wars end, there is too much circumstantial evidence to just claim that this was a failed attempt and the end of the trail. As we follow a possible trail further I hope to show you otherwise.

We did make an attempt to develop some of the more conventional Nazi technology without success. (The Avro car and the flying Pancake are examples). I believe all we discovered was the left over junk of early development and failures. The scientists we obtained were probably the ones who were not successful or incomplete in their projects and deemed expendable by the fleeing Nazis.

The inconsistent stories from captured or acquired scientists and engineers from Paperclip can be easily explained like this: You are a highly paid specialist working on a project with a secure government contract, life is good. Suddenly your boss kills himself, there is a walk out from all the employees at the factory and a new company is in the process of a hostile take over. They are only looking to acquire key people to continue business. Embellishing your resume, you struggle to make yourself that key person (which you know you are not) and try to secure continued employment. A feeding frenzy for survival becomes the normal behavior of these surviving "leftovers" These inconsistencies then are just what anyone would expect.

Skeptics would like to make this the total rational end of Nazi UFOs. Many believe that the US now leads in the further development of our own craft. However there is another trail that has no tangible proof, only rumors. In spite of that there are suspicious actions and a few mysteries that create circumstantial evidence. My proof in believing in this trail comes from the Bible. I will now bring this all together to show the possibility of this other trail.

Part Six

Missing Mysteries

The Fleeing 3rd Reich and the Flight of the Technology of Flight: The trail South

It has been reported that over 2,000 SS officers disappeared; over 200 of the latest Model 21 submarines were not in their pens when the Allies overran Germany. They were never found. This model had a snorkel that enabled them to stay underwater undetected for long distances while charging batteries and replenishing the air supply. It was possible that a cross Atlantic trip to the South Pole could be made unnoticed. Admiral Donetz commented to submarine students at the German Naval academy,

> *"if the war takes a turn for the worse, a safe harbor has already been prepared."*

Did he have Neu-Schwabenland in mind when he said that? At the end of World War II, over 200,000 German citizens were unaccounted for. Many were conscripted Ukrainian women meeting Aryan requirements for breeding with SS men. This figure already accounted for internment deaths, POWs and MIAs. The Germans were articulate in record keeping. The entire German Reichstag Bank disappeared! *Guinness Book of World Records* states this as being the largest unsolved bank heist in history. All of these mysterious loose ends appear to indicate an evacuation and relocation of an entire Government. Retreat to fight another day or maybe you won't have to fight by using a different strategy.

Antarctica: Secret Nazi Base 211 and the opening to a Hollow Earth?

Soon after Hitler came into power the expedition and partitioning of an area of the Antarctic was claimed by the Nazi's and renamed Neu-Schwabenland. Their enemies or their fellow countrymen never understood these actions and occult motivations. Throughout the war submarines continued bringing equipment, supplies and men to this area. Submarines that were captured in southern areas possibly in route to the Antarctic were reported to have as many as 50 people in them compared with what was normally an 8-10 person crew. It has been speculated that an underground complex was built. From operation Redoubt, (The tunneling and placement of a huge underground complex in the Swiss Alps.) We do know the technology was there. Gleaning technology from captured Nazi equipment the United States developed our own Iron Mountain complex. Part of Nazi ideology included Dr. Horbiger's eternal ice theory. He claimed that the true Aryan peoples belonged in a much colder climate and would thrive there. Hitler's goal was to section off a portion of land for an Aryan Empire. This empire was to be an example for the rest of the world to follow and desire. In keeping with these ideas, the Antarctic may well of been chosen for this purpose. They believed also that Thule the true Aryan capital was located from an entrance point somewhere in the North Pole. Believing that a reversal of polarity took place in our past, the Antarctic would now be the logical location and entrance to this mythical inner world. There is a prophetic text of scripture that would indicate these events are a part of end time fulfillment. The prophet Amos declared,

> **"Though they dig into hell, from there my hand shall take them; though they climb up to heaven, from there I will bring them down;"**
> **Amos 9:2**

In context the Nazis are now fugitives, fleeing God's judgment. There is every reason to understand this as a literal prophecy and not some allegorical statement. We will look further at this text later for now it is important to see movement in two directions: Heaven (space/time) and hell (an inner earth). "Why would anyone desire to dig into hell?", you might ask. If you believed some of the ideas of Bulwer-Lytton and Blavatski you would desire to dig into this area in search of allies. In the mind set of the Nazi's Theosophical ideas, they believed themselves to be the diluted genetic strain of a subterranean super race, which held the power of Vril. Their goal was to form an alliance with their underground "brothers" obtain the knowledge of the Vril to form new super weapons and lead the World into a New Age for the Aryan. At the same time by the elimination of the other races they would regain their Psychic powers. They did act seriously upon these crazy sounding beliefs by securing a portion of the Antarctic, and perhaps attempting to "dig" into the earth in search of allies, they actually found them! Hardly an overt desired action, to dig into hell, but by accident the end result may well have accomplished just that.

An Unholy Alliance?

Here is the full text from Amos:

> **"Though they dig into hell, from there my hand shall take them; though they climb up to heaven, from there I will bring them down; though they hide themselves in the top of Carmel, I will search and take them out thence; and though they hide from My sight at the bottom of the sea, from there I will command the serpent, and he shall bite them;"**
> **Amos 9:2-3 KJV**

Traditionally, it has been said that this text is only figuratively speaking about extremes in heights and depths that are impossible for man to actually achieve. However, the possibility exists that it is a literal prophecy of a future even. The details of sending the serpent to bite at them remove the figurative language, making it very literal.

Notice that if taken literally, these fugitive people are headed in two directions. They dig into hell, and hide themselves at the bottom of the sea, which means the abyss or a subterranean domain. They also ascend into heaven. It does not say they try or make an attempt. They do it! Even then God is in control and will eventually bring them down. A point made is the fact that they accomplish both tasks for a time.

No other time in the history of mankind could anyone fulfill or even desire to fulfill this prophecy except the Nazis. Ascending into heaven is more than a space program, as we have already come to understand. It is the ability to travel inter-dimensionally through time from the eternal to the linear.

In the Hollow Earth section, You will find the scriptural evidence for a literal hollow earth. Job describes this hollow earth, with openings at the poles now covered over as a stone on top by the polar ice caps. One is covered until the end of time but the other is "broken into". This text could be the Biblical evidence of the Nazi escape into an inner earth via the Antarctic.

Notice that God sends the serpent to bite at them. In Hebrew, the word for "*bite*" also means to **"pay interest on a loan"**. If this verse were describing a literal snake, biting would be the only meaning to make sense. However, the Hebrew word **Nachash** for *serpent*, does not mean a mere snake. The **Nachash** originally meant "an **upright shining creature** with the characteristics of a snake". In the chapter about Grays, you will see a line up with scripture that in five points line up perfectly with the alleged description of the Gray type Alien. In light of this understanding you can see this paying interest on a loan makes a lot of sense. It may suggest that the Nazis are being used or allowed by God to play a part in an alliance with the serpent. This paying interest is the willingness of the Grays (fallen Angels) to apply their own agenda and technologies to the Nazis for their own ends. This alliance is none other than the prophesized one mentioned in the Bible and the Book of Enoch between man and fallen angels!

Past translators could never have understood this text of scripture until events begin to line up with the original selected wording. This is a pretty accurate description of what happened right after WWII. Laughed at rumors and wild sounding claims may have a Biblical reference to their realties in this text of scripture alone.

From Overt War to Covert Infiltration:

After suffering such a great loss from WWII, the new strategy would be to retreat to a fortress of defense and utilize what you do have to change your enemy from within. With a personal relationship and alliance with the forces of darkness a position of superior strength is made believable to your enemy perhaps by staging a "crash" to get their attention. Then follow up soon after with random UFO sightings and "Alien" encounters. Their warnings and messages turn a political philosophy into a religious movement within the very camp of your former enemy. These surrounding events leading up to the first recorded UFO crash and retrieval becomes a milestone of deception and infiltration. It also answers the question Why Roswell?

Next let's take a look at the Roswell event and perhaps look at it from what our highest level of Military and Intelligence officials might have perceived. I believe Roswell was no accident it was part of a long patient plan!

Chapter Four
Why Roswell?

Part one

The Crash Story

The Roswell story of a crashed UFO has been one of much controversy and very difficult to sort out. Some of the problems creating this unclear picture are embellished stories, details with no conclusive evidence, deliberate false information proclaimed for personal gain by unscrupulous researchers and individuals seeking fame and fortune, and a large amount of disinformation distributed by our own government. To add to this, over fifty years have now gone by with most first hand witnesses deceased. Debunkers and the news media make the whole subject something on the lunatic fringe.

Yet in spite of these difficulties there does remain enough evidence that something out of the ordinary happened near Roswell in1947. In this account, I have stuck to details and the very basic elements that have survived most of the controversy and included details that are debatable for your awareness. My personal thanks goes to the aid of Dr.Stanton Freedman himself who offers the best first hand witness to this whole event

Wednesday, July 2nd 1947 Mr. and Mrs. Dan Wilmut sighted an oval shaped UFO flying overhead near Roswell New Mexico. Later that day William Woody and his father spotted a bright object with a red trail northwest of Roswell. At the same time of the Woody-sighting Mac Brazel, a rancher near Roswell New Mexico heard a loud explosion occurring out on his ranch. On July 3rd Brazel discovered the debris of an unusual wreckage on his ranch. Motivated by a reward for physical evidence verifying the existence of flying saucers, Brazel delivered some of the wreckage to Chaves County sheriff George Wilcox. Wilcox immediately contacted the Intelligence Office at Roswell RAAF.

Major Jesse Marcel, Intelligence Officer of the 509 Bombardment Group of the Army Air Corps (the only Atomic bomber wing in the US, based in Roswell), was sent with a CIC agent named

Cavett by the base commander Colonel Blanchard to check out the rancher's story on July 6. The Roswell Daily Record quoted Public Relations Officer Lt. Walter Haut, at Roswell RAAF:

"... the Intelligence Office was fortunate enough to gain possession of a disc thru the cooperation of one of the local ranchers and the sheriffs office of Chaves County"

On his way back to the base, Major Marcel took a few examples of the debris with him. He stopped by his home to show his family the debris. July 7th Wreckage debris is brought back to RAAF by the military. Following the announcement of the discovery the official account takes a sudden turn with the military going into full damage control to discount the story. July 8th The next highest chain of command to the local military authority in Roswell was General Ramey of Ft. Worth Texas the commanding officer of the entire 8 Army Air Core. He put an abrupt stop to the Flying Saucer story. Major Marcel is sent to Ft Worth and brought out before the press to reveal broken pieces of a weather balloon as Gen. Ramey explains away the original Headline story of the flying saucer as that of a "weather balloon". A retraction was also printed in the Roswell Daily Record on the 8th. In addition to the retraction, many other eyewitnesses were silenced with intimidating threats.

It wasn't until almost thirty years later Major Marcel, decided to end his silence. Major Marcel granted an interview with Physicist/ UFO investigator Stanton Friedman, whereupon Major Marcel stuck to the original story. Now the word is out and the public is aware that something indeed happened at Roswell in 1947. Other Roswell residents and military personnel also come forth, offering their accounts of the Roswell crashes. Eyewitnesses describe the wrecked flying vehicles shaped similar to our modern day SR-71 as well as seeing the remains of small gray bodies found at the sites. The local mortician in Roswell, Glenn Dennis, tells of a request by the Army base for child-sized coffins. Enlisted men recall transporting many large crates to Wright Patterson AAB. This base was known for back engineering foreign captured technologies. Pieced together, the collaborating eyewitness accounts add up to a story truly out of the ordinary. Years later, Retired General Thomas Deboise, second in command to Gen. Ramey, admits the weather balloon story was a cover and that the Roswell incident was given an above Top Secret classification. Despite the wide variety of theories that have evolved, the only thing for certain is that there was a cover up of an extraordinary event.

Throughout the Roswell incident, our government made every attempt to cover up the crash and to silence witnesses. Was this an attempt to conceal a secret technology from competing world powers, as some believe? Was it really Aliens who had an accident? Or was this part of a plan to undermine The United States of America at the highest level?

We have already understood that the United States was well aware of a possible possession of flying disc technology by the Nazis. As the world celebrated victory over the Axis Powers, the U.S. government had a guarded concern about Nazi Germany and what was already missing at the wars end. Based on intelligence gathered by the OSS, the US was well aware of the Nazi's Occult beliefs and the trail they pursued. Evidence alluded to the possibility of a massed colonization taking place from Germany to the Antarctic. Now let's back up and briefly review some events our Military and Intelligence officials were pondering just prior to the Roswell Crash

Part Two

A History you were never told; events leading to Roswell 1947.

The following is a series of events that might seem unrelated. They are bits of history that when put together, reveal the fearful background in the minds of our leaders leading up to the Roswell incident. In the early years after World War II, only our military leaders had privy to some of what are now easily documented events.

Summer of 1943: Project Rainbow was a government backed experiment that included Scientists, John Von Newman, Nicola Tesla, and Wilhelm Reich. Albert Einstein was also used as a consultant. Tesla's coils and Reich's understanding of "Orgone" were a part of this project. The Rainbow project involved the creation of intense electromagnetic fields and something went very wrong. This failed project was perhaps the first experience the US had that was similar to the later German research they would soon discover.

Winter-1944: While flying bombing sorties over Germany, Allied bomber pilots sight "Foo Fighters", which they described as small shiny glowing objects. The "Foo Fighters" were able to match the flight path of the bombers while disrupting the planes electronics and navigational systems. Furthermore they were capable of responding to sudden changes in flight patterns as well as attempts to shoot them down. Since they made no aggressive attacks they are only met with curiosity.

April, May-1945: Dr. Werner Von Braun (creator of the V-1 and V-2 rockets) along with the majority of his team of scientists from the Peenemunde missile complex surrender to American forces to avoid capture by the Russians. The relinquishment of this team whets the appetite for America to develop their own missile and jet programs.

June-1945: American forces enter the huge underground complexes at Nordhausen in the Alps. They capture V-1, V-2 and prototype V-4 rockets. Many experimental aircraft are discovered, including disk, and triangular craft. All featured either piston or jet powered forms of propulsion. Allegations have been made about the discovery of blueprints and documents describing an anti-gravity propulsion unit as well as plans for the peacetime exploration of space. At the same time, over 200 of the newest model 21 submarines are missing from their pens. The entire German Bank was missing! (*Guinness Book of World Records* lists this as the largest unsolved bank heist in history!) Over 2,000 Nazi scientists were missing and almost 200,00 people from the general population were never found. This figure did not included war dead, POW's and MIA's already accurately recorded and accounted for.

Fall of 1945: SS General Reinhard Gehlen, head of Nazi Intelligence-Eastern Division, surrenders to the Americans. He "cuts" a deal to pardon both himself and his staff in exchange for Nazi intelligence accumulated on the Russians.

The information garnered on the Russians, as well as the discovery of unknown research projects under development by the Nazis makes a profound impression on U.S. intelligence. With a desire to emulate Nazi intelligence and security, Reinhard Gehlen is enlisted to create the same operational system for the US. This results with the OSS evolving into the CIA. Part of this transition includes the release of hundreds of Nazi war criminals into America, posing as free citizens and operators in our own national infrastructure.

Late 1945: Following the surrender of Germany, U-boats U977 and U530 surrender to neutral Argentina. The U.S. sends a commission of high-ranking officers to investigate the acquiescence of the submarines. Both Captains were held in custody for two years and questioned about the whereabouts of Martin Borman, the body of Hitler, as well as a possible location of the last bastions of Nazis somewhere in the Antarctic. The commander of U977 Captain Heinz Schaeffer, was familiar with the Hartz Mountain complexes; the model 21 subs and had experience with patrolling the Antarctic. Following the grilling by the U.S. commission, Schaeffer was given over to the British for further interrogation.

December 1945 A squadron of Trainer planes disappears over what is to later become known as the "Devils Triangle". The planes that got "lost" somewhere off the Florida coast reported the same navigational disruptions that effected Allied bombers over Europe.

Late 1945,46 and 47: From the discovery of undetected and unknown technology that the Germans were working on, a race began to procure the scientists, engineers and remnants of projects and related paperwork. Russia, England and the United States comb Europe and South America. Projects Sunrise, Lusty and Paperclip pardon many Nazi Scientists and engineers, granting many American citizenship and positions of authority. In 1947 most are stationed at White Sands testing grounds or next door in Roswell New Mexico. To supplement their income they were encouraged to teach at many of our Universities.

Spring 1947 During a flight over Mt. Rainier businessman and private pilot Kenneth Arnold sights "Flying Saucers" flying in formation. The official term "Flying Saucers" is coined from this event. U.S. intelligence officials, with knowledge gained from captured Nazi documents showing similar craft, had to wonder if the sighted objects were not operational versions of the drawings.

February 1947: Operation High jump, a major expedition to the Antarctic, is set in motion. Admiral Byrd, our only expert on the Antarctic, commands the expedition. The convoy is equipped with 13 ships including an aircraft carrier, two PBY reconnaissance planes and 4,000 ground troops. There is not one special research ship among them. The entire convoy consisted of typical military support ships for combat readiness. The public is told that this was a scientific expedition to "test" military equipment in extreme cold conditions; the expedition is outfitted for 8 months. This would not seem unusual except that the expedition maneuvered like a military assault. They made a two-point landing converging on the area named "Neu-Schwabenland" by the Nazis. The expedition returns to America a few weeks later after suffering heavy losses of equipment. A Chilean newspaper announced a ship to shore conversation with Byrd who warned that in the future we would have to contend with aircraft that could fly pole to pole in a matter on minutes. Washington censures Admiral Byrd to be silent about the failed operation when they return. Like Roswell, a cover up ensues with only rumors and myths to follow.

July 3rd, 1947: The wreckage of the now famous Roswell crash is discovered and then covered up by the U.S. Military. Mixed signals from the military indicate the lack of any foreknowledge by our government officials. The fact that it was days before Brazel reported the debris, and there were no Government actions taken until it was made public, indicates that this was not our own failed research. An obvious contingency plan would have tracked and extracted the crash before it ever hit the press as was the case in Kecksburg Pa. The U.S. was taken completely by surprise!

Until the crash, the minds of U.S. intelligence were fixed on finding the Nazis and their amazing technology. However, now because of the crash at Roswell, the U.S. Government is aware of a possible alliance between the Nazi's and "Reptilian Gray aliens". Our Military believed they now faced a horror bigger than they could ever have imagined. This fearful position could have made them reconsider everything, including opposing the fleeing enemy who now appear to have the upper hand! A willingness to negotiate the best favorable terms for our own interests may have resulted due to the Roswell crash.

A select few aware of these facts may have started the trend to reprogram the American people toward a theosophical world view. This change of world view would help the public to eventually accept an alien presence while denying everything at the same time. A dualistic plan of "plausible deniability" becomes the game to be played out on the public. I do not think any of the U.S. officials ever considered that they were actually dealing with an unholy alliance of fallen angels.

1952: Following Operation High jump Admiral Byrd became a major proponent to establish the Antarctic as a nuclear test zone. In 1952 a bill was on the Senate floor to establish this site. Weeks before the vote, the Capitol was buzzed by many UFOs flying in a typical German formation. As interceptors were dispatched to confront them they simply "blinked" out. Once the jets returned to their bases, the UFOs reappeared. This happened several times the same day. Shortly after this event the bill was dropped from the Senate floor. This presence may have caused a stalemate between the powers of the US and the Last Bastion of Nazis in the Antarctic.

Part Three

Striking Horror into your Enemy!

Equipped with these facts, look into the minds of our leaders. You may begin to understand the fear that must have gripped their minds as they pondered these events.

1. From our own failed experiments we understood at least in principle, the reality of electro-magnetic anti gravity "occult either physics". This was something long rejected by the western world.

2. We aggressively searched for the Nazi technology and experts involved through Operation Paperclip. We found some, others were taken by allies, and others are still missing.

3. From captured Nazi drawings and prints, we knew that the recent reported "Flying Saucer" sightings resembled these prints.

4. We understood the possible Antarctic last bastion hold out of Nazis in exile as a possible colony. We tried and couldn't stop them.

5. Now, after Roswell, we think we now know why, The Nazi's were aligned with "Aliens"

Did this event cause a willingness to negotiate and compromise our previous position as the total victors of World War II? Did our very Judeo-Christian faith and western world-view begin to crumble in the minds of our leaders? Did they feel they had to re-educate and prepare us as a nation for this reality of a change? Did this begin to impact our educational systems, our news media and every faucet of our society? History would indicate yes. In the following years things began to change drastically in America. Infiltration was already taking place on two fronts from Operation paperclip and the Roswell incident.

Nazi UFOs become Alien Aircraft: The Transformation Begins

In the early 50's, the trail of Nazi UFOs and its occupants, Gray and Nordic, continued to appear throughout the World and in particular, America. This interconnectedness cannot be written off as mere coincidence. UFO Contactees were people who claimed to have encountered UFOs and their occupants. Unlike the later abductees, the Contactees retained the full memory of their experience. The Contactees of the 50's reported the occupants as tall with blond hair, blue eyed Caucasians. Their crafts matched the plans discovered at the Nordhausen complex. They often were heard speaking German or English with a heavy German accent. The warnings and messages were of a global theosophical outlook

The first "lost time" abduction experience of Barney and Betty Hill occurred in the early 60's. Barney identified a "Captain" with the little Grays. While under hypnosis he is asked why he can identify one of the occupants as a Captain. Barney responds because of his hat and uniform, and then in a panicked voice, as if he suddenly recognizes his captor he cries out, "He's a Nazi!" These events clearly implicate Nazi German technology as a product of an alliance with the occult. To the open minded objective investigator, it also indicates that this Nazi trail of UFOs does not end with the junk leftovers found at wars end. These events only reveal a continuation of developed technology and a change of tactics to "change the hearts and minds" of their enemies from within and meet their final objective, A New World Order! We will learn more details in the Alien section.

Closing thoughts on Man Made UFOs

The UFO Crashes

Why are there so many UFO crashes? We started getting reports shortly after WWII beginning in 1947 at Roswell through the mid 60s, with Kecksburg being one of the more recent. Are we to believe that these craft come light years across the span of space to our little planet, only to crash in a desert? Are these crashes from a disruption of simple radar, as one writer reported, or not paying attention to the terrain and pounding into a dirt mound as reported by another?

Stan Deyo, author of *The Cosmic Conspiracy*, Adventures Unlimited 1994, points out that UFOs from the nineteen-fifties look like the styles of the fifties, while flying saucers of the nineteen-eighties look like the style of the eighties. I might add the latest, greatest being the new triangle type of the nineties. Are we to believe that "Aliens" are defining their technologies to the present cultural styles of earth? And every decade they continue to develop? Does not the evidence strongly suggest that these are earthbound craft in a progressive research and development process in keeping with other developed craft, with occasional crashes?

Rumors of underground bases jointly manned by "Aliens" and humans working on human genetic hybridization with "aliens" and development of our own anti-gravity aircraft may not be unfounded. Now if "Aliens" have fully developed craft able to skip across the universe, why don't they just give us a blueprint, some material or formulas and let us have at it. There would be no development necessary, as the technology is already there, is it not? No, based on circumstantial evidence there is a development of technology being performed that is earthbound.

So Why Does the US have Rockets?

The final thing to ask is, if United States is developing such craft, why have rockets and a space program as we have now? Two reasons perhaps. One, it would be a good way to have a smoke screen. The other is that now Satan and his Angels are cast down to this planet. This grid makes for a fast time traveling, dazzling, and performing object in this earthly sphere. But it might be locked into this atmosphere. That could be why the Bible says Satan is the prince and power of the air.

We have discussed the complete story of the Flying Saucer as the Lying Sign. In a very physical sense, an occult based development of real technology to imitate the inter-dimensional travel of God and angelic orders, i.e. the ability to "ascend into heaven". \

The Lying wonders which accompany the signs are the moral and ethical messages proclaimed by the occupants of the flying saucer which in various forms is Theosophy. This message and its infiltration into our society is what we shall look at next. To make a proper connection, much of this understanding center on understanding our enemy and the closing events at the end of WWII. How we understand this in light of Bible Prophecy will determine our ability to understand other major events surrounding UFOs.

Chapter Five
Hitler and WWII in the Bible?

Part One

Wars and Rumors of Wars

No other time in the known history of mankind has there been such turbulence than in the 20th century. Having two major world wars and a tense period of a "Cold War" for half a century, this could be what Jesus meant when he stated,

> **"And ye shall hear of wars and rumors of wars: see that ye be not troubled: for all these things must come to pass, but the end is not yet.**
> **Matt 24:6**

The War in a Nutshell?

The next text of scripture accurately describes the European Theater of WWII.

> **" But he shall have power over the treasures of gold and of silver, and over all the precious things of Egypt: and the Libyans and the Ethiopians shall be at his steps.(battle of El Alamein stopped the African campaign right here!) 44 But tidings out of the east (Russian front) and out of the north (Normandy D-Day Invasion) shall trouble him: therefore he shall go forth with great fury to destroy, and utterly to make away many. (Hitler's Scorched earth policy) 45 And he shall plant the tabernacles of his palace between the seas in the glorious holy mountain;(The US not Israel!) yet he shall come to his end, and none shall help him. (Accomplished April 30th 1945 in a bunker in Berlin)**
> **Dan 11:43-45 43**

Much of this text is not understood because of the term **"Holy Mountain of God."** Most scholars agree this is either Mt. Zion or Jerusalem in Israel. There is however a "New Testament" definition that can also be applied. The word **"Mountain"** can signify a fortification or kingdom, which is a typical Biblical symbolic use. Mt. Zion is interchangeable with Holy Mountain and referred to as Jerusalem, the tribe of Judah (Ps78:68) and anywhere the people of God are congregated.(Ps74:2)

In New Testament terms this could be the United States a Nation where Christians have congregated! This concept with many scriptures to support this idea is discussed further in the America in Prophecy chapter. For now it is only important to realize that because of this miss-identification of the "holy mountain of God", this text about WWII has gone undetected for what it is saying.

When this military leader (Hitler) comes to "his end", The *"tabernacle of his palace"* is taken to a place between the seas. Mt Zion as Jerusalem is not between seas, America as a New Testament Zion, is. Tabernacle can mean a "tent" in its broadest use but also means "the body or inhabitants within the tent". In this sense, the Palace represents the very seat of Nazi authority and kingdom. The inhabitants of his kingdom that made him strong would be the creators of "secret knowledge" and the keepers of this "secret knowledge." These inhabitants would be the Scientists/Engineers and the Intelligence operatives that helped make Nazi Germany rise to its power.

Therefore Daniel 11:44,45 describes Operation Paperclip which relocated the Nazi scientists and engineers to Roswell, New Mexico as well as the Nazi intelligence officers through the Gehlen agreement. This idea is also cross-referenced by the prophet Amos:

"though they hide themselves in the top of Carmel, I will search and take them out thence;

In Old Testament times Carmel would usually mean Mt. Carmel in Israel. However if this is in fact a prophetic word pertaining to the future, A New Testament interpretive value could be placed upon Carmel. Carmel means a "garden land" or "a planted land to produce fruit". As you will see in the America in Prophecy section, this could be in reference to America as the gathering place for the seed of Jacob. (The lost ten tribes). If Carmel can mean a nation whose role is this "garden land" to produce the fruit of the Gospel of Christ, this is a fulfillment of the prophetic promise Jesus mentioned in Matthew 21:

> **"Therefore say I unto you, The kingdom of God shall be taken from you, and given to a nation bringing forth the fruits thereof."**
> **Matt 21:43 (KJV)**

I am not a believer of "replacement theology". This kind of New Testament interpretive value only explains prophetic texts for the "time of the gentiles" There will be a time when everything returns to Israel including the promises and God's grace, but that will be when Israel as a nation accepts her Messiah Jesus Christ.

In the original languages this "hiding" is forced as if a fugitive. It also can mean hiding by blending in. Where do they hide? At the top, this top in context here can refer to a preferred esteemed position in society! If Amos was speaking of a literal end time prophecy using New Testament interpretive values, we then have an accurate account of fugitives fleeing in two directions. One group hides in a fortress of defense underground, (as stated before) the other group blends into the highest levels of society in the "garden land" and tries to reach into heaven. This text could describe Operation Paperclip, the merging of many Nazi Scientists/ Engineers and Security officials into the US. The NASA space program and other special black operative programs gleaned from the Nazis, results in "reaching into heaven". Once again the line up is more than a coincidence.

The other implication to Daniel 12 is that this military leader Adolf Hitler was the Antichrist. This always gets people in a stir. I will mention this more later. Try not to assume too much yet.

Part Two

Beast Empires of Daniel: The Nations of WWII

In this section of Daniel, only one Aramaic word is used to describe "Beast". In this context the Beasts are Nations. There is a man called a "little horn" by Daniel and John in Revelation calls the same a "beast". This same event in Daniel, cross-referenced with Rev 13 and 17 however, has three different Greek words used for Beast. Described are both nations and a man. It is important to see this overlapping of scriptures in order to get a full description of just who is involved.

"... I saw in my vision by night, and, behold, the four winds of the heaven strove upon the great sea. And four great beasts came up from the sea, diverse one from another".

Dan 7:2-8

1. "...The first was like a lion, and had eagle's wings: I beheld till the wings thereof were plucked, and it was lifted up from the earth, and made stand upon the feet as a man, and a man's heart was given to it.

2. "And behold another beast, a second, like to a bear, and it raised up itself on one side, and it had three ribs in the mouth of it between the teeth of it: and they said thus unto it, Arise, devour much flesh."

3. After this I beheld, and lo another, like a leopard, which had upon the back of it four wings of a fowl; the beast had also four heads; and dominion was given to it.

4a (The Kingdom) After this I saw in the night visions, and behold a fourth beast, dreadful and terrible, and strong exceedingly; and it had great iron teeth: it devoured and brake in pieces, and stamped the residue with the feet of it: and it was diverse from all the beasts that were before it; and it had ten horns.

4b (The Man) I considered the horns, and, behold, there came up among them another little horn, before whom there were three of the first horns plucked up by the roots: and, behold, in this horn were eyes like the eyes of man, and a mouth speaking great things.

Revelation 13 describes an overlapping description of the last beast empire. It further defines this last empire so we need to include this.

"And the beast which I saw was like unto a leopard, and his feet of a bear, and his mouth as the mouth of a lion: and the dragon gave him his power, and his seat, and great authority."

Revelations 13:2

Traditionally, this text has been taught to be four Kingdoms following the Babylonian Empire and is rightfully explained as such in the scriptures. However there is enough evidence to indicate that a much later interpretation could and should be applied under the rule of duplicity. In context, this is a last day scenario, which would include last day kingdoms. Typical of many of the Prophets, is a twofold message addressing the present and then trailing off to a future prophetic one. A couple of examples are; Isaiah in addressing the King of Babylon, who then addresses Satan, and Ezekiel addressing the King of Tyre, speaks to Satan. Jeremiah speaking of Historical Babylon trails off to speak to a future Babylon in a figurative sense. In keeping in this same pattern we find the overlap describes the powers of WWII!:

1. England/ United States:

The Lion has always been symbolic of England. The wings of the eagle are symbolic as the United States breaking away from English rule. After this separation, England develops a doctrine called British Israelism.

This was a doctrine whereby England saw herself as a modern day "Spiritual Israel." The doctrine claims that the lost ten tribes of Israel made their home in England. They became the "New Testament" chosen people to convert the rest of the world to Christianity.

Unfortunately, powerful greedy people used this excuse to justify the huge expansionism of the Imperialistic British Empire. Much of the "conversion" was to a British cultural standard with the elimination of the "host" countries culture. Many of these countries were defenseless third world nations and the "Good News" of this kingdom was forced upon them with no choice in the matter.

The end result was a distorted image of Christ and distaste for "Christianity". This all happened after the independence of America. These "Heavenly ideas" were motivated by human ways with a human heart, which the Bible further defines as deceitfully wicked. (Jer17:9)

In this human minded attempt to do the work of God, good intentions turn to bad results. This doctrine has recently been further distorted and adopted by Neo-Nazi and other survival groups to suggest that the Caucasians of Anglo decent are the "chosen" people of God with America playing the spiritual role of Israel. This is a false doctrine with a wrong premise and conclusion having some elements of truth sandwiched in between. We will address this further in the America in prophecy chapter.

2. Russia

The bear has long been the symbol of Russia. Notice that the bear lifts itself up on one side. God does not do the lifting but she raises herself on one side. This could be symbolic of the extreme leftist doctrine of Godless Communism and the raising of Russia to a world power by it.

There are three ribs in her mouth. The unusual aspect of this is the appearance of the vulnerability of the three ribs in the bear's mouth and yet they are dictating to the bear what to do! Ribs could be referring to the fact that as Eve was taken out of the rib of Adam, these three are connected or a part of the bear itself. This could imply a genetic connection. There has been much speculation that after the fall of Germany in World War II, a pact was made on the highest levels by the allies to secretly develop technology captured at the wars end. Massive funding needed would be provided by staging a "Cold War" that would allow clandestine development without public knowledge. Of course there is no hard evidence for this kind of speculation. A BBC documentary aired in Australia called *Alternative 3* addresses this very idea. After airing once it was pulled from the airwaves. This documentary can be purchased through Adventures Unlimited Books. The sudden "fall" of Russia does create an even more suspicious circumstance to ponder. This text of scripture could indicate that there might be a basis of truth behind such a suggestion.

Suppose these three ribs do share the same heritage and genetic bond as the bear. On the surface they appear to be held at bay by the bear when in fact they are in control. These could be the rest of the Allies, Britain, France and the Untied States. A pretty accurate picture of the post war power structure! The bear is told to go and devour much flesh, which is just what Russia did after World War II.

3. Germany

Germany has been described as the Leopard because of the Blitzkrieg tactics of WWII. There are four wings of a foul upon its back. Foul are birds raised or hunted for food. Wings are suggestive of something in transition or movement. The suggestion could be something nurtured and fostered in Germany that moves and influences to somewhere else. These four wings could line up with the four birds mentioned in Job 39. On the surface, this whole chapter reads like a demented *Animal Planet* commentary that is pointless and makes no sense at all. The animals are totally out of character with their natural state and interacting in nonsensical ways. So what is the point of the whole chapter? Nothing is in scripture without reason or design. Logic would dictate that something more exists here. Job 39 is possibly symbolically defining something prophetic. By going back to the original language and using some of the correct variables for word meanings a very sensible and realistic story unfolds. In brief for our most current references to the fowls in Job 39 we have:

The Hawk which flies to the extreme south (Antarctic) in a position of a defensive fortress with ivory cliffs, could be describing the last bastion of Nazi's relocated in the Antarctic! The Peacock who, as an arrogant aristocrat influences and supplies the Stork with "feathers of flight" may have several types of members. The major corporate backbone of Nazi Germany, now turned Globalist; such as I.G. Farben, Krupp Works and Thyssen Steel may be some of these "Peacocks" that continued on to influence the worlds thinking. Another part of this group would be the Aristocratic European families and American Industrialists that funded and brought into existence the Nazi vehicle. The third and largest group could also be in reference to operation Paperclip and Lusty. The NASA space program can explain the mention of giving "feathers of flight" to the Stork, which was the direct result of Paperclip and Nazi scientists.

The Eagle and the Hawk are the military and technological parts of this "trade". The Ostrich who forgets her young becomes the result of the successful infiltration and influence upon the "Stork" for the price of procuring technology and a new intelligence system.

The four heads of the Leopard are the four stages of power given as four Reich's. Germany, through the Hapsburg's was the controlling and influential part of the Holy Roman Empire for most of its duration starting with the coronation of Otto I in 962, the First Reich.

Kaiser Wilhelm and the Pan German movement of World War 1 being the Second Reich, and of course Adolf Hitler and the Nazi's as the Third Reich. So where is the Fourth Reich? The successful infiltration and clandestine takeover of the United States as a catalyst through the United Nations to produce the "New World Order" there is the fourth Reich.

Dominion was given to the Leopard. Germany has been an invisible hand of power behind the scenes within the Holy Roman Empire from the very beginning. Germany fostered the Illuminati the alleged center of all secret societies. They were part of the fostering of the U.S. and German industrial alliance of merged corporate structures which began at the end of WWI and are still thriving today. Germany's still thriving Occult Nazi regime has turned from a political movement based upon blood and race into a religious movement based on a spiritual perception called "The New Age". All of these connections continue to influence and hold world power and dominion.

The Last Beast Empire of Daniel: U.S./U.N.=New World Order
A Melting Pot of Humanity

Daniel says this last Beast Empire is different from all of the others. Revelation however says that this Empire has characteristics of the other three. It is a composite of the other ones, and yet it is different from the all of them. It is described as dreadful, terrible and strong exceedingly.

Not to sound redundant, we go to the original language to understand these words as meaning, "an object of fear or respect, well equipped, in the sense of being able to supply and reproduce its needs and resources and surpassingly strong and more powerful than anyone else". This nation has the swift power and rapid deployment abilities of the blitzkrieg tactics of Germany. It speaks of a noble intention like Great Britain's Imperialism. It also has the determination to smash opposition and devour much flesh like Russia. The dragon also supernaturally powers it!

Last Empire Receives Supernatural Power

Rumors of back engineering "Alien technology" at places like Area 51, with its beginnings at Roswell might be the actual means of obtaining this "power". This act starting at Roswell is actually more of an opening with a "key" to the bottomless pit. (Rev 9:1) The Greek word for "key" has a consistent Biblical use in a figurative sense as understanding and knowledge. This would make the key something to comprehend! The dragon (represented by Little Grays?) are supplying their power. Perhaps by supplying the Physics from the eternal realm! This would be the enticement to delve further into the depths of Hell itself. (All in the name of science of course.)

In Nebuchadnezzar's dream of the final empires represented by the statue, Daniel further describes this last kingdom also.

> **"And the fourth kingdom...41 "Whereas you saw the feet and toes, partly of potter's clay and partly of iron, the kingdom shall be divided; yet the strength of the iron shall be in it,**
>
> **Dan 2:41**

Daniel says that the kingdom is **divided**. By the original language this implies that there are two phases to this kingdom. They were once at variance with each other. One remains strong and united, the other becomes shattered and broken up, but they become as one in the end. This again describes the infiltration that happened by Nazi Germany into the US. What Nazi Germany started, The United States as a catalyst carries on through the U.N.! The unseen hand behind this kind of transformation is the rich elite Globalists than funded and supported the whole global agenda from the start.

Within this last Kingdom mentioned also is the very strange activity of, **"They shall mingle their seed with men."** This is a genetic hybridization of the human race that happened before the Great Flood that re-appears again within the last empire. All cultures record this "Golden Age" period when god-men walked the earth. Only the Bible mentions that this was a horror. It happens again in this last kingdom but this time without a relationship of marriage. This time it is clinical in a lab, outside the mixing of any relationship in the form of "alien abductions".

Nazi Germany under the direction of Dr. Joseph Megenele began the study and experiments of "Twinning" This was the first modern day attempt to clone the human being and "purify" certain genetic traits. Today the same activity is claimed about "Alien Abductions" with the removal of sperm and eggs, extraction of fetuses that may explain this text of scripture! It all happens within this last empire. The Alien section will cover this thought extensively and completely, I promise. For now let's look at a few scriptures and consider Adolf Hitler. It can make one wonder if cloning could make a dead leader come back to life.

EIGHT EMPIRES of Rev. 17 and Dan 2. Nebuchadnezzar's Dream

1. **EGYPTIAN EMPIRE**

2. **ASSYRIAN EMPIRE {Existing before Nebuchadnezzar's Dream}**

3. **BABYLONIAN Head of Gold 605 - 539BC**

4. **MEDIAN-PERSIAN Breast and Arms of Silver 539 - 331BC**

5. **GRECIAN Belly and thighs of Brass 331 - 168BC**

6. **ROMAN Legs of Iron (2 legs = 2 phases) 168BC - 476AD (Holy Roman Empire) 800AD - 1806**

7. **NAZI (Iron Mixed with Clay Pt 1.) The Scattered: "and when he comes, he must continue a short space." And the beast that was, and is not, even he is the eighth, and is of the seven, and goes into perdition." Rev 17:10,11**

8. **U.N. (U.S. as Controller Pt2) N.W.O. The Strong: " and the ten horns which you saw are ten Kings which have received no kingdom as yet; but received power as Kings one hour with the beast. These have one mind, and shall give their power and strength unto the beast" Rev 17: 12,13 Empires 7 and 8are both the complete Revived Roman Empire in two parts opposed yet ultimately**

the same of Dan 2:41 "And whereas you saw the feet and the toes, part of potters clay, and part of Iron, The Kingdom shall BE DIVIDED...so shall the Kingdom be partly strong and partly broken."

Chapter Six
The Horse and His Rider

Part One

Was/Is Hitler the Antichrist?

The Scriptures mention the spirit of Antichrist and an individual. The many scriptures that are assumed to mention this individual do not bear the title in their context. In the same manner, many scriptures referenced as the coming messiah do not necessarily mention a name or title to that effect but do allude to the coming messiah. What confused the Jews was the fact that these scriptures were describing the same person with two separate appearances. The same pattern may exist for the Antichrist with the same confusion experienced by the Church's lack of identification.

Although the following scriptures I will share with you point to the obvious, I hold to the fact that this is an unconditional prophecy that has much left to be fulfilled. Although I am personally 98% convinced of Hitler being the Antichrist based upon scripture, things could be different. Future unconditional prophecies must always be treated with this kind of caution, allowing for a margin of error and the human factor. I claim no special direct revelations to the personal identity of Hitler being the Antichrist. This is in the "wait and see" folder of my own files. Allowing this possibility does make a lot of other scriptures and events fit into this very complex puzzle.

The aftermath of Hitler is still with us today. The whole New Age movement is the "religious" side of Nazism and a "New Testament" version of Theosophy. Their followers are actually the modern Nazi's of today. This is not a moral judgment on them. Nor do I group these people with the atrocities and hatred of the former political movement which was the "Old Testament version of Theosophy. Nazism had an appeal and looked good at first. It reared the ugly side only after it became widely accepted. Embracing this same philosophy, even as a religion, will only come to the same conclusions, another Final solution.

This spirit of Antichrist is far more important to detect and reveal as we shall see. For now let's look at few scriptures that could describe two separate appearances of the Antichrist.

Part Two

Antichrist in Two Appearances, the Same but Opposite of Christ's Two Appearances?

> **"The beast that you saw was, (alive) and is not, (is dead) and will ascend out of the bottomless pit and go into perdition. And those who dwell on the earth will marvel, whose names are not written in the Book of Life from the foundation of the world, when they see the beast that was, (alive) and is not, (dead) and yet is. (Alive again!) 9. Here is the mind which has wisdom: The seven heads are seven mountains (Kingdoms) on which the woman sits. (false religious system) 10 There are also seven Kings. Five are fallen, one is(Roman Empire) and the other has not yet come. And when he comes, he must continue a short time. (12 year Nazi Empire?) 11. "And the beast that was (alive) and is not, (dead) is himself (signifies a person, not a nation) also the eighth, perdition. (Total destruction.)**
>
> **Rev 17:8-11 NKJ**

According to this scripture, a ruler of one of seven prior empires dies and comes back from the dead. Ascending from out of the bottomless pit, he becomes the ruler of the last 8th empire. Many fearful of the implications that a dead man returns to life, malign the Scriptures to say that it is figuratively speaking of a kingdom i.e. the revived Roman Empire. The descriptions include a first person noun which can only mean an individual person. There is no other way to interpret this text of scripture. Two appearances by one man!

Now let's look at some of the other scriptures that describe this same leader in what I believe describes two appearances.

1st coming

> **"And I saw, and behold a white horse: and he that sat on him had a bow; and a crown was given unto him: and he went forth conquering, and to conquer."**
>
> **Rev 6:2 (KJV)**

1. Conquering and to conquer - A militaristic leader that would make war and conquer peoples and land.

> **And in the latter time of their kingdom, when the transgressors are come to the full, a king of fierce countenance, and understanding dark sentences, shall stand up. 24 And his power shall be mighty, but not by his power: he shall destroy wonderfully, and shall prosper, and practice, and shall destroy the mighty and the holy people.**
>
> **Dan 8:23-24**
> **(KJV study bibles**
> **render this as**
> **"people of the holy ones".)**

2. A fierce Countenance - his very look and presence will radiate with intense emotion

3. Understand "dark sentences."- a workable knowledge of the occult. Literally, this is an understanding a riddle or puzzle so complex that no man could figure it out on their own. This is not just a dabbling in astrology but the ability to extract an applied physics of the eternal realm into our linear one. Much of Hitler's agenda was to restore the people and the technology that existed before the flood. He viewed this as the golden age; others viewed this as the pre-flood world.

4. Destroy wonderfully- A horrific destruction that would always be remembered in history ie WWII and the 50 million left dead.

5. Destroy the holy people- If the popular accepted rendering is correct, "people of the holy ones" is a term that would be used for the Jews sometime after 70AD. This would be a description of their mass execution- the Holocaust. It can be said that Stalin killed more Jews than Hitler. But Stalin killed many different people indiscriminately out of a paranoid fear which even included most of his seasoned military staff. Hitler's extermination of Jews, not understood by historians was not just blind hatred for the Jews. The Theosophical Occult beliefs took social Darwinism to its most logical conclusion, the pragmatic elimination as a sense of survival for the Aryan. Himmler is quoted as stating to the SS camp guards that the disposal of the bodies in ovens was a sacrifice to God!

> **"And I saw one of his heads as it were wounded to death; and his deadly wound was healed: and all the world wondered after the beast."**
> **Rev 13:3 KJV**

6. Deadly head wound healed - It is said that Hitler committed suicide with a bullet wound to the head. This would make him the only world leader of the other six empires who died in this manner during a war. His body was never found.

> **...that they should make an image to the beast, which had the wound by a sword, and did live.**
> **Rev 13:14 KJV**

7. "Wound by a sword" - This does not necessarily mean a literal sword but rather this was a term commonly used to refer to something happening in battle or during a war.

His reappearance at his second coming includes these startling events

2nd coming

> **"Even him, whose coming is after the working of Satan with all power and signs and lying wonders,"**
> **II Th 2:9 (KJV)**

8. Signs- In the Greek, this is always a "supernatural event". Usually some startling sudden presence from the skies! I suppose UFOs could be included in this context!

9. Wonders- In context here, this is an overlapping of the same event. In the Greek it is the "moral or ethical message accompanied with the event that is emphasized". It takes no great imagination to see how this fits the description of UFOs and their messages of hope, promise and warnings.

Scripture Says What it Means, Means What It Says

These are just a few of the Scriptures to describe the Antichrist. Revelation 17 is pretty clear that this is a man, a ruler of one of seven empires, who dies and comes back to lead the final last empire before the return of Christ. This text of scripture removes the argument of a single coming or of different "Antichrists". One guy two times. Same but opposite of what Christ did. He is described as a beast which could indicate a mixed human/fallen angel bloodline or the second appearance as the man of sin, an unnatural re-creation of life a clone possibly. In either case beast is signifying something unnatural.

A Common Myth

A preconceived Church Myth is that of one appearance involving an assignation with a third day resurrection. This is not even alluded to in the scriptures. My challenge to that thought is show me Chapter, text and verse, Where is it? As popular as this idea has become within the Church it is only a speculation relying on no scripture to back it up.

A Dead Leader Comes Back to Life: A Satanic Resurrection?

"Hell from beneath is moved for thee to meet thee at thy coming: it stirs up the dead for thee, even all the chief ones of the earth; it hath raised up from their thrones all the kings of the nations. All they shall speak and say unto thee, Art thou also become weak as we? art thou become like unto us? Thy Pomp is brought down to the grave, and the noise of thy viols: the worm is spread under thee, and the worms cover thee."
Isaiah 14:9-11 (KJV)

This text of scripture is very obscure in its surface understanding but look at what happens by using other correct variables in this text. I have to include that the traditional understanding of this text is that of Satan's fall, (from a pre-Adamic perception). Others see this as the eventual throwing of Satan into the "pit" at the end of the tribulation period and before the 1,000 year earthly rein of Christ.

However, by the specific language used this suggests a life once used up and descending into hell. The idea of two separate appearances of the Antichrist in the same manner as that of Christ is only recently beginning to be understood by the Church. In the book, *The Sign by Robert Van Kampen,* Crossway Books 1992 the author expounds with excellent documentation this very thought with Hitler as a conclusion. Now let's see this scripture using other possible variables from the original languages:

> **"Hell from beneath is excited for you, to meet you at your coming: it wakes up the dead for you, even all the chief ones of the earth; it has raised up from their thrones all the Kings of the Nations. All they shall ask you, "Are you also become weak as we? Are you become like us?" Your majesty and glory is brought with you down to the grave, and the clamor of your spent life: The man is spread out into the place of Christ's as a garment."**
> **Isaiah 14:9-11 (UJWV)**

I have this text and a few other key texts in a breakdown on my web site, echoesofenoch.org so that you might check out my conclusions. This rendering if accurate, is actually describing the same but opposite resurrection power applied to the Antichrist as a satanic version. This mortal possessed man (possibly a hybrid) now deceased, completing the first half of his mission, descends into hell and moves into a redemptive role producing the same resurrection results of Christ's! You must realize though that this is just a cheap imitation of the real power of God. Nevertheless it does produce short termed similar results. Cloning may be the technology applied to accomplish this very task. Remember it was SS Dr Joseph Mengela who first started working on "twinning". This was the Nazi term for cloning.

I must also include the fact that I am not so foolish as to think Hitler would reappear wearing a Nazi uniform, hair combed in reverse, with the same silly mustache. He will be a deceiver, and clandestine, from a fortress of defense, weave his illusion of truth until a time to make his presence known. When a generation has accepted the beliefs of Karma, evolution, reincarnation and principles of Tao, the time will be right. Probably a very modern contemporary leader with much disciplined New Age beliefs, he would not be detected for his real past. Remember this is all done in the same but opposite pattern as what God has done. Christ is described as the "firstborn of many brethren," Romans 8:29 Isaiah here speaks of the Antichrist in the same manner as well as that of Revelations 17 - One man two times. Hitler may have been this foretold man, and the Nazis his vehicle. Regardless of weather he was or not, his message of Theosophy is something we are still dealing with. This is the spirit of Antichrist and this is what we allowed into our country.

America Made the Same Mistake Ancient Israel Made. NO SPOILS OF WAR!

The very thing Moses, Joshua and Caleb were warned about in their conquest of the "promised land", was something America should have taken heed to as well. This warning was the wisdom of not taking the people and religious artifacts into their own country. The influence of the philosophies of the conquered culture would contaminate them from within! This was exactly what the US did at the end of WWII!

> **"And the city shall be accursed, even it, and all that are therein, to the LORD...And ye, in any wise keep yourselves from the accursed thing, lest you make yourselves accursed, when you take of the accursed thing, and make the camp of Israel a curse, and trouble it."**
>
> **Josh 6:17,18**

The "spirit of Antichrist"

The United States has become infiltrated by accepting the former enemy as spoils of war through Operation Paperclip. Another influence has been the many UFO sightings bearing the same Nazi message from "Aliens". This message is what we need to understand in the broadest sense as defined by the Bible.

In addition to a specific individual that is called the Antichrist, the Bible describes an abstract idea or movement that opposes God and inspires men to rebellion against God as well.

> **"Little children, it is the last hour; and as you have heard that the Antichrist is coming, even now many antichrists have come, by which we know that it is the last hour".**
>
> **I John 2:18**

In this above scripture, we see that an individual is recognized as one who will come, but then the Apostle John conveys the idea that many antichrists have already come. By this, he states we know that it is near the time of Christ's return. John was remembering Jesus' words when he told the disciples the sign of his return,

> "For many shall come in my name, saying, I am Christ; and shall deceive many...And many false prophets shall rise, and shall deceive many"
>
> **Matt 24: 3,11**

What makes the "spirit of Antichrist"?

John further defines why these people are called false prophets and antichrists.

> "And every spirit that confesses not that Jesus Christ is come in the flesh is not of God: and this is that spirit of Antichrist, whereof ye have heard that it should come; and even now already is it in the world"
>
> **I Jn 4:3**

A most pivotal point is centered on the person of Jesus. To come in the flesh is to understand that God became man. John emphasizes this statement again.

> "For many deceivers are entered into the world, who confess not that Jesus Christ is come in the flesh. This is a deceiver and an antichrist".
>
> **II Jn 1:7**

For God to become man, a relationship of the triune nature of God is understood. This is why the Old Testament name for God is in the plural. To be the Christ or Messiah, is to be the manifested truth in the flesh. (John1:1) This relational position and ministry is also emphasized by John. ***"Who is a liar but he that denies that Jesus is the Christ? He is antichrist, that denies the Father and the Son."*** I John 2:22

Antichrist Opposes the Uniqueness of One

Anything less than the proper identification of the person, position and ministry of Jesus is of the spirit of Antichrist. Many today think this is an unfair non-inclusive and narrow minded statement. God is a jealous God and rightfully so. He became man in only one person and made the ultimate sacrifice, Himself. No one else did this act of love and grace toward man. No one else rose back from the dead to give eternal life by a simple act of faith in response to His act. It was God's Love alone, not dependant upon our goodness or lack of it, not dependant on our gnosis or intellect. Any other concept or alteration of this

91

character is to rob God of who He is and what He alone did. This is why in Jesus' own words; He made what many would accuse of being the narrowest minded, non inclusive statement ever,

> **"I am the door: by me if any man enter in, he shall be saved, and shall go in and out, and find pasture... Verily, verily, I say unto you, He that enters not by the door into the sheepfold, but climbs up some other way, the same is a thief and a robber".**
> **John 10:8-9, 1**

> **"I am the way, the truth, and the life: no man comes to the Father, but by me".**
> **John 14:6**

By these statements of Jesus Himself, you are left without any other interpretation. He was not an energy consciousness, a prophet, or teacher; He was God in the flesh. As a well known Christian Author Josh McDowell puts it, "He was either Lord, Lunatic or Liar!" You have no other choice; anything else is the movement of the spirit of Antichrist.

Counterfeit Offers

Satan offers so many other ways, systems, principles and methods that appeal to our intellect and rebellious nature that it is very confusing. Most that follow other things are not doing this out of a desire to follow Satan. They are doing so out of ignorance. They have been seduced and deceived by not knowing the truth. They don't realize the warnings in the Bible, and perhaps never went to a church that properly represented the real Jesus. That is why this spirit of antichrist is already active in the world to seduce and deceive everyone from the simplicity of God's love, including a deception and seduction within the "Church". This movement then is anything that does not proclaim the proper deity of Jesus.

666 Key to the Identity of Antichrist but What Does It Mean?

Much has been written and speculated about this number. It is associated with a monetary system and identity of the coming Antichrist. Is the mark a literal tattoo dependant upon a form of a new computerized monetary system? We have assumed this belief until it has become doctrine. Some have claimed that the use of Gematra (a Jewish way of assigning a numerical value to each letter in the Hebrew alphabet) would add up to the name of the Antichrist). Nero actually does! I would like you to consider another possible way to look at this.

Here is the main text for this mark of the beast.

"And he caused all, both small and great, rich and poor, free and bond, to receive a mark in their right hand, or in their foreheads: And that no man might buy or sell, save he that had the mark, or the name of the beast, or the number of his name. Here is wisdom. Let him that hath understanding count the number of the beast: for it is the number of a man; and his number is Six hundred threescore and six."
Rev 13:16-18

Some understanding about this number might be much simpler than what many want to make of it. In Biblical numerology numbers have a consistent use and meaning. Six is the number of man and three is the number of God signifying the three personages of one God. Six in a triple fashion is simply man becoming God. It is man's total self reliance excluding God in three ways.

1. **Man's Religion ; Monism**- A belief that God is in all, all is in God therefore we are a part of God and we can become God as we "tap" into this universal consciousness. This is the Religion of Man in its simplest element. It is the worship of the human as divine. It is expressed in almost every variation within all other religions. Man becomes God instead of God who became a man. Man is divine without a personal God. This is the mockery of God's Spirit, the first **6**.

2. **Man's Science as Truth manifest on earth** - Not necessarily true science but assumed science that excludes a creator God. Evolution becomes our creator, we being a product of chance and the process of "natural selection" where the stronger survive. A universe where elements assimilate into higher more complex forms over eons of time is proclaimed by "scientists- priests". No proof or evidence exists but this is stated as a "scientific fact". It excludes a divine creator who made everything unique and complete within itself. If we came from protoplasmic goo and became a monkey, a caveman then modern man, you could also see the need to continue on to something even higher than our present form. This accomplished of course, without a creator

God. This comes from man's own understanding of our natural universe and the "powers" to control it. These truths based upon our own natural five senses, is the mockery of the manifested truth on earth, the son of God...a second **6**.

3. **A One World Government-** A unified earth with national identities erased, along with specific religions and culture. A government celebrating man as the highest order in the universe with the ability to control his own destiny apart from the involvement of a personal accountable God is also proclaimed. This is the mockery to the will of God the Father...the third **6**.

God and Mankind completely Re-defined

Religion, Science and Government in these three are what defines man. Our moral and ethical practices as motivated by our concept of God as Religion, our perceptions of reality by our five senses in science, and our expression of the other two with the formation and active involvement through Government. With man's natural touch to each of these areas excluding a personal God you get **666**. This is the spirit of Antichrist and perhaps for the ardent follower, his "mark" on your life!

Taking the Mark

To receive a mark in the forehead or the right hand has a consistent figurative use elsewhere in the Bible as that which you believe in your mind and that which you apply in your life (by your right hand). (see Rev 9:4, forehead, Ps 78:54 hand) If you accept in your mind and apply into your life the three lies of man's self reliance, could this be the mark? It would be a rather nondescript invisible way of accepting this mark. If someday it becomes necessary to embrace these ideas to function in society and at the cost of rejecting any personal accountable God, you have already accepted the spirit of Antichrist and maybe even the mark of the beast

Theosophy The Anti Gospel of Hitler:

The heart and mind of our enemy

It is important to see the historical rise of Theosophy and Adolf Hitler to understand the intense religious movement Nazism actually was. The occult based climate in Europe created by Theosophy and inspired by their messiah Adolf Hitler burned this religion into their very hearts and minds. This level of commitment was just as intense as the same but opposite as the experience of the first Apostles who carried the Gospel message of Christ. The acquired Nazi scientists and intelligence officers as Satan's apostles would convey this same philosophy as a New Testament version of Nazism upon an unsuspecting American public as The New Age of Aquarius.

While I describe Hitler as the type or role of Antichrist I am not proclaiming any title upon him. I am showing how the same but opposite pattern fits his life and the theosophical message he embraced. As I also bring prophetic scriptures into view, some might actually pertain to this very important period of history. This evidence should be considered without any prior preconceived thoughts to get a fresh and different view. Venture out from these preconceived ideas taught to you in the past and realize that prophecy is progressive in being revealed and we just cannot teach future events as dogmatic absolutes. I am not saying that any are right or wrong just that several variables should be put into your mind as a wait and see category. In this flexibility there is a safety to not do what the Jews of Jesus' time did as they looked upon all their hopes and desires and then with their preconceived notions put him to death on a Roman cross. Next we will look at the story of Bad News for Mankind the Anti gospel of Adolf Hitler. In this we shall see just what we allowed into the very infrastructure of our own country.

Theosophy: the message of the spirit of Antichrist

A Fullness of another kind

> *"But when the fullness of the time was come, God sent forth his Son,"*
>
> **Galatians 4:4**

In this scripture we are to understand that when Christ came as the Messiah the first time, much transpired to carefully insure the right place, people and preparation in the hearts of mankind was coordinated to make a successful mission for Jesus.

In a same but opposite pattern, a fullness of another kind was made almost fifty years before Hitler came on the scene in Germany.

The Dawning of a New Age

At the end of the 19th century, society was going through major social and economic changes. The emergence of the industrial revolution produced resources and prosperity unheard of before. Populations shifted from peasant, rural people to sprawling cities and urban centers that created a cosmopolitan society. People were confronted with new technologies and wonders, the gramophone, automobiles, telephones, electric lights, moving pictures. These technological wonders gave certain validity to the revolutions taking place in "Modern Science", Charles Darwin's Theory of Evolution, and the new sciences of the mind called Psychology. Much of this new science challenged traditional religious thinking through de-mystifying and rationalizing.

Extending beyond this we had the first greatest Science-Fiction writings of Jules Vern and HG Wells who also stimulated the imagination to reach for the very stars themselves. So much change in such a short time and all at the end of a century.

H.P. Blavatsky and Theosophy: The Anti-Moses who gave the written Word.

The stage is set for accepting the unorthodox

For many individuals whose traditional beliefs and values were upset and displaced by all of this, Theosophy offered a melding of ancient religious ideas combined with borrowed concepts of modern science and speculative fiction. It swept the nations educated elite not only in America but even more in Europe with its biggest acceptance in Germany and Britain. The Occult practices had gained acceptance with the elite from mere entertainment to serious initiation. This was a "fullness of time" in another direction. America and Britain were being prepared for the New Age but the rest of Europe was being made ready like a plowed and planted field for the New Order.

Who was Helena Blavatsky?

The Theosophical Society was formed in 1875 by Helena Petrovina Blavatsky, a Russian mystic born of Nobel class and her close companion Colonel Henry S. Olcott. In 1879 this Society was based in New York. In 1888 she wrote her most famous book, a huge two-volume text, The Secret Doctrine. Recently, the Los Angeles Times called her "A godmother of the New Age Movement." Her official Biographer, Marion Mede said of her,

"......she paved the way for contemporary Transcendental Meditation, Zen, Hare Krishna's; yoga and vegetarianism; karma and reincarnation; swamis, yogis and gurus."

Madame Blavatsky claimed an exclusive authority on the basis of her occult knowledge or gnosis. She also claimed her initiation into the doctrines came from two exalted mahatmas or masters called Morya and Hoot Hoomi. These dwelt in a remote and secret vastness of the Himalayas. English author Sir Edward Bulwer-Lytton also heavily influenced her. His Novel, The Last Days of Pompeii (1834) was perceived by her as a narrative of the impact of the Isis cult in Rome during the first century AD. Her first book was Isis Unveiled (1877). In 1879 she moved her headquarters from New York to Madras India. It was there that she wrote the Secret Doctrine based on the Stanzas of Dzyan, which she claimed to have seen in a subterranean Himalayan monastery. This book is alleged to be a pre-flood text revealing a very different world than what we know of today. Much of this part of her life is in dispute and claims of plagiarism and of being a charlatan have followed until today. Claims have been made of her use of drugs also. Her "significant other" relationship with Henry Olcott was also a whispered rumor in her day. Just what one would expect as a satanic version of Moses, a rule breaker with a rule breaking book.

It really doesn't matter about her personal character or how she wrote her book. The end result is still the same; this one book has done much to influence and change the course of human history.

Secret Doctrines: The Bible of Theosophy

The Secret Doctrine can be summarized by three basic principles:

1. A God who is omnipresent, eternal boundless and immutable as the instrument Fohat, an electro-spiritual force which impresses the divine scheme upon the cosmic substances as the "laws of nature" this concept entitles mankind as the highest form of government of Self Rule. The **6** of Government

2. The rule of periodicity whereby all creation is subject to an endless cycle of destruction and rebirth. These rounds

always terminate at a level spiritually higher than the starting point. This is the **6** of Science

3. A fundamental unity between all individual souls and the deity, between microcosm and the macrocosm exists as the concept we call monism. This leaves man as the highest source of a progressive existence and ascendance into the God-man realm. This is the **6** of Religion

The first Volume Cosmogenesis, outlines a scheme whereby the divine being, manifests itself in three phases creating time, space and matter. All the rest of creation occurs in conformity with the divine plan passing through seven rounds of evolutionary cycles. The first four cycles depicted by fire, air, water and earth are downward from a higher level to a lower one displaying the fall. The last three depicted by the "ether" are upward movements ascending into a higher form displaying the redemption and restoration cycles.

The second volume, Anthropogenesis describes in further detail the seven cycles of humans in cyclic patterns of cosmic, physical and spiritual. According to Blavatski, mankind is in the last of the fifth cycle, on a planet ending the fourth cosmic round. A new Era or beginning of a new cycle awaits mankind and the earth.

Theosophies Calling of the "Chosen"

The particular story of the last cycle of the fifth root race reads like the same but opposite of Deuteronomy. According to the Secret Doctrine, the leaders of Atlantis were hybrid god-men with super human abilities (Genesis 6 fallen angels). The other residents willingly accepted their leadership. Some were selected for special breeding and seven races developed. From these a few became monstrous and grotesque. Others developed great magical powers. Their speech was intimately connected to the forces of nature. Their words could advance the growth of plants, tame wild animals and bring about physical healing. Their words could also bring destruction to their enemies. They soon developed the overwhelming greed to control and dominate everyone and everything. In order to preserve mankind, a master root race was created to survive the coming great flood. This new race was not made from a refinement of the others but separate and new, derived from the god's themselves. This new race was created in the bitter cold of the mountain regions where they developed ruggedness. Those who were selected to be the leaders were isolated and trained under uncompromising discipline. Everything that confronted them physically on earth was directed by "invisible powers". They were told to dedicate themselves without reservation to their service. Above all they were taught to respect and protect the purity of their blood.

The other races upon seeing this new race maturing went to war. The root race wins the war but realizes they have lost all contact with the spiritual realm. To correct this, the god-men give the race a mystic religion, the oracle of the sun. They are given the sun wheel sign as their personal symbol. The leaders became the mediators between the masses and the unseen invisible powers of the spirit world and the material world. The race was then led off Atlantis before the flood by the great Manu, the last of the sons of god or god-men. Their migration took them through Europe and Asia and into the Gobi desert, from there to the top of the Himalayas in Tibet. There on top of the world, at Shambala, the sun oracle was founded to mastermind and direct the seven civilizations of the post flood age.

By now you are almost to a tear drop, lump in the throat, feeling warm and fuzzy all over or you are scratching your head wondering who would ever believe this kind of story and how could this impact or change anything. The social climate was perfect to receive this conglomerate message with excitement. This master root race was the Aryan the sun sign was the swastika and the religion was Theosophy. The rest as they say is history!

Theosophy a mixture of eastern religions.

Theosophy is a mixture of Buddhism, Hinduism and Taoism. In this mixture were the recipe for spiritual chaos and the potential for a holocaust.

From Buddhism, the concept of reincarnation diminishes life as not being singular and therefore not so precious. From Taoism, absolutes of right and wrong are reduced to situational ethics. Whatever fits for the time is ok because as they teach there are no absolutes. (Hmm isn't that an absolute statement?) From Hinduism, the act of karma and retribution creates the cast system of the uncompassionate attitude that you get and have gotten what you deserve because of your past life and bad karma. On the flip side of this is the fact that you can be entitled to self indulgence with wealth and riches, guilt free without sharing because of your good karma from a past life.

With the overall concept of God as an impersonal power or force with ascended masters, angels or extra-terrestrial beings who "guide" mankind and truth being relative, the stage is set for the spiritual chaos which led to the "Final Solution".

Theosophies Integration into Europe and German society

Blavatsky's Theosophy was first introduced into Germany in 1894 where it soon gained a wide acceptance and was integrated into many variations within existing secret orders such as the Knights Templar, Golden Dawn, Freemasonry, Rosicrucian's, Ordo Templi Orientis, Thule Society, Illuminati, and many more. Here are some influential people who as Patriarchs and prophets helped pave the way for Theosophy as a spiritual movement

Patriarchs and Prophets

Guido Von List - a contributing "prophet" and Patriarch. List was a writer who was the first to mix German volkish ideology (Nordic Mythology applied as a lifestyle) with Theosophy and the occult. Much of his well published books helped to create the Germanenorden. This was the very beginnings of the Pan-German movement which helped bring about the "Great War." (WWI) It also helped foster the Nazi party much later. He created a Nordic religion called Wotanism. Part of this religion included his interpretations of the Icelandic Edda and Runic symbols. He was the first to assign mystical values to the Ancient Runic symbols which are still practiced by many pagans and New Ager's today. In 1891 List discovered a prophetic verse in the "Voluspa" which promised a messianic figure would come and set up an eternal order. This was the "Starke von Oben" which means, "the strong one from the skies". He believed Hitler to be this prophetic promise.

Jorg Lanz Von Liebenfels a protégée of List, He created Theo zoology and the publication Ostara. The young Adolf Hitler read this publication and was mentored by Liebenfels.

Karl Hausehofer was another Patriarch. Along with Dietrich Eckhart, Hausehofer mentored Hitler into the political aspects of the movement He developed his geo-political ideas of Lieberstorm or living space; this was combined with Guido Von List's studies of Nordic mythology and ruins. They laid claim to the fact that wherever ruins or the swastika was found, Germany had a legal claim to that land. The use was so wide spread that a global dominance was figured from the golden age, therefore world dominance was justified. This concept also inspired the Eugenics program of mercy killings of the disabled and retarded ending in the final solution. Haushofer made several trips to India, studied the ancient Vedas, lived in Japan where he was initiated into an esoteric Buddhist society "The Green Dragon". He later served as a connection to bring many Tibetan Lamas into Germany as SS officers on an advisory staff at Himmler's castle in Wewelsburg. When allies overran the castle in 1945 they found over 1,000 monks in German uniforms lying burned to death in ceremonial circles of suicide.

Huston Stuart Chamberlin was an English occult author who wrote "Key's to Human History, The rise and fall of races". He mentions the Teutonic race as the Aryan. He believed in a personal mystical connection to the pan-German movement. Of Hitler he said, Hitler is an awakener of souls, the vehicle of messianic powers.

Friedrich Nietzsche was a sort of Prophet laying down the laws of behavior for Dominance and control. He prophetically stated. "...a coming elite would rule from whom this superman would spring. He and those around him would become, "Lords of the earth". He died in 1900 without seeing his vision fulfilled.

Aliester Crowley claims an encounter with an alien entity Awiaz in Cario in 1904. Crowley has claimed at times that Awiaz was actually the Devil. This Aiwaz communicated a scripture to Crowley in the voice of three Egyptian gods that became known as the Book of the Law: the gospel of the New Age, also known as the Aeon of Horus. Within the writings is a mention, **"I am the Warrior Lord of the Forties."** Could that have been a prophetic description of the greatest battle ever to be experienced at the hand of the Horse and his rider? Satan has his own supernatural empowerment and revelations even though they be lies!

Charles Darwin - As the first "Scientist- Priest" He was the prophet who gave the concept of evolution as a new way to look at creation and existence without God. This Theory of Evolution is a root concept to set up and deceive all of mankind. This belief will compel a desire for people to be "something else or more through continual evolving". Through this false science and technology, promises and products will be accepted as the only "logical" choice.

Wagner - Prophetic artist through artistic expression of music, he gave an emotional appeal to the celebration of the chosen elite. Teutonic Knights, Wotanism, Nordic mythology and veiled occult themes filled his operas.

In all of this Hitler did not just happen. People, ideas and events were just as carefully orchestrated to make ready his appearance as the opposite of Christ. Occult initiates were more than ready to embrace Hitler as their Messiah as they had many such "Promises and signs" foretelling them of his appearance

Theosophy became The Pan-German movement of WWI

Fringe science, ancient myths, folk lore and esoteric occult practices melded together to form a belief in a chosen race the Ayran which based on bloodlines and genetic purity would help to bring about this New Era of change.

In its broadest sense, this philosophy was the Pan-German movement which was eagerly accepted by the European elite of the old aristocrats, the new industrialists, artists and the intellectuals of the day. With the onset of World War I and the Kaisers Second Reich, the Germanic peoples rallied together in the belief that a new Germanic empire would herald in this new golden age.

Watering the planted seed

In 1917 at a coffeehouse in Vienna, an unknown turning point took place within occult and secret societies. A clairvoyant Maria Autche met with influential leaders of the Thule Society and the Knights Templer. Included were Baron Von Sebottendorff and Karl Haushofer. In a séance it was revealed that they would prepare for a "new leader" that would bring in this New Age. This meeting inspired many occult lodges and secret societies to work together toward this goal. This came at a critical time because months later Germany was to lose the Great War. These few would help keep the Pan German movement alive during the rough times ahead.

A vision maintained

As Germany lost the war and became a fragmented state of cities whose remaining self control was threatened by the Communists, only the occult lodges and secret societies whose members included the elite of Germany stood in the gap of this threat and kept the Pan German vision alive. The Communist's biggest mistake was the execution of seven members of the Thule Society on April 30th 1919 among these was a Prince Von Thurn, a well connected aristocrat with blood relations among the crowned heads of Europe. This event rallied the people in Munich coupled with 20,000 members of the Free Corp, (a Para-military unit and extension of the Thule organization and part of the Germanorden organized by Baron Rudolph Von Sebottondorf) to successfully overthrew the communist presence in Munich and solidified their structure to ensure no more communist expansion would overtake Germany. This was the first time in history that a military group assembled under the swastika singing a swastika song veiled with occult meanings. Most of the elite of all of Europe saw this organization as the only power able to resist this threat to their personal empires and were quick to support them. Many were fellow initiates and sympathizers and others were ignorant of their occult beliefs or overlooked them for the sake of self preservation.

Thule Gesellscaft beginnings of the Nazi elite

After this great military success, the Thule Gesellscaft organized a two pronged strategy of political activism. The Thule Society will do the organizing; will make the right connections among the society figures, wealthy capitalists and the intelligencia. They will stock pile the weapons and organize the free corp. units. They will remain the invisible controlling hand upon the other arm of attack. This other branch was the German Workers Party renamed in one year, to the well known National Socialists German Workers Party. This group will have no overt involvement with the Thule Society. They are to recruit members from the middle and lower class working people and meet in beer halls. From this group would come the Brown Shirts, a rough and tumble collection of working class peoples formed to patrol the cities and protect the people. From the Thule society, the Free Corp would become the Order of the Black Sun commonly known as the SS or Storm Troopers, the elite. It was in this preparation that Hitler came upon the scene.

Now the birth of Hitler was on the wise:

More than an eerie coincidence, in 1889 Franz Von Stuck painted a picture of Wotan the god of destruction. 1889 is the same year Hitler was born. Hitler was an admirer of Von Stuck and knew this picture well. The resemblance is uncanny. Did Hitler pattern his looks after this picture, or was this another prophetic sign of the coming "son of perdition". The next decade as Hitler was developing into the beast he would become; Theosophy was becoming the cement of the new movement. **"Wotan God of War", painted by Von Stuck in 1889 the year Hitler was born**

Calling of the Corporal

Two prophetic occult events happened in the same year in 1917. One, at a Vienna Coffeehouse where an important annunciation took place during a séance, "Germany was about to receive her messiah." Another revelation was also happening in a military hospital. A corporal in the German army suffering the effects of a mustard gas attack received an annunciation. A little voice in his head declared that Germany would lose the war but he was "selected by God to be Germany's messiah" with a destiny to fulfill, he would be used to unite Germany and usher in a New World Order. This corporal of course was Adolf Hitler.

Hitler is sent out.

In 1928, the group Edelweiss of Austria announced the coming of a New Messiah. In England, Sir Oswald Mosley of Bellamy gave out that Germany had been "touched by the Light"

The Final preparations for Hitler as Messiah were declared throughout occult Europe in this manner.

Adolf Hitler meets Dietrich Eckhart A different voice crying in another wilderness.

Dietrich Eckhart was the one to make straight the way for Hitler. He was a satanic opposite of John the Baptist. An original member of the Thule Society and several other esoteric societies, he owned his own newspaper with a wide circulation. He was an international socialite and coffeehouse darling. It is through him that conventional history records, Hitler learned his ability to orate. Claims have also been made that it was through Eckhart that Hitler was introduced to the elite of society and international monies including Americans like Henry Ford of which it is claimed, channeled funds to support the Nazi party in the early years. What is not mentioned is the fact that Eckhart, a renowned Satanist belonging to the Ordo Templi Orientis of Aleister Crowley fame, had claimed to receive a satanic annunciation at a séance in which slain Thulist Prince Von Thurn appeared. It was declared that Eckhart was destined to prepare the vessel of Lord Matreya the Antichrist. Upon seeing Hitler for the first time he stated, Here is the one for whom I was but a prophet and forerunner. On his death bed in 1923, he stated, "Follow Hitler! He will dance but it is I who have called the tune! I have initiated him into the Secret Doctrine, opened his centers in vision and given him the means to communicate with the Powers. "Do not mourn for me I shall have influenced history more than any other German." Dietrich Eckhart was Hitler's "spiritual" mentor. Hitler dedicated Mein Kampf in his memory among others honored.

I would like to comment here that the occult practices claimed in these events may have been real but were perpetrated by demon spirits pretending to be these other people.

Who Did Hitler think himself to be?

Wolfram Von Eschenbach published an epic poem Parzival sometime between 1195 and 1216. The poem was a story of Percival and his search for the Holy Grail. The poem was steeped in occult mystical symbolism and Buddhist philosophy. Hitler believed the main characters of this story represented the leaders of Ninth century Europe. He also believed the story was in reality a prophetic one to be replayed on world history in the twentieth century. According to the testimony of Dr. Walter Stein, a close acquaintance of Hitler, Hitler believed himself to be the reincarnated character Landulph of Capua and ninth-century Lord of Terra di Labur, possessor of the "spirit of antichrist". True or not, in the mind of Adolf Hitler, he believed himself to be the Antichrist. Of course he saw himself as a liberator for the "chosen" Aryan, and really the good guy with a hard task to perform with God (the electro-spiritual force type.) on his side. In his mind he was bringing the Aryan back to the golden age of the gods when in fact he was trying to bring back the world before the great flood!

Worship accepted

Hitler accepted worship and even changed holidays and events from Christian to Pagan worship. Calendars would emphasize the winter and summer solstice and disregard Easter and Christmas. They were still celebrated, just not publicized. At one of the Nuremberg rallies a giant photo of Hitler was captioned with the words, "In the beginning was the Word." Some even changed the Lord's prayer replacing Hitler's name for God. In the book "Hitler's Cross" by Erwin W. Lutzer, He cites many examples of the deification of Hitler. An important book worth reading, he explains the infiltration of Nazism into society and even the church. This book is a good warning for American Christians in today's society.

Some quotes with religious overtones by leaders and citizens of Nazi Germany.

> *"Just as Christ made his twelve disciples into a band faithful to the martyr's death whose faith shook the Roman Empire, so now we witness the same spectacle again: Adolf Hitler is the true Holy Ghost."* **-Hans Kerrl, addressing SA leaders, Brunswick, 19 November 1935**

> *"God gave the savior to the German people. We have faith, deep and unshakeable faith, that he [Hitler] was sent to us by God to save Germany".* **Hermann Gööring (***Hitler's Elite, Shocking Profiles of the Reich's Most Notorious Henchmen," Berkley Books, 1990*)

> *"No matter what human beings do I shall some day stand before the judgment seat of the Eternal. I shall answer to Him, and I know he will judge me innocent."* **-Rudolf Hess, in a statement to the Nuremberg Tribunal,** *(Hitler's Elite, Shocking Profiles of the Reich's Most Notorious Henchmen," Berkley Books, 1990)*

> *"With all our powers we will endeavour to be worthy of the Fuhrer thou, O Lord, has sent us! "* **-Rudolf Hess, address to political leaders, Munich , 21 April 1938 (Rolf Tell,** *Sound and Fuhrer*)

> *"I swear before God this holy oath, that I shall give absolute confidence to the Fuehrer of the German Reich and people."* **-Heinrich Himmler, reminding his hearers about the oath taken by all SS men as well as by the military forces** *(Hitler's Elite, Shocking Profiles of the Reich's Most Notorious Henchmen," Berkley Books, 1990)*

"We have a feeling that Germany has been transformed into a great house of God, including all classes, professions and creeds, where the Fuhrer as our mediator stood before the throne of the Almighty". -Joseph Goebbels, in a broadcast, 19 April 1936

"We believe on this earth in Adolf Hitler alone! We believe in National Socialism as the creed which is the sole source of grace! We believe that Almighty God has sent us Adolf Hitler so that he may rid Germany of the hypocrites and Pharisees." -Robert Ley *(quoted in Frankfurter Zeitung, 23 July 1936)*

"He who serves our Fuhrer, Adolf Hitler, serves Germany and he who serves Germany, serves God." Baldur von Schirach (speech to Hitler Youth, 25 July 1936)

"Blessed are the pure in heart, for they shall see God. The way has been shown to us by the Fuhrer." Dean Eckert, sermon at Tegel, North Berlin, 10 February 1935 *(Rolf Tell, Sound and Fuhrer)*

"Look at a marching troop of German youths and realize what God has made them for. They are warriors by nature and their calling is to rule". Walter Stapel, *The War Against the West, Bibl 1, 30, p. 609, London 1938*

This was the religious overtone as quoted by Nazi leaders and average citizens who lived in this Third Reich climate. It is obvious from these quotes that true Nazism was more than a political movement or philosophy it was a religion! This mind set, this ideology, is what Operation Paperclip and the Gehlen organization unleashed into the highest levels of our Defense Departments various intelligence divisions, into our highest levels of Corporate America and into our highest levels of the Academia in our learning Institutions. Together, the very infrastructure of America was infiltrated by these religious zealots!

The Occult Significance of April 30th 1945 :

Suicide or a Hopeful Expectation of a Resurrection?

Perhaps not just a cowardly act to escape, April 30th was one of the highest "power point" days in the Celtic Druids calendar of Sabbat known as Beltane. (Derived from Bel or Balam ancient Canaanite god, and alternate name of Satan) This was also the Nordic celebration, Walpurgisnact and Modern Wicca's day of love and fertility. A chilling realization with this occult day is another holiday that floats around the calendar and in April 30th 1945 it fell on this same day, GOOD FRIDAY! Could this also be another hint to an intersection of the same but opposite pattern? It is more than coincidental!

The Druids had an emphasis of rebirth as the cold wintry weather made way to the replenishing of crops in spring. In Austria and Germany, some ancient lore possibly includes the practice of an individual human sacrificed in a fire to signify the gloom and ill of winter passing and the re-birth of spring. Modern day Wicca's deny human sacrifice in spite of archeological evidence stating otherwise. Wicca's practice this night and day as a party or orgy celebrating love peace and fertility. This suicidal sacrifice was done in pairs by Hitler and his new wife Eva Braun, Gobbels and his wife with Karl Haushofer and wife. This was also done in accordance to an ancient Cathari and Druid rite of "Endura". This was the Tao principle of the female and male of yin and yang coming together in completeness as one entity as a sacrifice. There were specific occult reasons for everything they did. Perhaps to a fulfillment of laws from another direction and dimension!

Here is a ritualistic poem about Walpurgisnact that is almost prophetic:

Midnight of Walpurgisnacht
I baptized myself in a sea of discontent.
I leapt from the bank of life
Into a river where no mortals roam,
There I breath no more.
Daybreak after Walpurgis,
my body floats in a sea of content.
nestling, I slept in mothers arms.
I struggle not with the forces that howl,
But embrace them

Undisturbed, I sleep, cradled, dreamless, unmoving.
Gales and torrents wash over me.
When the storms break, waters settle, light will shine.
I will awake to a new age.
Then home I will be.

Awake to an new Age?, the Coming one?. Here is a quote from a 1940 version of the Great Invocation:

Come forth, O Mighty One.
The hour of service of the Saving Force has now arrived.
Let it be spread abroad, O Mighty One.
Let Light and Love and Power and Death
Fulfill the purpose of the Coming One.

Hitler, being the occult initiate was well aware of this "prayer". He wasn't dying to escape; he was sacrificing occult style to come back again! Just before Hitler went into his bunker and killed himself, his aid asked, "What should we do next?" Hitler in a monotone voice stated, go west and wait for the coming one." His last words were in reference to this prayer and the coming man! This ended the Old Testament version of Theosophy as The Third Reich. Next, after a resurrection, the New Testament version of Theosophy would arise, The Age of Aquarius... This "New Age" would have it's dawn in the West in America!

Next we shall see that just as Rome felt she had defeated her arch enemy the Jews in the destruction of Jerusalem in 70AD, she forever changed the empire from within by taking the very essence of Judaism into herself by the fleeing refugees who were Christian Jewish believers of Christ. Within decades, the Roman Empire became the Holy Roman Empire, which for better or worse as pagan as it was, it did contain the remnant of true believers within.

The United States replayed the same scenario at the end of WWII as we shall see next.

Chapter Seven
America in Prophecy

"Behold you shall call a nation that you knew not and nations that knew not thee shall run unto thee because of the Lord your God and for the Holy One of Israel for he hath glorified thee."

Isaiah 55:5

Is America in the Bible?

The name America or The United States is not in the Bible. If God was to reveal names of future countries before they came into existence, man's inclination would be that, if it was favorable, every new country would be named as such or in a bad sense, no country would ever be named that way. Because of this, if America were in the Bible it would not be so obvious. Just as Jesus spoke in parables with the understanding revealed only to those willing to hear, the same would be of many future events, including the people and nations involved. The key to understanding would only be unlocked by God's Spirit when it became necessary to know.

America in the "End Times"

Probably one of the most common thoughts concerning America in the scheme of end time events is that America is not even mentioned in the Bible. If that is the case, it would mean that America is not even an influential World power during the ending of the Age and at the time of Christ's second coming. The logical deduction assumed by some evangelical Christians today is that judgment will take out the United States before other events ever take place.

Some suppose that we are the Babylon (in a spiritual sense) mentioned by the prophet Jeremiah in the 51st chapter. Evangelist Jack Van Impe has long speculated that we are this Babylon. While I agree with him in part, I am not so soon to write my country off with just this identification. There was a positive calling for America, ordained of God, before the current falling away we are now experiencing.

Part1

A Transfer of God's Kingdom: A Kingdom once removed

We need to start with the transition point of Law and Grace. This was during the earthly ministry of Jesus at his first appearance. Jesus made this startling decree while speaking to the Jewish leaders of Israel's religious community the Sanhedrin as recorded in Matt 21:43,

> **"Therefore say I unto you, The Kingdom of God shall be taken from you and given to a nation bringing forth the fruits thereof."**

In context, Israel (including Judah) rejected their Messiah and because of this, the Kingdom would be taken away and given to another nation. Plain and simple God would remove his presence from Israel; it would go to another group of people that would bring forth fruit.

In 70AD Titus and the Roman Army accomplished this task. They burned the city down, killed the residents and plundered the Temple. They further defiled the inner chamber of the Holy of Holies by placing a statue of Zeus there, on the ramparts of the outer wall; each legion flew their unit's banner. This could not have been more symbolic of the departure of the Glory of God and a horrible mockery to every Jew. Titus ordered every stone of the Temple torn down just as Jesus had warned would happen almost forty years prior. This was the prophetic and symbolic act to show the departure of God upon the nation of Israel and the Jewish people. (For a time anyway) The Kingdom was given to someone else somewhere else.

Another Nation Promised

The Prophet Isaiah saw this as he foretold in Isaiah 55:5 ,

> **"Behold you shall call a nation that you knew not and nations that knew not thee shall run unto thee because of the Lord your God and for the Holy One of Israel for He hath glorified thee."**

The Holy One of Israel is one of the many names of Jesus. These are a people who are not a nation in Isaiah's time, all other nations not even familiar with Israel will run into it because of the God of Abraham, Isaac and Jacob and the Holy One of Israel. Jesus.

Clearly, this is a future Christian Nation. Just why these people are running into this nation is because He has glorified this country. Glorify means to gleam, to make beautiful, to explain or make clear. America's immigration policies have allowed people from all over the world to become a part of the "American dream". The first thing they encountered was Ellis Island and the Statue of Liberty. The inscription says it all,

> *" Give me your tired, your poor, your huddled masses yearning to breathe free, the wretched refuse of your teeming shore, send these, the homeless, tempest-toss to me. I lift my lamp beside the golden door."*

No other country from the time of Jesus to the present comes close to the fulfillment of what Isaiah spoke of. The golden door is that which opens to opportunity in a land based on individual freedom and the pursuit of happiness.

Law Vs Grace A Key to Identity

We cannot identify America with any keys of identification until we realize there was a change in some terms from The Old Testament into the New Testament. This is the idea of Law verses Grace.

Some prophetic events are "mixed up", others are not even noticed because of this type of miss-identification. We have placed Old Testament interpretive values upon a New Testament age. In doing this, we do not recognize where some major prophetic events are happening. At the same time we are looking in directions with anticipation where nothing is happening.

Seed of Abraham

A good example of this New Testament redefinition of terms is the "seed of Abraham". This term was used to identify the Hebrew bloodline of the Nation Israel going back to Abraham the Patriarch.

"And if ye be Christ's, then are ye Abraham's seed, and heirs according to the promise."

Gal 3:29

Here we see The Apostle Paul describe the "seed of Abraham" as being in a spiritual sense. Every Jew understood this as their catch phrase to identify their heritage and promise. Suddenly Paul overturns this long held concept with a New Testament definition. By this we see that the old term no longer applies to the New Testament time of Grace. It now means a whole different group of people, not based on bloodlines but by faith in which they believe.

"There is neither Jew nor Greek, there is neither bond nor free, there is neither male nor female: for ye are all one in Christ Jesus."

Gal 3:28

With this understanding the seed of Abraham now and forever will be based upon faith In Jesus for whosoever will, not just Hebrews based on their bloodlines. This becomes what is called prophetically, "the time of the Gentiles".

" I will also give you for a light to the Gentiles, that you may be my salvation unto the end of the earth."

Isa 49:6

This change in terms for God's people also has a change in terms for their location.

What or Who is "Zion"

Other terms have also changed. Zion was the name for the Mountain near Jerusalem. It has been used for the name of Jerusalem, the city of God. (1 Chron 11:5) It can also mean wherever the people of God are congregated.

"Remember Your congregation, which You have purchased of old, the tribe of Your inheritance, which You have redeemed-- this Mount Zion where You have dwelt."

Ps 74:2

This may not be speaking about an Old Testament situation at all. In a New Testament sense God now dwells in the hearts of men not in temples made of stone. (1Co 6:19) This congregated people have been redeemed. This clearly indicates that this text is speaking about a time after the finished work of Christ.

This then could be speaking of a New Testament group of people, Christians not Jews. The Apostle Peter gave this definition of the "church body of believers"

> **"But ye are a chosen generation, a royal priesthood, an holy nation, a peculiar (purchased, not weird) people; that you should show forth the praises of Him who has called you out of darkness into his marvelous light:"**
>
> **1 Pet 2:9**

This would be a group who would have the same pattern and "type" as in the Old Testament. God once used the name Zion for the Tribe of Judah

> **"But chose the tribe of Judah, the mount Zion which He loved".**
>
> **Ps 78:68**

This same pattern could be carried over into the New Testament times only with another tribe. The Bible does single out two tribes in this manner.

Part Two

The Lions Whelp: A Tribe Nation

The Patriarch Jacob while on his death bed gathered together his twelve sons (who represented the heads of the twelve tribes to become Israel) and began to prophesy concerning what would befall each tribe in the last days. (Genesis 49)

Moses just before his death blessed the twelve tribes of Israel. (Deut 33) This blessing was a prophetic promise to each tribe. Combining these two events can give us a clear picture of the tribes and their roles in history and the promises to them.

Of Judah it was said,

> **"Judah is a lion's whelp: from the prey, my son, thou art gone up: he stooped down, he crouched as a lion, and as an old lion, who shall rouse him up? The scepter shall not depart from Judah, nor a law-giver from between his feet, until Shiloh come, and unto him shall be the gathering of the people be."**
>
> **Gen 49:9,**

Two tribes, Judah and Dan were told that they would be a "lion's whelp". The Hebrew word **"Guwr"** means "a cub still abiding in the lair". It is derived from the root meaning **"a traveler who turns aside from the road".** In this sense it is a cub turned aside or on its own, yet still a part of the family unit. This is a rather poetic way of describing a tribe nation that is separate, yet still a part of God's **"family"** providence and plan.

Judah

In the time of King David, Israel was split into two with the new tribe nation Judah. From David on, all succeeding Kings were of the tribe of Judah until Jesus came in which time the "scepter" was taken away. This "scepter" was the sign of authority and leadership. Shiloh is prophetically speaking of Jesus who "gathered all to Him." In the appendix I have quoted Dr. Henry M. Morris' commentary in, *"The Genesis Record"* Baker House Publishing 1976, which is worth viewing for an in-depth understanding. The main point being that the term "lion's whelp" refers to this tribe nation role that the tribe of Judah was to experience.

Dan

Dan is also called a lion's whelp. In identifying this term as a Tribe Nation, we can see that another tribe Dan, would become a tribe nation of apaert from Israel but part of the family and providence of God also.

> **"And of Dan he said, Dan is a lions whelp: he shall leap from Bashan."**
>
> **Deut 33:22**

To leap from Bashan is to take a sudden or violent leap from Lebanon. This leap can be explained by the Assyrian captivity by Tiglath-Pileser in 734 BC. The ten Northern Tribes were carried off into captivity and never returned to Israel. The tribes of Judah and Benjamin and a small portion of Levites remain from that time on as "Israel" in the nation of Judea. This is known as the

Diaspora by modern day Jews. This leap we will see was part of a plan that would cause Dan to eventually become a "tribe Nation".

Judah and Dan are Singled Out

If there is some kind of a shared promise for Judah and Dan to experience such a great role, we might expect to find something that would allude to this connection or prominence.

It is interesting to note that in the building of the Ark of the Covenant; only two craftsmen were chosen by God through Moses to do the work. One, Bezaleel who's name means **"in the shadow of (as in protection) God"**, is from the tribe of Judah. The other name, Aholib meaning, **" tent of his father"** came from the tribe of Dan.

Notice the names of these two. Judah as being protected and tent would mean in the sense as a dwelling or vessel for God. I do not think this was by accident. Everything in the Bible has an amazing interconnectedness and meaning. Judah has been protected and preserved by God as a foundation and Dan as America has been the tent safe haven for His Church to proclaim the Gospel as the vessel.

It would appear that both tribes, Judah and Dan would, as independent nations yet belonging to God's "family Israel", be in service to accomplish God's will. They would both fulfill the role as a Lions Whelp.

Another interesting fact is that when Dan moved northward to Lebanon, they captured a city named the Lion and renamed it Dan. According to this implication from the Bible, Judah would be the first to be used and then replaced by Dan who would be the last.

Another interesting fact is the four faces on the Cherubim flanking the Ark of the Covenant. On one side is a two faced Cherub with the faces of a Lion and a Man. On the other is the face of an eagle and a bull. This could be alluding to the strange duality of the tribe of Dan. From the "Lion of Judah" comes the man, the Son of God. From the eagle comes the bull. The bull was always symbolic of Ballam who was Satan.

The eagle was the symbol of the tribe of Dan! It has been speculated by many that the "son of perdition" or Antichrist would come from the tribe of Dan in part because of this symbolism.

Yes there is a pattern of Dan and Judah being singled out for something special in the way of service to God.

Part Three

All About Dan.

Dan was the fifth son of Jacob. His name means , "to Judge" or "to set a straight course". As a tribe of Israel, while on the march or moving, Dan's position was the last.(Num2:25) When the tribes were encamped, Dan's position in relation to the Ark of the Covenant was on the upper right hand side or the **"side of the North"**. This position may have important prophetic meaning as you will see later.(Num10:13)

Dan was also the designated meeting place, angelic or human, for all the other tribes to congregate for military or spiritual assemblies.(Num10:13). This idea of being the meeting place also has important prophetic meaning. Each tribe was given a standard or symbol of the Zodiac and a banner or flag that represented their tribe.

Dan was given the sign Scorpio,(from the Egyptian symbol the serpent). Finding the serpent repulsive as symbolic of Satan, Ahiezer replaced the serpent with its natural enemy the eagle as their symbol. The colors of their banner were red and white.

The Danites were also a seafaring people living on the coast. (Judges 5:37.) Their neighbors the Phoenicians and the Philistines also were seafaring peoples. The Bible later records Dan as being in company with the Phoenicians, and prophetically there will be some relationship with whomever the modern day Philistines are.

Part Four

Similarities of Dan and the US

I would like to consider some of the similarities between Dan and the United States. The United States is the "hindmost of Nation empires."(Jeremiah 50:12) Dan was the last in procession.

The United States first had a flag with a snake on it with the saying, "Don't tread on me." That was changed to the National Symbol of the Eagle. As already stated, Dan changed from the serpent to the eagle in the same pattern of the U.S.

The American flag has Red and White stripes with a standard of blue to signify a New Constellation in the Heavens with 13 stars. Dan's banner was colored Red and White. The Levitical priesthood was the tribe of Levi, they were never counted as one of the tribes. In this understanding, Dan being the last of tribes would have been #13 if you counted the Levites.

The Eagle on our national crest has in the left claw the defensive side, 13 arrows in its claw. Now if we were added as one of the tribes of Israel (after the dispersion) we would be the thirteenth. In the Eagle's right claw (signifying righteousness) the Eagle holds an olive branch. Our founding fathers meant for this to mean peace and it does, but the olive tree is the national symbol of Israel. We have the branch of it on our symbol which as Paul stated, in Romans 11:24,25 describing the church proper as the **"grafted olive branch"**.

The Great Seal on the face side or the side of the Eagle, which holds the banner in his beak, says,**"Out of many One."** The tribe of Dan was the place of gathering for the rest of the tribes in the Old Testament.

Interesting too was the fact that they were located on the," sides of North" in relation to the ark of the covenant. As the Bible has stated in Ps 75:6 promotion comes from the North. This is the seat of Heavenly authority in Mt Zion within the New Jerusalem which is located on the sides of the North.

> **"Beautiful for situation, the joy of the whole earth, is mount Zion, on the sides of the north, the city of the great King**
>
> **Ps 48:2.**

The earthly geographical location as mentioned many times in the Old Testament is Jerusalem in Israel. However in the New Testament, believers borne of God's Spirit in Christ are called Zion. Heb12:22,23. This would make the Christian Nation if founded by the descendants of Dan, the gathering point for the rest of the tribes and the Spiritual, "sides of the North".

> **"For promotion comes neither from the east, nor from the west, nor from the south. But God is the judge: He puts down one, and sets up another."**
>
> **Psalms 75:6-7**

Remember that the name Dan means "to judge or set a straight course". In a spiritual sense this nation would be one given authority and power of influence. If all of these scriptures point to America it would mean that we would be the point of attack and desire for a clandestine takeover by Satan as stated in Isaiah 14:13 as one of the five points to his plan,

"I will sit also upon the mount of the congregation in the sides of the North."

From these scriptures we can see a New Testament spiritual "sides of the North". These are Christians as the people of God dwelling in the modern day camp of Dan; called The United States of America.

Part Five

The Garden Land and Jacob's Seed
The plan of God: scatter to re-gather in Dan

Why would God scatter the people to re-gather them later? This is mentioned by Isaiah in 28:21 as God's "strange work." In context, God is describing the planting of a crop for harvest and expounding on His authority and design to place the "seed" where He desires. He is planting His seed into the entire world into all the races and cultures.

In order for God to make a change from Law to Grace, and create a "fullness of time, for Jesus to come and offer to anyone the promises by faith in grace, a genetic "mixing" of his "chosen" had to take place. In this sense God was doing the same but opposite of what happened in the flood. He started his own hybridization with His seed. One that was produced by Abraham and Sarah having a baby supernaturally well past child bearing. In this act of almost 700 years prior to Jesus' appearance, this mixing broke a "bloodline" border or barrier. Now everyone from everywhere could have a chance to come into the presence and have a relationship with God.

This is what was meant when it was said that, **"in the fullness of time God sent his son" Gal 4:4**

The Whole World is Seeded

The Prophet Amos describes the fact that Israel would be dispersed into all the earth.

> **"For Lo, I will command, and I will sift the house of Israel among ALL NATIONS, like corn is sifted in a sieve, yet shall not the least grain fall upon the earth."**
>
> **Amos 9:9**

Racists from any vantage point would not like this part of scripture because it clearly declares that Israel will be dispersed in the whole world. This in not an exclusive statement just like the "whosoever will" of the New Testament is not exclusive. This includes anyone and everyone! Again in Isaiah 27:6,

> **"He shall cause them that come out of Jacob to take root: Israel shall blossom and bud, and fill the whole face of the earth with fruit."**

In these verses we begin to get an understanding of a separation of Jacob and Israel.

Ps 22:23 indicate this further.

> **"Ye that fear the Lord, praise Him, all ye the seed of Jacob, glorify Him, and fear Him, all ye the seed of Israel."**

Jacobs seed is told to explain, make clear and proclaim Him, the same thing Isaiah said a nation would do some day, and Israel is told to revere God. Even in Israel's rejection of their Messiah, they still revere what they do know of God. This kind of separation describes the tribes of Judah and Dan as the nations of Israel and America.

The Scattering

This separation of "the seed of Jacob", from Israel proper can be explained by a captivity and release of the ten northern Tribes. The Assyrian empire under Tiglath-Pileser laid siege to the Northern coast of Israel in 734 BC. The ten Northern Tribes were carried off into captivity and never returned to Israel when they were finally released. The tribes of Judah and Benjamin and a small portion of Levites remained from that time on as "Israel" proper.

This is known as the Diaspora by modern day Jews. In Tel Aviv, Israel in the Museum Of Jewish Diaspora there is a display of a compilation of all myths legends, historical and cultural evidence for the whereabouts of these tribes. There is a CD, "*Sambatyon, Myth of the Lost ten tribes*" taken from this display with amazing evidence that covers all races and every corner of the earth.

One of the most incredible claims was that of a Portuguese explorer in the late 1600's. He describes observing a South American Indian tribe conducting a ritual sacrifice of a lamb upon an alter high up in the Andes. Included in the ceremony, they recited the "SH'ma" in Hebrew! This is a prayer taken from Deuteronomy 6:4 Hear O Israel: The Lord our God is one Lord! Every Continent and every race has evidence of Hebrew culture and religious practices. The Berbers, Ethiopians and Ibos of Africa, The Chiag-Min of Tibet, the Sindia of Japan, the Karaites and Khazars of South Russia and Turkey , Yemenis and Abyssinians of the Arabic world, the Ganges of India, the Kareens of Burma, even many American Indian cultures have claims to a Hebrew influence. Clearly, the ten northern tribes have spanned the globe and intermingled with the rest of the peoples of the earth as the prophecy proclaims.

Re-Gathering in Israel?

So where is Jacob's seed re-gathering and why? That is a question that should be answered using New Testament interpretive values and not Old. Tradition would tell you that this re-gathering is in Israel with the Jews. In 1948 when the Jewish state of Israel was reinstalled, the peoples to re-gather then were primarily from Europe. These were the remnant Jews from the destruction of 70AD. They were also the Israelites who returned from captivity being from the tribe of Judah, Benjamin, and part Levite. Now these are Jews returning to Israel but not like the return of Jacobs seed prophesied in the Bible. This is not to diminish Israel and her role in God's plan. Everything will end up in Jerusalem and in the valley of Megiddo. What happens before that might be a bit different from what is known or expected.

Re-Gathering of "Jacob's Seed" A first step

If the United States of America founded by Danites, is a gathering point for Jacob's seed, it would mean that this re-gathering has been taking place for almost 300 years. The unique start and vision our founding fathers had and sensed as destiny would be raised to a world power by God's grace to fulfill Isaiah's vision mentioned in 55:5. There are two re-gatherings that will eventually unite all of Israel proper once again.

This next scripture helps to understand a re-gathering in Israel and somewhere else.

The dialog here although coming from the prophet, is between God the Father and God the Son,

> **"It is a light thing that you should be my servant to RAISE UP THE TRIBES OF JACOB and RESTORE THE PRESERVED OF ISRAEL.**
> **Isaiah 49:6**

This is a description of two different actions taking place for two groups of people. The United States as the collection of Jacob's seed is being raised up to a world influential power. This was actualized in WWII for America. To, "restore the preserved of Israel"? This happened when in 1948 the Israeli flag flew over

British occupied Palestine for the first time since 70AD. Who were the residents? The Jewish survivors of the Holocaust, The preserved of Israel!

Part Six

Mystery Babylon: Home of Jacob's seed?

The seed of Jacob is re-gathered and we see them again mentioned by the Prophet Jeremiah. Of all places they are in Babylon! Now this is not the Babylon of Jeremiah's time. So typical of the prophets, is the ability to see and address beyond the present situations and trail off into a future situation. This is the case here in the 50 and 51st chapter of Jeremiah. Extracted from the text is the evidence that makes the Babylon containing the seed of Jacob very different from the one of Jeremiah's time.

51:13 -dwells upon many waters, Historical Babylon is not surrounded by waters, America is.

50:12 -the hindermost of nations, and her mother sore confounded, Historical Babylon had no "mother country" and certainly was not the hindermost of anything. The United States would consider England as her "mother country". She will become ashamed of us at some point in the future.

51:53 -Babylon should mount up to heaven. The United States desired a space program and compromised ourselves greatly with the Nazis at the end of WWII to have one.

51:7 - Babylon hath been a golden cup in the Lord's hand, which made the earth drunk. Historical Babylon was never a "golden cup" in the Lords hand. To be a golden cup is to be a godly vessel. In this case one that turns bad and makes the world drunk with lies. Cf/w Rev :17:4

These phrases could not be speaking about historical Babylon. I agree with Jack Van Impe that this is a future Babylon and one that could only (so far) refer to America. In light of this, the above scripture is telling us that there is a portion of Jacobs's seed in the midst of Babylon.

This "spiritual Babylon" is ready for judgment. What was once a nation raised up to let the world know of the realties of a personal loving God has changed from within to become the woman riding the beast. This golden cup is now being filled with madness (New Age Movement) that leads people away from God. The enemy now usurps the influential power given by God.

> **"I saw a woman sit upon a scarlet colored beast, full of names of blasphemy, having seven heads and ten horns. And the woman was arrayed in purple and scarlet color, and decked with gold and precious stones and pearls, having a golden cup in her hand full of abominations and filthiness of her fornica- tion: And upon her forehead was a name written, MYSTERY, BABYLON THE GREAT, THE MOTHER OF HARLOTS AND ABOMINATIONS OF THE EARTH."**
> **Rev 17:3-5**

In contrast to this, Jeremiah describes Jacob's seed (using my paraphrase to bring out the full-intended meaning).

> **"The inherited part of Jacob is not like them (Baby- lon) for he is the pre-ordained purpose and plan of all things and Israel is the scepter (or mark of au- thority) of his heritage and inheritance."**
> **Jer 51: 19**

In the minds of many American Christian believers this describes our position or sense of destiny and our relationship with Israel. This influence has created the determined feelings toward Israel to stand with her since 1948. We also recognize Israel and Judaism as part of our heritage and in a sense "family". This is of course in contrast to the other residents of America who God refers to as "Babylon", who think, feel and believe very differently about America.

God in His mercy, will appeal to His own and tell them,

"My people, go ye out of the midst of her, and deliver ye every man his soul from the fierce anger of the Lord."

Jer 51:45

"Come out of her , my people, that ye be not partakers of her sins, and that ye receive not of her plagues."

Rev 18:4

Where do they go, if they are in fact leaving America and being called out?

Re-United Israel: The Second Step

"Therefore fear thou not, O my servant Jacob, saith the Lord, neither be dismayed, O Israel: for lo. I will save them from afar, and thy seed from the land of their captivity, AND JACOB SHALL RETURN, and shall rest, and be quiet, and none shall make him afraid."

Jeremiah 46:27.

This I believe speaks to us today. The United States of America was to be given a golden cup to be a light to the world. God would draw the nations and His seed into it because of God the Father and the Holy one of Israel, Jesus. A Christian Nation is born!

The other part of His plan: to restore the preserved of Israel. In 1948 those Jews that survived the Holocaust of Nazi Germany went to their spiritual home - Israel! Two decades later Jerusalem is restored and Israel is made near complete in the geographical sense. I believe in the near future America being this chosen nation in the time of the Gentiles, will retake lost ground and reclaim her heritage and inheritance. America will then experience a revival unparalleled in all of history. During or shortly after that will be a persecution like never before as a second holocaust. We as a nation may even turn against Israel. God will finally punish America and many Christian refugees will flee to the only other "home" that they would identify with: Israel! We know that Israel and all of Egypt will experience a national repentance and accept Christ. This evangelism will be the result of a well trained and tested through the fires church which is also a part of the seed of Jacob and part of the lost ten tribes returning to their spiritual home Israel. In these events Israel is re-united with all 12 tribes. They are not Hebrews under the Law of Moses, but a mixture of people who are Christians under Grace with faith in the Messiah Jesus!

The beginning of the fall of the American Empire

If Dan is America, we have a future end time prophecy about Dan as this tribe nation America.

> **Dan shall be a serpent by the way, an adder in the path that biteth the horse heels, so that his rider shall fall backward. I have waited for thy salvation, O LORD. Gad, a troop shall overcome him: but he shall overcome at the last.**
> **Gen 49:17-19 (KJV)**

This scripture is telling us that Dan as a serpent will be an obstacle to the horse and his rider which is a reference to the antichrist mentioned in Revelation 6:2. He bites at the horses heel that makes the rider fall backward. This language is the same that is used in Genesis 3 describing the first coming of Jesus as the Messiah and his sacrificial death. IN this sense, Dan would be instrumental in stopping the vehicle of the antichrist resulting in the end of his first appearance or death. A flood of fortune will overwhelm Dan but he will overcome it in the end. Gad is the name of the Canaanite god of fortune and the name of one of the twelve tribes. This fortune may be in the form of the spoils of war and in our case the end of the Nazi régime, the death of Hitler and the spoils of Paperclip and the Gehlen organization, our undoing.

America is The Spiritual "Sides of the North"

Satan had stated in Isaiah 14 as one of the five I will's

"I will sit also upon the mount of the congregation, in the sides of the north:"

Isa 14:13

America is an earthly representation of the "sides of the North". Our duties were to be a safe haven for all Christians, to proclaim the Gospel to the entire world. Raised to be the most influential country in the world we were to be the golden cup in the Lord's hand. But we became a Harlot with a cup that made the world filled with madness.(Rev17:4) How did we come to this? We took the spoils of war into ourselves and began to change from within. The message of our war booty was the message of the spirit of the Antichrist. Now here are the vivid details of just what happened. Keep in mind I present only a small fragment of what actually happened as an example.

Chapter Eight
The Selling out of America: Operation Paperclip and the Gehlen Organization

> "...And he shall plant the tabernacles of his palace between the seas in the glorious holy mountain;......"
>
> **Dan 11:44p**

Now let's put meat on the bones from the skeletal framework that the Bible has given us. Here are some examples of the particulars of how we took the enemy into ourselves.

Part One

Step 1: The Dulles Brothers

A name that is almost synonymous with Operation Paperclip is Allan Dulles and his brother John Foster Dulles. Contemporary history remembers Allan Dulles as one of America's top spy masters. Both brothers were international corporate lawyers. John Dulles worked for the powerful Wall Street Law firm of Sullivan & Cromwell. This firm has a long standing record of supporting and representing the financial interests of I.G. Farben, Krupp Works, Thiessen Steel and other major German industries.

The German banks that were the major providers of the Nazi machinery were linked with many American corporations and business interests. This activity went back to the days of the Paris Peace Conference of 1919, which determined reparations Germany would make from WWI. John Dulles was one of the State Department's most important representatives. He was able to use his clients to weave a German-American industrial complex to help Germany repay their debt and at the same time create opportunity for American businesses. Innocent sounding at first but this was treasonous by the time Hitler came on the scene and business adjusted in a shell game and continued on as usual.

Allan Dulles entered the U.S. Foreign Service of the U.S. State Department as a junior intelligence officer in Bern, Switzerland. Both enjoyed a position of accessibility above their posts, as Uncle Bert, Robert Lansing was U.S. Secretary of State appointed by then President Woodrow Wilson. In addition their cousin was Nelson Rockefeller. It was 1917 in Switzerland that Allan Dulles made friendships and contacts with international businessmen, insurrectionists and rival nationalists. This was the time and place for shifting powers in a neutral country that served as a forum for negotiations and agreements. It was from this beginning Allan Dulles raised quickly to a major leading roll as an OSS officer during WWII. His long established business and legal contacts enabled him to develop a spy network that crept right into Berlin, most of Europe, parts of Asia and Northern Africa. Aft the end of WWII, Allan Dulles was stationed in Berlin. His job was to oversee U.S. intelligence evaluations of German business and political leaders to determine Nazi war criminals. With his brother John's efforts they thwarted many legal attempts to bring to justice many pro Nazi businesses and corporate heads. Allan Dulles even gave a guaranteed de facto asylum to the highest SS officer to survive the war, SS Obergruppenfuhrer Karl Wolf. In addition many on his staff and aids were also protected from prosecution. Wolf was Himmler's most senior officer, adjutant and Chief of Staff. He was one of the twelve initiates to partake in the Nazi rituals at Wewelsburg castle. He arranged SS transfers of slave laborers to I.G. Farbin, Kontinentale Oil and other major companies and the major sponsor of the mass extermination at Treblinka. Allan Dulles would later become the head of the newly formed C.I.A. composed of ex Nazi SS officers which he helped bring into this country. John F. Kennedy would also fire him for the Bay of Pigs mess and for dealing with other agencies traitorously. Oddly enough Allan Dulles would be a member of the Warren commission investigating the assassination of Kennedy. He was also a Director of the C.F.R. Commission on Foreign Relations. John Dulles was a board director for I.G. Farben. It takes little effort to discover the many conflicts of interest in the two brothers business and political life

Part Two

Step 2: SS General Reinhard Gehlen

In March of 1945 General Reinhard Gehlen the Senior SS Intelligence Officer for the eastern front along with a small group of his senior staff microfilmed the vast holdings on the USSR from the intelligence section of the German Armies General Staff. They packed the film in water tight steel drums and buried them in the Austrian Alps. Then on May 22, 1945 Gehlen and his top aids surrendered to an American Counter-intelligence Corps. Gehlen immediately asked for an interview with the commanding officer and offered the United States his intelligence staff, spy apparatus, and the files for future service. Not only did The United States take the bait, our intelligence community was assisted by Gehlen in the redevelopment of our own intelligence system. Gehlen was sent back to Germany and worked with Allan Dulles to set up the German branch of the newly developed C.I.A. Hundreds of Army and SS officers were quietly released from internment camps and joined with Gehlen in "Operation Sunrise". Later many of these were given U.S. citizenship and became a part of the newly formed Central Intelligence Agency in Washington, D.C. under Operation PaperClip. By the time the Federal Republic of West Germany became a sovereign state in 1955, Gehlen's Bureau became the official intelligence arm of the Bonn government. The actions of Allan Dulles and Reinhard Gehlen set precedence for many other such acts of reconciliation and partnerships.

The Pentagon, Symbol of Restructuring US Intelligence and the New Presence.

A new building was already in progress to help facilitate the new branches of the C.I.A., the N.S.A. and other re-organized defense departments called the "PENTAGON"! Why a pentagon? Is this name another "coincidence" or a prophetic re-awakening of the Philistine presence? Remember, the Philistines had the Pentapolos; a five city fortification of defense for their land. The Pentagon can also have another connection to the possible prophetic indication of Satan's desire to sit on the sides of the North in the Mount of the Congregation, the five point plan signified by the Pentagram. This is more than a coincidence. Could this be a sign of Satan's infiltration into the US? A sign not made by human design but perhaps by God's mercy to us, a simple way to see what has happened. This is just what Satan meant as recorded by Isaiah 14

" I will sit also upon the mount of the congregation, in the sides of the north:"

Isa 14:13 (KJV)

Satan's desire is to sit in the seat of power and authority on this earth not in God's Heaven. He does not want God's heaven he wants his own eternal place made from the linear one he helped to set up. To sit on the sides of the North as a judge and determine world policy is an earthly plan and part of His five-point plan. This is to infiltrate and sit in the camp of Dan (the sides of the North) as the new judge. It begins with a corrupted intelligence community at the center and very heart of our nation! A hidden government within the government. Funny Washington, DC is on the northern right-hand side from the center of our continent. This is the same location as the camp of Dan in relation to the Ark of the Covenant located in the center of the other tribal camps. The whole situation mirrors the Old Testament procedures.

Von Braun and 1ˢᵗ crew from PaperClip

Part Three

Step 3: Operation Paperclip and Lusty

Operation Sunrise turned into operation Overcast as Dr. Werner Von Braun and about 115 scientists, engineers and technicians "surrendered" to allied forces approaching into the heart of Nazi Germany.

Dr. Von Braun was the chief scientist overseeing the technical operations of rocket productions and launchings at Nordhausen and Peenemunde. Most people recognize Von Braun as the main architect of N.A.S.A. and our own space program. What you may not know was that he was a Nazi SS officer who wore the Death's Head Cross and bones on a Nazi uniform. This was quickly played down as being an honorary position and not one of commitment to the Nazi agenda. If founding and building a new terror from the skies that indiscriminately kills large amounts of innocent people is not a commitment to the Nazi agenda what is? Parts of his duties were to utilize the forced laborers sent from the death camps. Many of these died being worked to death. Just prior to Von Braun's admission to the United States, Pentagon's Joint Intelligence Objectives agency Director Wev wrote the director of U.S. European Command a blunt letter.

"There is very little possibility that the State and Justice departments will agree to immigrate any specialist who has been classified as an actual or potential security threat to the United States. This may result in the return to Germany of specialists whose skill and knowledge should be denied to other nations in the interest of national security. Therefore it is requested...that new security reports be submitted where such action is appropriate."

These changes allowed many Axis "scientists" into the United States. June 20th 1945 the U.S. Secretary of State Cordell Hull approved the transfer of the German rocket specialists. They were stationed at Ft. Bliss Texas and later most were transferred to newly built complexes of research and development in Roswell New Mexico. Dr. Von Braun convinced the U.S. through the Assistant Secretary of War John J. McCloy to admit his boss SS General Walter Dornberger. The problem was he had already been charged with war crimes. He was in charge of the entire Nordhausen concentration camp and underground compound in the Hartz Mountains. 20,000 inmates were worked to death under this man's command.

In his position of office it is said that McCloy blocked the executions of many Nazi war criminals. He was also the overseer of the concentration camps in California, which interned Japanese-Americans during the war. In 1949 he was made high commissioner in Germany and pardoned war criminals such as Alfred Krupp of Krupp munitions, a German corporate giant, and Dr. Hjalmer Schact. John McCloy was also on the Warren Commission investigating the assassination of JFK, He also became head of the World Bank, head of the Chase Manhattan Bank (The Rockefeller's), the Ford Foundation and chairman of the Council of Foreign Relations. He also co-authored Department of State publication #7277, "Freedom From War: The United States Program for General and Complete Disarmament in a Peaceful World." He was part of an elite "good old boy system" as a Globalist with a One World vision.

Soon the limit of 350 scientists was filled. The urgent need for many more experts was needed before they fell into Russian hands. As the result of this urgent need, President Truman approved Project Paperclip in the spring of 1946. Under Paperclip, the United States could recruit 1,000 additional Axis scientists, along with their families, and offer them eventual citizenship. Although the program was to exclude war criminals and "ardent

Nazis", if officials felt a person vital to a project, they would alter his records to allow his eligibility. In this manner Von Braun, Dornberger, Klaus Barbie (ex Gestapo chief) and well over 1,000 Nazi's and their families were allowed entrance and citizenship. As elite scientists with education and unrestricted movement in our society, it didn't take long for many to excel into prominent positions within our society.

Dr. Werner Von Braun became the head of N.A.S.A. He was also made the official spokesman for Disney. Is it any wonder that Disney, once an icon of American traditional values, spews out indoctrinated New Age Cartoons and Movies? Or that it has taken up a political support for "alternate lifestyles". Like the Hitler Youth before, Disney helps pave the way for a generation to accept the New World Order.

SS General Kurt Davis headed the Marshall Space Flight Center. He was also released from prosecution of war crimes.

SS General Dornberger became a senior executive of Bell Aero systems, a Division of Textron! This company worked on Top Secret technological projects for the government some of which were the development of Intercontinental Ballistic Missiles!

SS spy, George Bookbinder was an operative of the Gehlen organization who later became the President of the Rand Corporation. Claims have been made that the Rand Corporation is heavily involved with government contract work building underground complexes across the United States assisted with I.T.T. and the Krupp family.

Otto Von Bolschwing an ex SS intelligence officer and part of the Gehlen organization. He came a long way in America. In Germany he developed an import/export business, owned a coal-mine and was involved with several drug companies. As an SS officer he worked with several German branches of General Electric and Standard Oil (now Exxon). It is said that he was in charge of important funds that came through Nazi connections with Allen Dulles in the Schroeder Banks of New York. He later came to the United States as a member of the Gehlen /C.I.A. He got a job with Alfred Driscol, former Governor of New Jersey and president of Warner-Lambert Drug Company. Later he joined the Trans-International Computer Investment Corporation (TCI) in the Silicon Valley, California and became Vice-President.

Dr. Sidney Gottlieb was the head of the CIA Chemical and Biological Warfare program, a part of the MK Ultra mind control experiments using LSD in the 50's. Although he was an American, he was heavily influenced by the many ex-Nazi scientists under his leadership. This influence allowed the Nazi mind control experiments preformed in the death camps to continue on as part of gleaned American technology. The program was illegal to American law so the headquarters were located in Canada at McGill University.

The system and people that allowed much of this to happen was a "good old boy" system that included friends and family and co-workers of Dulles and others bound by memberships of various Secret societies such as the C.F.R. Builderbergs, The Tri-lateral Commission and the Club of Rome. All of these have Global goals and are only a front for their occult "Parents" the Illuminati, Rosicrucians, Masons and Theosophist to name a few. Many were the same financiers who supported the Nazi machinery from the very beginning!

Frank Wisner was OSS head of the Office for Policy Coordination which became the Plans Directorate of the C.I.A., headquarters for covert warfare employing Nazi collaborators. Frank Wisner once worked for Allen Dulles as a Wall Street lawyer.

Only the tip of the Iceberg.

Many books with excellent documentation have been written about Paperclip and the gathering of Nazi intelligence and scientific personnel, as well as the gathering of technology. In the Bibliography, I provide a list of books to further research. So many more interwoven links could be mentioned but I hope in this brief description you might begin to see the scope and implications of just what has happened. I believe that just one person with determination can make a difference. Imagine if you magnify that by several thousand! Of the least amount from these various programs, say 1,350 ex Germans from Nazi Germany came to live in influential positions in America. Many were encouraged by our Government to take up teaching positions at many of the Universities within America to assist themselves in their research and personal financial help. Abraham Lincoln made a statement that should have been a warning to us,

"The philosophy of the schoolroom in one generation will be the philosophy of government in the next."

The sensitive and secretive positions most of these people held would have to speak to any thinking person that most were determined Nazis with a zealous mission from their messiah! What about their families? How many have been indoctrinated by the Hitler Youth to be the next generation of Nazi leaders? We have made the same mistake that Old Testament Israel made. We treated these people and their technology as spoils of war and took it into ourselves. For the last fifty years we have slowly been transformed by a Nazi fifth column into becoming the Fourth Reich.

Part Four

So What is Next in America?

Leading the way with her Canadian and English allies, the strong middle class Judeo-Christian America is the only nationalistic power standing in the gap of the New World Order. Our national identity as an Independent Free American with certain inalienable rights is something we will not be willing to give up. Our strong base of a middle class social economic power provides a check and balance to the extremes of class struggle politics. The influential power we enjoy today is the result of our united faith and moral practices which struggle to maintain a godliness and right relationship with our creator God. If we depart from this process, we will lose our rewards as a nation.

Understanding this, we see the areas to be attacked. These targets are, the middle-class economy, our national identity and sovereignty and our Christian heritage. The trend since the 50's has been an outward attack on private owned farms and small business that are being eaten up by international corporations. Economic programs which cater to the elite rich and pamper the poor with a lack of accountability and penalize any one with ambition to become more continues to be imposed upon the people. This breaks down the economic balance that the middle class provides. They become the invisible poor as they get lost in between the cracks of aid and assistance. This creates a have and have not society with nothing in between. The mighty Roman Empire fell from within in this same manner.

The moral and ethical beliefs, practices and laws that made us this great Nation are being overturned into a socialistic situational ethics state of mush. The good are made to look evil as moral issues are turned into human rights issues. We now embrace the eastern philosophies and unsound ethics that have made other nations impoverished and decadent.

9-11 was a hook in our jaws leading us to a path toward Globalism. Americans have to be provoked to get involved with the affairs of other nations. By being forced to respond to terrorism on a global level we set the precedence for the United Nations to follow suit.

As the rest of the world gets tired of America playing the role of International Police, the whole process will backlash upon ourselves. I see enough subtle and overt events happening inside America that will eventually create some kind of internal chaos leading to a fractioned society of groups fighting each other for political, religious and racial differences. The justification by the U.N. to intervene will be presented to a world that will be very desirous to hold us to the same standards we held the terrorists to. The events no matter how hypocritical and contrived they may be will result in the collapse of the America we once knew into a combined occupied UN malignancy which becomes the New World Order. In this time we may have help from above, an intervention of "white spirits" from the heavens. We will see this part of the plan more in the Alien section.

Let's see just what the Nazi New Age Lie is and how it is working in America and throughout the world. We will see Theosophy in its most deceptive manner in three forms. The messages of the Aliens, The message of New Age Leaders is actually the same message and plan of Adolf Hitler repackaged and made presentable to a unsuspecting public.

Chapter Nine
A Global Conspiracy to believe a Big Lie!

Part one

Conspiracy Theories: Just for the Paranoid and Reactionaries, or a Biblical fact?

When I was a young Pastor twenty years ago, I used to become irritated whenever "conspiracies" were presented as fulfillment of Bible Prophecy. As a theme to many of the writings, sermons, teaching tapes, radio and TV media, and conspiracy theories usually created both fear and the urgency to "do something". Often that something to be done was either unclear or left unsaid, leaving the listener hanging on a cliff. As a result, the individual needed to rely upon their own strength and resources to "get ready" for the upcoming hard times. Militias and splintered off communal groups headed for the mountains, dug underground and stored supplies for the coming "hard times". These extreme reactions only helped to take away any credibility to some very real warnings that were being proclaimed.

Reflecting back, I believed it was offensive to think that people would run down this country with accusations that clandestine activities were carried out by our Government against the American people. I used to think that this rash of new conspiracies was a left over from the Anti-War Protest years. Frustrated Hippies having nothing else to rebel against found their new source in conspiracies. Also, the idea of having no actual control over policies because "they" already determined the outcome of such matters in secret meetings was offensive. Each individual can and does make a difference so there can be no conspiracies against the people. Or can there?

Close Encounters of the Weird Kind.

My ministry looked more like a survival group than a church since many came from the "outlaw biker" background. Because of this we had been approached by several organizations that wanted us to hook up with them. As I studied the group's beliefs, I had concluded that these people knew enough about assumed Bible prophecy to make themselves dangerous to themselves and to others in the name of doing good for God and Country. What they lacked was the trust and faith in a personal God that could direct their lives without strife and fear.

Over the next twenty years our culture underwent a further breakdown of traditional Judeo-Christian values. At the same time, the New Age/Occult explosion replaced itself as the new world view. In light of this I have to admit that I was wrong in turning a deaf ear to all of the claims of a global conspiracy. My last twelve years of study devoted to the UFO/Alien Abduction phenomena has opened up a "Pandora's box" of cover ups and conspiracies. I have now been left with no other conclusion based on my research than in fact, yes a World conspiracy really does exist! While I now agree with many of the warnings proclaimed by the different fringe groups, (many of whom are being motivated by fear and strife), I have to differ with their response to the reality of this global conspiracy. You can realize these truths and have peace not paranoia. Again we go back to what the Bible has to say about it.

It really doesn't matter what you or I think about conspiracies. Let's take this out of speculation and find out what the Bible has to say about a conspiracy. Even more important, if there is a conspiracy, how should we feel and how do we react?

A Biblical Logical Fact.

A conspiracy is both Biblical and also very logical. If a One World Government is to ever come about as the Biblical Prophetic claims declare, it certainly will not happen by coincidence or chance. A great amount of planning and careful building must be implemented to deceive the whole world into this kind of unity. Even more important is what we are expected to do in light of this.

The Bible gives us a clear "code of conduct" in light of these fearful conspired events. The faith to follow those orders comes from a time tested relationship in a God that can and will provide for each one of us no matter what fearful things might be going on around us. But what does the Bible have to say about them and more important how are we to respond? Is there a balance? Can you believe in the realty of a global Conspiracy to a Big Lie and not behave like a reactionary Paranoid? Yes! We can find a balance and have peace of mind in the midst of all of this. Let's take a look at the Biblical and logical understanding of this Conspiracy.

The "god" of this World.

"In whom the god of this world hath blinded the minds of them which believe not, lest the light of the glorious gospel of Christ, who is the image of God, should shine unto them."

2 Cor 4:4 (KJV)

In 2 Co 4:4, the Bible tells us that Satan is the god of this world. *World* means "the system or arrangement of this entire present universe".

When "god" is used with a small "g" it signifies an imitation or copy of the real thing. It is something done over or repeated. In this application, Satan is not the real God but an imitation. He assisted man in his fall into a linear existence. He set this system up; he has a plan for it. He is able to place people and events accordingly. Just as God works through people, Satan likewise must work through people along with his angelic minions.

He has a Plan.

"For the mystery of lawlessness is already at work: only he who now restrains will do so until he Is taken out of the way."

II Th 2:7 (NKJV)

Paul stated in 2Th2:7 that a Mystery of Iniquity was already actively at work.

This Mystery of Iniquity is actually a five point plan to eternalize this linear dimension into an eternal state. It is outlined through the Prophet Isaiah in Isa 14:13,14. Many Christians believe Satan to be an already defeated foe randomly creating chaos and bringing down as many with him as possible. But, he has fallen is falling and will continue to fall until thrown into the Lake of Fire! We need to understand that the entire linear history of mankind is an on going fall! Linear time is in itself, the "ripple effect" of one wrong decision. This present arrangement was a set up for a particular purpose and reason. It involved this five point plan right from the start.

Satan is much more dangerous than an enemy without hope. We are told that **"a fire burns within him".** **Ezk 28:18** This fire means insanity! In spite of his vast intellect he will always come to the wrong conclusions because his sin and separation from fellowship with God caused him to go insane. He has hope of victory. He thinks he will beat God at his own game! He will do the same but opposite of everything God did in hopes of producing his own heaven or eternal state. As part of this plan he must use mankind and work through them to achieve his goal. The Bible does tell us that an attempt to create a One World Government will be made just prior to Christ's return and is in part, the reason for His return. It is only logical to understand that such an endeavor just doesn't happen on its own. A very sophisticated and elaborate plan would have to be implemented in a clandestine manner. To believe that such an attempt could be accomplished spontaneously or in some happenstance fashion is ridiculous!

The Plan is conspired: The Elite Ten give all for one.

Excuse the redundancy but to flow the Scriptures together several texts have already been mentioned but they flow as an overall plan. For the sake of continuity I briefly include them.

> **"The beast that you saw was, and is not, and will ascend out of the bottomless pit and go to perdition. And those who dwell on the earth will marvel, whose names are not written in the Book of Life from the foundation of the world, when they see the beast that was, and is not, and yet is.**
>
> **"Here is the mind which has wisdom: The seven heads are seven mountains on which the woman sits. There are also seven kings. Five have fallen, one is, and the other has not yet come. And when he comes, he must continue a short time. "And the beast that was, and is not, is himself is also the eighth, and is of the seven, and is going to perdition.**
>
> **"The ten horns which you saw are ten kings who have received no kingdom as yet, but they receive authority for one hour as kings with the beast. These are of one mind, and they will give their power and authority to the beast."**
>
> **Rev 17:8-13**

In Revelation 17th Chapter, we are warned that a "Beast" who was alive and died, will come back to life, ascending out of the bottomless pit to rule this final One World Empire. In context we are told that this "Beast" was a leader of one of seven prior Earthly Empires. Jesus told John in his time that 5 have already been past, One is, (The Roman Empire) and one when it comes will appear for just a short time, then this dead ruler comes back to lead the final Empire just before the return of Christ.

His power will not be his own, The dragon gives him his power. (Rev 13:4) Which is in a sense a supernatural power. He also receives a very natural power from ten people! The Bible tells us that there would be a conspiracy from a small elite group of men that would assist the Antichrist:

> **"And the ten horns which you saw are ten kings, which have received no kingdom yet; but receive power as kings one hour with the beast. They have one mind, and shall give their power and strength to the beast."**
>
> **Rev 17:12,13**

These are ten powerful people we are told, are not leaders of a kingdom or country but have the resources and power that even exceed that of nations! They are the rich elite families that have maintained power for centuries. There are some newcomers, but these are ones who have power and influence that reach beyond national boundaries. With their vast resources and wealth, they willingly provide them for the man of sin and his agenda. This means they are in league together to accomplish a goal.

According to the American Heritage Dictionary the word "conspiracy" means to join or act together, to plan or plot secretly, simply plot, design or scheme. This text is not necessarily describing a ten nation confederacy as supposed by many but is in fact referring to an alliance of same minded powerful people with the desire to achieve a common goal through one man -- the Antichrist. These are Globalists! They are the Leadership of Globalist organizations such as The Counsel of Foreign Relations, The Trilateral Commission, The Builderburges, The Club of Rome, The Illumaniti. Many of the old money Americans, aristocratic European families and oil rich third world families are members who actively support and contribute to the One World cause.

The United Nations is fast becoming the New Global Police force. There are plans already drawn to partition the world into ten sectors for this New World Order!. Is that the reward to the ones who invested everything to this cause? Are they to become the future area Leaders in the New World Order? According to the simplicity of this Scripture it must be! That my friend is a Conspiracy! There is no other way of defining this text of scripture. Ten rich powerful people make a pact and pool their resources together to help set up this final last ruler. It can only be accomplished by conspiring together secretly. The only "proof" is here in the scriptures. A good conspiracy is one with no evidence. This one will work for a short while so we cannot expect proof or what proof is shown will not be believed by the majority. For the skeptic, I hope you can now see that your argument is no longer with "paranoid people" and reactionaries, it is with the Word of God. And the proof, only time will tell. For further reading on the Global Conspiracy I highly suggest reading, *Des Griffin's, The Fourth Reich of the Rich, Emissary Publications 1979*. And *Ralph Epperson's The Unseen Hand, Public Press 1985*

A Time of a Great Deception.

The Bible predicts that there will be a certain point in time when a great deception will come upon all of mankind. This deception would be the end result of an elaborate lie woven in the fabric of time that goes all the way back to the Garden of Eden. Paul called it the Mystery of Iniquity. It is a plan inspired by Satan, conspired by man and allowed by God to fulfill His ultimate will.

> **"...That ye be not soon shaken in mind, or be troubled, neither by spirit, nor by word, nor by letter as from us, as the day of the Lord is at hand. Let no man deceive you by any means: for that day shall not come, except there come a falling away first, and that man of sin be revealed, the son of perdition...For the mystery of iniquity doth already work:...Even him, whose coming is after the working of Satan with all power and signs and lying wonders. And with all deceivableness of unrighteousness in them that perish; because they received not the love of the truth, that they might be saved. And for this cause God shall send them STRONG DELUSION, that they should believe a lie."**
>
> **2 Thess 2:2-11p,**

This great falling away, in the Greek, **apostasia** actually means, "to stand apart or away." This scripture refers to those that may profess to be Christian, but have never made a heart surrender and commitment. In this sense they elect to "stand apart or away" from the truth. However, they do not go astray in many different directions but are all gathered together by a strong delusion. Understanding this action, you have two belief systems, two seeds and only one choice. Jesus describes this separation in the parable of the wheat and tares (Matt 13:25-40).

2 Thessalonians 2:1-12 (Jim W's unofficial paraphrased version).

> "Let no man deceive you by any means: for that day will not come until there is first a gathering of those that refuse the truth, and the man whose nature opposes God, missing the true goal and scope in life, disobeying a divine law, shall be revealed. The offspring not only by birth, but by the very nature of the exclusion of salvation (John 5: 43) Who opposes and exalts himself above all that is called God, or that is worshiped: so that he as God, sits in the holy place of God, showing that he is God.(cf. Rev 13:3 17:8) Don't you remember when I was with you I told you these things? And now you know the Spirit restrains that he, (the anti-Christ) might be revealed in his own opportune time. For the secret of a divine rule broken, is already actively at work. And only the Holy Spirit who now restrains the awareness and understanding of this hidden action restrains, until out of the midst it comes. And then shall the lawless one be revealed, whom the Lord Jesus shall destroy by the Spirit of the mouth, and bring to no effect by the outshining of his presence, of him whose presence is according to the operation of Satan. Even him whose coming is after Satan with all inherent power, exercised authority by permission working miracles with strange, startling appearances in the sky, bearing an ethical message. And with all deceitfulness of following a wrong way which falls short of the divine law in them that perish; because they received not the unconditional gift of love of the manifested truth. (Jo1: 1 1Tim3: 16) that they might be saved. And for this cause God shall send them a wandering error, that they should trust and act upon a lie: that they might all be damned who did not rely and trust in the truth but had a hopeful expectation in a wrong way."

A common preconceived notion of Thessalonians 2:10 assume that unrighteousness refers to people committing continual civil acts of violence resulting in a state of anarchy. When using the original language to its fullest definition, a very different slant can be clearly seen. The unrighteousness committed were acts against God, not the current social structure. It is not what they are doing against the state, but against the laws of God which are incorporated into the state social mores. They are deceived! We are further warned in the scriptures that there would come this time in the last days when traditional values and morals of the Bible would be made to look evil while new alternative social views would be made to look good.

"Woe unto them that call evil good, and good evil; that put darkness for light and light for darkness; that put bitter for sweet, and sweet for bitter! Woe unto them that are wise in their own eyes, and prudent in their own sight!"

Isaiah 5:20

When we as a society redefine moral laws stated in the Bible as human rights issues that impose repressive and restrictive actions against violators of those laws, we have just called good evil and evil good.

Part Two

The Dawning of the New Age of Aquarius
A Gathering together away from Christ.

The New Age movement is that gathering together of those who have already stood apart from the truth. This belief system existed in various forms in all the other prior earthly empires. Only in the last One World Empire would it be completed to its full maturity. The preparation for this lie to permeate throughout the world and be accepted at least by general principle is crucial. Along with this acceptance is the tearing down and developed disdain against Judaism and Christianity for its non-inclusiveness and rejection of the One World Agenda. When this Theosophical world view has overshadowed the Judeo-Christian world view within the minds of the general population the time will be right for the reappearance of the Antichrist!

A Fishnet Structure.

Leaders in the many varied organizations considered being New Age are the first to insist that none of these various groups are connected by any centralized organizational body or are a part of any conspiratorial movement. They are in many cases telling the truth as they understand it. Author Constance Cumby sites in her book, *The Hidden Dangers of the Rainbow*, that the structure is based upon networking." Networking is not a passing fad; it is the key to success for the New Age Movement. "Mrs Cumby's view is verified by Author and New Age leader Marilyn Ferguson. In her book, *The Aquarian Conspiracy,* she states;

> *"The Aquarian Conspiracy is, in effect, a SPIN (Segmented Polycentric Integrated Network) of SPINS, a network of man networks aimed at social transformation. The Aquarian Conspiracy is indeed loose, segmented, evolutionary, and redundant. Its center is everywhere. Although many social movements and mutual-help groups are represented in its alliances, its life does not hinge on any of them."*

Though many New Age groups deny any conspiracy, leaders like Marilyn Ferguson dispute this claim. She points out the fact that most of the New Age groups share many assumptions. It is in this that collusion exists among these groups. Ferguson actually boasts about the goals of this New Age Conspiracy:

> *"Leaderless but powerful network is working to bring about radical change in the United States. Its members have broken with certain key elements of Western thought, and they may have broken continuity with history.... Broader than reform, deeper than revolution, this benign conspiracy for a new human agenda has triggered the most rapid cultural realignment in history. This great shuddering, irrevocable shift overtaking us is not a new political, religious, philosophical system. It is a new mind - the ascendance of startling world-view."*

This "new mind" and "ascendance" of a "startling world view" is the same thing New Age leader, John White proclaimed :

"The difference is inward, in their changed mentality, in their consciousness... Homo noeticus is the name I give to the emerging form of humanity."

The entire movement by their own words is a transformation of society with the central focal point in the creation of the "New Man" for the New Age based no longer by blood alone but a mental consciousness change of "ascendance".

This fishnet structure is a way of slowly changing or "transforming" a people or nation without them even noticing. It is not a sudden or abrupt change but as Ferguson states it,

"Cultural transformation announces itself in sputtering fits and starts, sparked here and there by minor incidents, warmed by new ideas that many smolder for decades. In many different places, at different times, the kindling is laid for the real conflagration- one that will consume the old landmarks and alter the landscape forever."

Jesus compared the end-time events as happening like a woman travailing in birth. Contractions and the pains progressively get more intense so the woman builds a tolerance to the increased amount of pain. It's like the Lobster in the water that is slowly coming to a boiling point. Slowy and progressively the lobster is cooked before he ever knew what was happening. This is exactly what has happened to the United States in the last fifty years and in turn with our influence, the entire world!

This Strategy for Structure was drawn up in the 1920's

Networking becomes the strategy of applying a constant barrage of loosely linked concepts with a common theme. Presented through the media, these themes suggest itself as the new truth to an unsuspecting public, while tearing down and discrediting old standards and traditions. The entire population becomes embarrassed or unsure of their old values as they become receptive to these new truths. This kind of movement can only be effective if every aspect of society has been secured to control what is put out to the public.

A well-known inmate whom I now quote drew up these plans in Landsberg Prison in the early 20's,

"When a movement harbors the purpose <u>of tear-</u><u>ing down a world</u> and <u>building another in its place,</u> complete clarity must reign in the ranks of its own leadership with regard to the following principles: In every really great world shaking movement, pro-paganda will first have to spread the idea of this movement. Thus, it will indefatigably attempt to make the new thought process clear to the oth-ers, and therefore to <u>draw them over to their own</u> <u>ground, or to make them uncertain of their previ-</u><u>ous conviction...</u> If propaganda has imbued a whole people with an idea, the organization can draw the consequences <u>with a handful of men...</u> The better the propaganda has worked, <u>the smaller the orga-</u><u>nization can be;</u> and the larger the number of sup-porters......<u>this core alone shall exclusively lead</u> <u>the movement,</u> that is, <u>determine the propaganda</u> <u>which should lead to its universal recognition, and,</u> <u>in full possession of the power, undertake the ac-</u><u>tions which are necessary</u> for the practical realiza-tion of its ideas......It must not only <u>occupy all the</u> <u>important positions of the conquered territory</u> with the basic core of the old movement, but also <u>con-</u><u>stitute the entire leadership.....</u>The second task of propaganda <u>is the disruption of the existing state</u> <u>of affairs and the permeation of this state of affairs</u> <u>with the new doctrine,</u> while the second task of or-ganization must be the struggle for power, thus to achieve the final success of the doctrine...The most striking success of a revolution based on a philoso-phy of life will always have been achieved when the <u>new philosophy of life as far as possible has been</u> <u>taught to all</u> men, and if necessary, later forced upon</u> <u>them,...</u>This, however, in turn occurs for the most part only in mutual struggle, since it is less a ques-tion of human insight than of the play and <u>workings</u> <u>of forces</u> which can perhaps be recognized from the first, but cannot forever be guided...All great move-ments, whether religious or a political nature, must attribute their mighty successes only to the recog-nition and application of these principles, and all lasting successes in particular are not even think-able without consideration of these laws."

......from Mien Kampf, by Adolph Hitler.

This New Age "transformation" of society and man is the same agenda and vision of the Antichrist Adolf Hitler! The New Age movement is following Hitler's tactics as outlined in *Mein Kamph*! He is not in a hurry, he has all the time in the world but be assured his time is running out in God's plan.

"The Plan" is structured by an elite few

Just as Hitler described in *"Mein Kamph"*, there is in a sense a Hierarchy of leadership within the New Age. They are all Globalist's as this is part of the Agenda. According to Alice Bailey's writings,

> *"The Plan is the organized program of the spiritual Hierarchy to get a selected portion of mankind to the next evolutionary level. Since quality is vital for starting the next "root- race", only selected "star seed" people are designated to make the quantum leap into the next level of human transformation, but even these need careful preparation by more advanced spirits lest they "burnout" in the transition."*

The Plan is quite lengthy, and proposes many global changes. Here are some names of the most influential leaders, some are deceased but their writings have been added to The Secret Doctrine like add-ons to a New Age "Bible" of Doctrines and strategies for implementation.

These additional books begin to reveal an overall plan:

1. *Revelation: the Birth of a New Age* by David Spangler - describing the 'Luciferic initiation' as a New Age requirement

2. *The Open Conspiracy, Blueprints for a World Revolution* by H.G.Wells - calls for "destructive criticism of personal-immortality religions" (Judaism and Christianity)

3. *The Critical Path* by Buckminster Fuller - plans for undermining monotheistic religions by use of computers.

4. *The Armageddon Script* by Peter LeMesurier - plans to stage a "second coming of Christ" to satisfy Christian expectations

5. *The New Genesis: Shaping a Global Spirituality* by Robert Muller - calls for the New Age to begin in 2000,

6a. A couple of ancient texts, *The Aquarian Gospel* (Gnostic writings) and *Urantia* (author unknown) the later describes the "star seed" ET incarnate souls on earth ideas.

6b Other recent books have been additional How to books for the Plan.

The Manual for Co-Creators of the Quantum Leap. By Barbara Marx Hubbards

7. Alice Bailey's many books: *Externalization of the Hierarchy, The Rays and the Initiations, Education in the New Age, and The Problems of Humanity*.

The specific stages of the Plan were "transmitted" in detail through Bailey from the Tibetan Master, "Djwahl Kuhl" beginning in the 1930s. Much of this was shared only with inner-circle disciples until 1975, when the New Age leaders received instructions (clairvoyantly) to go public. Bailey's guide confirmed Helena Blavatsky's message, in *The Secret Doctrine*, that open implementation of "the Plan" would not be possible until "the end of the 20th century," when the generation then coming of age "will inaugurate the framework, structure and fabric of the New Age." Most of the agenda can be found in Alice Bailey's, *Externalization of the Hierarchy*.

It is an Interwoven Network.

As predicted by Bailey, the New Age movement has permeated the structure and fabric of 21st century society. Our public schools, corporate America and various Government agencies have incorporated the New Age into their systems. For example, *"World Core Curriculum"*, written by Robert Muller is acknowledged to be based on "the teachings set forth in the books of Alice A Bailey by the Tibetan Teacher, Djwhal Khul." This book is promoted by the UN and has entered the public school systems. Industrial giants such as General Motors, AT&T, Chrysler Corporation, Exxon Oil, Lockheed, and Blue Cross-Blue Shield require their managers to attend New Age seminars.

Shortly after her book circulated, the Department of Defense invited Marilyn Ferguson as keynote speaker at their annual dinner in 1982. Other agencies who have adopted teachings and texts are the National Institute of Mental Health, and the Department of Health, Education and Welfare. This is taken from a list from over 20 years ago! The influence and lists have grown considerably since. Certain popular "spirit guides" being channeled today are seriously considered by the United Nations, through an unpublicized group called SEAT, the "Society for Enlightenment and Transformation. These spirits include: Kryon, Lord Maitreya and "The Group". I refer to the on line book, *The Rainbow Swastika* by Hannah Newman and *The Hidden Dangers of the Rainbow* by Constance Cumbey for far greater detail about this elaborate entwining

New Age Credibility Gained: The Transformation.

Concurrent with the influx of New Age philosophy into today's culture, business and professional leaders throughout the world are accepting the New Age thoughts and principles with evangelical fervor. As a result of being taught at corporate levels in seminars, people are finding effective and desirable results with their job performance. This only reinforces their belief in the New Age system.

Through the practical applications of these new alternate methods of visualization, meditation, holistic healing and the like, the individual, after experiencing effective results usually delve further into other New Age practices. Many of these practices are supernaturally empowered by millions of demon entities that are working hard to give credibility to the New Age. These include, "channeling", psychic readings, spirit guides, and many other occult practices that God severely warns about in both New and Old testaments as coming from the rebel enemy of God and mankind; Satan.

As they begin this new level of "contact" real supernatural workings are experienced, that in most cases, they were never aware of before. "Open minds" that have rejected the truth will believe anything after experiencing this "new power" in their lives. Unfortunately most become convinced of their rightness and superior level of initiation based upon experience alone. Because something is real does not make it automatically good or right!

Further support for the New Age comes from the appeal for "Ancient Wisdom". In the lack of understanding our own past history according to the Biblical account, this knowledge gap has created a great misrepresentation and perception about the past. First the traditional secular view as given by modern scientist-priests is a distortion of half truths which contain many gaps and questions unexplained.

Recently we have many new "fringe science researchers" who have discovered hidden truths that attempt to fill in those gaps and explain what has never been understood before. These discovered truths are real but the manner in which they are perceived by these researchers are contrary to a Biblical description and become a cement to explain an even greater distortion of the past, which becomes a part of the big lie for the future! I can explain this transformation going back to Babylon.

Babylonian Roots: Ancient Myths and Their Practices Turn the Tables of Truth!

The ancient Sumarians, Babylonians and Assyrians all believed in pantheism. This is a belief system composed of many of the same gods and goddesses. The gods and goddesses of pantheism all interconnect in one way or another. These cultures believed the earth to be a goddess, a living entity and in a monistic sense connected to all of matter. Mankind was to be a work force for the gods and was subject to the constant changing whims and disputes between the various gods.

Unlike the Living God of the Bible, the gods of pantheism project the same flawed behavior that mankind does. Enlil is a short-tempered god who was responsible for the great flood. He created mankind and possessed the power to speak things into existence. Enlil is compared to the Old Testament God of the Hebrew Bible. The Hebrew derivative is El, which is the generic name for God in the Old Testament which shares the same etymology with Enlil.

Aruru is the mother goddess who assisted Enlil, she was later replaced by Ishtar. Ea or Enki was a god sympathetic to mankind. He was the Lord of all wisdom and incantations (like the serpent). The ram' 's head or a goatfish symbolizes him. His son Marduk (symbolized by the Bull) later usurped Enlil ''s position as head of the Pantheon. Marduk was the head of the Anunnaki, who are the underworld gods who came from heaven. They have been described by ancient Sumarian texts as being "white god's" from the skies. Furthermore, the Anunnaki received instructions to build Babylon. Credit is given to the Anunnaki for giving man science and culture.

Ancient Babylonians also believed in magic and charms, which they carried with blends of substances in pouches. As part of their cultural heritage, they practiced a form of holy prostitution and performed human sacrifices. Despite their barbaric practices, they were also the focal point for international trade and commerce, with a banking system similar to our own!

This culture also had the oldest know writings that predate the Bible by at least a thousand years. Because of this, many modern professionals in the scientific community automatically give them credit as being more accurate than the Bible, without considering the source and moral condition of the Babylonian society. Many go so far as to claim that the writers of the Bible gleaned accounts from them as opposed to being inspired by God. In America today, even some liberal seminaries teach this as fact.

A Shell Game Against the Truth

How could any modern sophisticated person today believe or give any credence to such childish sounding tales and myths? Part of the reason may be the misconception that our past is primitive. Science and archeology has been willing to ignore certain anomalous artifacts. However, willful ignorance leaves much to be accounted for.

Zechariah Sitchin states that the myths and legends of gods from the skies are in fact an actual historical remembrance of extraterrestrial visitation and intervention. Sitchin claims that the tenth planet, Nibiru, is on a 3,600-year orbital path opposite the earth, which removes it from detection. According to the same tablets interpreted by Sitchin, this planet serves as home of the Anunnaki, the "white gods" from the skies. Furthermore, Sumarian myth says the Anunnaki now live underground within the earth.

As a Hebrew scholar Mr. Sitchin could be considered an authority on the Bible, in fact he uses Biblical references to progress his claims. The word "Elohim" is the most commonly used name for God in the Old Testament. It refers to the supreme God in the plural sense. He cites a passage in Genesis 1:26 where God (Elohim) says, "...... let us make man in our own image." Speaking as a Hebrew scholar Sitchin claims that the Elohim are actually the Anunnaki, whom he claims are the extraterrestrials. Therefore we are a product of their intervention. There is a Biblical allusion to the Anunnaki, but it is not the Elohim.

Elohim is the implication of the three part triune nature of God. Even the Old Testament mentions the three parts of God.

Father and Son is mentioned in Isaiah 55:5,

> *"...... nations knew not thee shall run unto thee because of the LORD thy God, and for the Holy One of Israel......"*
>
> **(KJV)**

The Spirit is mentioned in Ezekiel 36:27,

> *"......and I will put my Spirit within you, and cause you to walk in my statutes...... "*

In addition, there is a text of scripture, Deuteronomy 6:4, that every Jewish person alive today both knows and recites as prayer,

> *" Hear O Israel: The Lord our God is one Lord."*

In this verse **Echod** is Hebrew for one; its meaning is in the sense of a composite one. The same word is used in Genesis 2:24 when the man and woman come together in marriage, they are no longer two but one flesh. God and man made in the same image of God refers to this same concept. According to the Bible we have a three part existence; a body, a soul and an exclusive part that only God can create or control; our spirit. One then is a composite one.

The Biblical reference to the Anunnaki is completely different than what Sitchin is trying to pass off. The Sumarian Anunnaki, who came from heaven and now live underground, share the same word etymology as the Biblical **Anakum.** in Numbers 13:33 and the Nephilum of Genesis 6. They were the fallen angels who came from Heaven, were judged and sentenced, they now reside in Hell (inside the earth). This description parallels the Sumarian myth of the Anunnaki! These are the bad guys not God as Elohim, (and we are not their descendants). In this twisting and false representation of Scripture good becomes evil, and evil becomes good, just like the Bible said it would be.

While some of the research of Zechariah Sitchin may be interesting and valid, he grossly misunderstands the Scriptures and falsely misrepresents them to prove his unfounded beliefs. (Whether ignorantly or innocently, I do not know). In doing this he places himself in a position of being a blasphemer. He is leading many on a wrong path away from a loving God to their destruction. Unlike any other culture, the Hebrews also used a plural form to denote an importance to a concept, person or emotion. This is well known amongst Bible scholars as an established truth. What appears to be some "new revelation" by Sitchen is only a gross disregard for known established truths by fellow scholars. One such scholar who has offered to debate the issue publicly is Mike Heiser, who is an Ivy League Scholar. Sitchen has never responded to his offer.

In his book, *"The Gods of Eden,"* William Bramley takes it one step further. He suggests that the Elohim created man as a work force and has created religion in particular the Christian religion to keep the creation submissive to his will. The Ea or the serpent took pity on mankind and desired to give him wisdom to be equal with the "gods". Bramley also believes that aliens have played the role of "gods" in our past.

The rest of his book explains how the suppressive Christian church through the Elohim was responsible for all wars and plagues and human suffering. Jesus was a creation of the aliens to secure complacency upon the human race. Paul's conversion was an abduction experience and the entire church was a controlled organization by them. Secret societies are alien controlling posts set up by Ea or the serpent to control and direct esoteric knowledge and keep the Elohim in check. In these various beliefs, there is a set up of good alien-bad alien with man in the middle.

In this amazing twist, God becomes the oppressor and Satan becomes the liberator! Seemingly foolish sounding ancient legends from our past are made believable and their doctrines acceptable as superior with the added explanation of aliens and their technology. And once again the Good is made Evil! and Evil is made Good!

"Scientific Proof" for the New Age?

Many valid scientists with impressive credentials working on "fringe" trends of research have been combined to help validate Theosophy. With scientific sophistication the monistic idea of "the oneness of all matter," is explained down to the point of quantum physics. Quite often prominent scientists accept and proclaim this as fact. Furthermore, their work is interpreted by active New Ager's and added as "proofs". The following example leads up to the idea know as the coming "Paradigm Shift".

The concept of synchronicity popularized by psychiatrist Carl Jung states that everything is related as an indivisible whole. When two events that seem to have no causal relationship, yet in close proximity of time seem related, you have synchronicity. A common example of this would be a time when you might be thinking about someone you haven't heard from in a long time and suddenly you run into that person within the next few days.

In 1964 the synchronicity principle received its alleged "scientific" support. J. S. Bell in Switzerland derived from his experiments that if identically charged particles fly apart and the experimenter changes the polarity of one, the other one is changed instantaneously, as though each particle knows what the other is doing.

Nobel Prize winning Belgian chemist, Ilya Prigogine's hypothesis is that the natural law of entropy (the Second Law of Thermodynamics), which states that all matter will eventually break down to its lowest elements in a state of disorganization) is counteracted by a higher law of Syntropy. This accounts for the evolution of higher, more intricate levels of organization and design. Prigogine claims that there is a natural organizing force (Blavatsky's electro-magnetic consciousness fohat?) behind the universe bringing assorted parts into increasingly more complex systems. This occurs by the dissipation of energy, which creates the potential for sudden reordering. In this sense, life eats up entropy. It has the potential to create a new higher order through the shaking up of old ones.

The "Hundredth Monkey" experiment conducted in 1953 by researcher Lyall Watson became a "living example" of harmonic convergence. Watson studied a colony of monkeys on the island of Koshima, Japan. The monkeys were given sweet potatoes to bring them out into the open for better observation. Before eating them one of the female apes began washing off the dirt by dunking it into the sea. She taught this to her offspring. Soon others learned this trick. When 100 of them began to practice this, suddenly the awareness overtook the entire colony, even to other islands and the mainland. After a film and three articles published in scientific journals, this became an imbedded fact. Afterwards Watson admitted faking his findings. In New Age circles, it is still used as "proof".

The basic idea is that when an idea is taught to enough people a "critical mass" is created and the release of that energy will reorganize everyone else into synchronism or harmony into the higher form. The magic number based on interpretations of the Mayan and Aztec calendars for this to take place for the human race is 144,000! This is an interesting parallel to Christian Eschatology. The Mayan calendar ends this great cycle at 2012.

Harmonic Convergence "Setup"

According to New Age thought, all life gives off vibrations or resonance and light or auras. To create harmony the life forms must be in harmony to the earth mother. In this matter the paradigm shift can occur with little resistance or problems. But what if... some do not conform or harmonize with the flow? What happens to this paradigm shift? They say that just as the rubbing together of two tectonic plates beneath the earth's crust causes earthquakes, the rubbing together of conflicting vibrations will also produce natural reactions to "mother earth".

This sure sounds like a set up to me. I know of one group of people who will never ever buy into this One World Theosophical world-view no matter what is blamed on them for their lack of acceptance or tolerance to it.

Part Three

Theosophy's Next Holocaust: The End Time Set up Against Christians.

Following are a few examples of implications or outright proclamations from many segments of the New Age Movement. Also included are the "filtered" and acceptable ideas coming from the majority within the UFO community. When you add these pieces together it is not so hard to project what course they will lead to or their grim conclusion. Added with the right series of events also alluded to or proclaimed by the same people, a growing threat is being directed toward Christians and Jews.

1. In Zechariah Sitchin's many books; a re-explanation of the creation of man is elaborately given as nothing more than a product of genetic experiments by extra-terrestrials. This educated, intelligent man who possesses many scholarly credentials is very convincing in his claims. Despite his vast resources and intellect, he does not even understand the simplest of Bible truths about God. He rejects the thought of a personal God, closing his mind to any hope of a Creator that loves him in spite of his rejection and lies!

2. Continuing in the fashion of Sitchin's groundwork William Bramley adds to the notion that Christians and Christianity were formed as a control measure by the Elohim. (In the sense of a group of bad aliens). They, (the Christians) are responsible for wars, plagues and persecutions of pagans and others of alternate beliefs. The Crusades, Spanish Inquisition, Holy Roman Empires and Salem Witch burnings being some of the "Christians" crowning achievements.

Bramley's book is presented in an elaborate and intelligent manner, but based on a wrong premise and devoid of the true meanings of the Bible. He also ignores another part of history; the martyrs who were real Christians that suffered and were killed by the hands of the same people he simply and loosely calls "Christian". By the time you read his version of early Church history, Christians and Aliens are almost one in the same. (At least the bad ones from his viewpoint.) Christ was created by the Elohim and Paul's conversion on the road to Damascus was an alien abduction. This suggests that the rest of the founding influence of the early church was formed not by God through man but by Aliens through man to maintain control and dominance.

3. This same thought was presented to Linda Moulton-Howe. Linda is the Director of Special Projects for CBS and produced the TV series *Sightings*. In the late 70's a side career was launched as she began to investigate cattle mutilations while working at a Denver affiliate. Now she is considered to be the nations top expert on this subject. In 1983 she left her job to work on an HBO film *UFO's: The ET Factor*. I will let her tell the story in her own words from her book, *An Alien Harvest*.

>**"I went to the Air Force Office of Special Investigations (AFOSI) at Kirkland AFB in Albuquerque, New Mexico. An AFOSI agent (MJ Richard Doty suspected member of "Avery" a dis-information govt. program) gave me some pages to read entitled "Briefing Paper for the President of the United States of America" about extra-terrestrial vehicles and alien beings. I was told that the government had decided to disclose information to the public about its contact with alien life forms. Further, I was told that several thousand feet of color and black and white film would be provided for the HBO documentary. That film was described as historic, shot between 1947 and 1964. The content concerned UFO crash-**

es, retrieval of dead alien bodies- and at least one live E.T...According to the briefing paper I read, the creature lived at Los Alamos until June 18, 1952, when it died of unknown causes...In 1983 the ET story that was outlined for me by the briefing paper and government sources said that the Gray aliens are responsible for our biological evolution through manipulation of DNA in already evolving primates on this planet. Various time intervals of DNA manipulation were specified for 25,000 15,000 5,000 and 2,500 years ago. Included in this government description of the Gray intervention in this planet"s evolution was their creation of a being 2,000 years ago to be placed here to teach Homo Sapiens about love and non-violence. I asked the AFOSI agent at Kirkland AFB if the briefing paper specifically meant Jesus Christ and he nodded his head."

She goes on to describe that an agreement was made between the United States Government and the Grays. We would allow "controlled" abductions of humans and cattle slaughters and build underground bases in exchange for exclusive access to receive and develop their technology. Another group was mentioned the Talls or Nordics. They were said to be the bad guys, having been losers in a 300-year war with the Grays. Now they tolerate each other. The story today goes that the Government was tricked by the Grays, the Nordics are the good guys and the government is powerless to stop the Grays.

Suddenly the plug was pulled and denial of any of these events followed. Linda never got her promised film. She has become suspect even by some of her fellow investigators. I have corresponded with her and find her to be a very pleasant and sincere person. I do not believe or share in her world-view, but I do believe she is a woman of integrity. I only pray she finds the real truth.

4. Television is the strongest media format for conditioning the masses. It is always interesting to see what is being said and what supporters are being created by it. Consider the very short-lived Television program "*Dark Skies!*" The intense announcer proclaims, "history is not what you think it is! They're here! And they are hostile!" In the show John Loenguard is a pilot turned Majestic operative. (Majestic is an alleged elite group of men overseeing UFOs and the Alien presence on earth.) He discovers that the Grays (who gave the United States an ultimatum to

surrender to them) have given a certain portion of the human population a hive collective consciousness implant by means of a parasite. Once inside the person, they become their mind controlled operatives. Before the individual embraces some sort of sphere of light the parasite can be induced out and freedom for the individual restored. Once these people accept or receive the "Light" there is no redemption, only death as a release from this horrible control.

When the program was going to be taken off the air, all on-line members to "*Dark Skies*" received an urgent E-mail memo from the producer. This Letter stated that it was important to remain on the air because the basis of the story was real. There was a real John Loenguard. He quit Majestic and wanted to go public and reveal everything. The story, being too fantastic to be believed, would be presented as a "fictional story". This collective hive consciousness is a running theme in many other sci-fi movies such as the Borg of *Star Trek* or the Ga-ou-uld of *SG1*.

These four examples are just a few of the many more subtle pieces being put out to the public. They represent a pattern of thought typical and consistent to the New Age and UFO community. They also represent a popular theme of Hollywood as well.

Now concerning the skeptic who would contest all of these allegations. I have no real evidence; I cannot prove any of this as being true. However, don't let your sacred quest for "proof" distract you from the main issue. It doesn't matter if it is true or not. Some of it just might be and maybe none of it is. The point is that it is being <u>presented as truth</u> to the public. Furthermore, what matters is that <u>people believe it is true</u>, at least enough of the right people to make a difference. No one could "prove" the rumors of what was happening to, "all those people being loaded in rail cars in Germany" either. Proof or lack of it, certainly didn't stop the Holocaust back then, and it won't again.

"Truth is not what is; truth is what people believe it to be". Adolf Hitler:

The main concern should not be whether it is true or not, but rather what is being implied as the truth. Put the pieces all together. This is what they imply, truth not being the issue, as this is part of the big lie:

- There is no personal God, only aliens acting as a god or misunderstood as being God.

- Aliens created man.

- Aliens created Jesus.

- If Gray aliens are bad, Christ and Christianity are just a controlling factor for them to impose their will upon mankind and suppress them. Therefore Bramely's twisted ideas would be right.

- If *Dark Skies* was a program based on truth, then who are the ones that were infected by a symbiotic collective consciousness that makes them follow and obey the alien agenda? The ones who "saw the light?" They would be Bramely's controlled Christians of course.

- If Christians refuse to conform into the harmony of the world order even at the cost of "causing natural catastrophes" then they must be the ones controlled by this alien entity and therefore causing the catastrophes.

- If there is no hope for them, as they have "seen the light" then regretfully, the only way to free them from this controlled rebellion is to ...kill them. With New Agers belief in reincarnation life will simply recycle itself so it is not all that bad, they will just come back free from the alien implant. After all the sacrifice of the few for the benefit of the many! It is us or them!

In this scenario, it is not so far fetched to realize that Christians may be accused of unknowingly accepting an alien entity into themselves and not the Holy Spirit of God! In a sense they are not far from the truth. Being born again we do receive a part of God, which is His Spirit into ourselves. Certainly nothing related to a Gray reptilian creature! But again it depends on how you look at it and whose seed you are.

Perhaps this sounds too incredible to be true now. You might believe this is just some paranoid speculation on my part? Perhaps, but this could be the future logic and rationale that produces the next holocaust by mercy killings. I certainly do not think the explosion of aliens and their consistent New Age beliefs by Hollywood is a coincidence. Neither are the role playing games that shape and mold these realties to our youth. All of this Intergalactic imagery just might play an important part of End Time events.

Part Four

The Extrapolation of the Gospel of Jesus Christ the Greatest Deception since the Flood!

This next part will be a brief possibility of how this big lie just might conclude itself. This is *only a guess* and not meant to be made into any doctrine. I base this guess on the patterns of the same but opposite from statements of those in the UFO and New Age Communities, as well as a few scriptures that might allude to this format. The only reason I would give any consideration to the mediums and their "channeled messages" is for a pattern of the same but opposite. Through the occult they have their own prophetic promises. Half truths but in this they tip off what the enemy is planning. In a booklet I have on the rise of Hitler based on the occult perspective, it reads out like a same but opposite Gospel story. In the same manner I see these "experiencers", mediums and contactees fulfilling the same role for another set up of events.

New Age Medium and UFO cultist, Ruth Montgomery states in her book "Aliens Among Us", that there is a coming shift of the earth's axis which will cause this "cleansing." The catastrophic events will destroy a large portion of life. Her "guides" have told her,

> *"that there will be flying machines to remove some of the earth people who are too valuable to be allowed to go into spirit, because of the need for their wisdom."*

This theme runs steady in UFO "Channeled messages" by various cult leaders.

Thelma Terrell of Durango, Co., channels messages from "Ashtar Command". They gave her the name "Tuella", of which she is more know as. [Tuella and Thule (name of mythical Aryan capital) both pronounced two-la. A pattern also in that the names of many of these channeled beings seem to be the same mythical names of heroes or names of demons.] "Tuella" states as received by her E.T. contact "Andromeda Rex" (Indiana Jones has nothing on this guy) that,

> *"The Great Evacuation will come upon the world very suddenly. The flash of emergency events will*

160

be as the lightening that flashes in the sky. Our res-
cue ships will be able to come close enough in the
twinkling of an eye to set the lifting beams in op-
eration. In a moment. Mankind will be lifted, levi-
tated shall we say, by the beams from our smaller
ships. These smaller craft will in turn taxi the per-
sons to the larger ships overhead, higher in the at-
mosphere, where there is ample space for millions
of people."

New Age writings by Alice Bailey, David Spangler, Angi Yogi,
H.G. Wells, The Theosophical Society, Rosicrucians, all describe a
coming "cleansing" action that will have to take place at a critical
point of this convergence or next evolutionary step up for Earth
and Mankind. David Spangler's quote is very ominous to any
Bible believing Christian or Jew,

"...those of us who refuse to accept the "Christ" will
be sent to another dimension other than physical
incarnation, out of physical embodiment, to anoth-
er level of vibration where we will be happier."

Abductees' accounts also indicate one or both evacuations of
certain people. Billy Meier and his Pleiadian encounters with
"Semjase" although slightly different (WWIII) mirror the same
warnings. With the strategies of staging a false Second coming of
Christ by Peter LeMesurier's *"The Armageddon Script"*, One can
almost see an entire end time traditional scenario taking shape.

Add a couple of scriptures that allude to these events and you
have the same but opposite events happening just before and
interwoven with the real events. Let's take a look at these
scriptures first. Then I would like to suggest an explanation of
this intertwining.

Thanks in part to the *Left Behind* series the traditional end time
events are becoming known even to non Christians or Christian
professing people who have never been taught anything about the
return of Christ by their "Churches". As part of these traditional
teachings comes the idea of the "Rapture". This is the sudden
removal of all Born Again believers in Christ assumed to be just
before the "Great Tribulation".

With this world wide expectation, imagine a scenario in which
there is a sudden removal or disappearance of many but not a
tremendous amount of people. Instead of being the "Born Again

Christians" it becomes the hierarchy and leaders of the New Age movement. At the same time a flap wave of UFO sightings are reported around the world.

A Possible Scenario: A Phony Rapture that Includes UFO's ?

With this sudden void of influence, two things begin to result. One, a Christian revival such as the world has never experienced before. The second, a Fake Tribulation period in which the tables are turned where good is evil and evil is good. This could begin with many sudden earth changes and natural catastrophes.. (It has been alleged with much support that H.A.A.R.P. is a project that could influence weather and produce some of these effects. In the appendix I will give a few books and sources for further research)

During this time the world will begin to piece together an understanding that the New Age is fulfilling Christian prophecy and replacing Christianity in the same manner as Christ was the fulfillment of Old Testament prophecy and replaced the Old covenant with the New Covenant of Grace. It can be why the New Agers say they want to eliminate Judaism, and adjust Christianity from its Jewish influence (or as they put it, its contamination)

This sudden new turn and direction for America's Christian revival incurs Satan's wrath and leads to an attack.(Third part of Washington's vision discussed in the Alien section) These threatened Nations, with an alliance of like minded nations lead to an-all out, short-lived war or attack on America. In response there is a "supernatural intervention". The "Christ" consciousness, Matreya and thousands of "angels" appear to deliver America and save the day. They come in the "clouds of heaven", or rather, nut and bolt UFOs.

In a space age Inter-galactic format, with good angel aliens and bad angel reptilian ones, man is in the middle. Bible prophecy, ancient myths, all other religious prophecies and occult myths are fulfilled. This results in the attempt to unite the World U.N. style. Christian resistance and refusal to accept this New Age becomes obvious. In a very convincing manner, Christians because they seem to prosper both spiritually and in the natural at this time are blamed for being the deceived ones who unknowingly took a mark. The Holy Spirit is explained and viewed as being an alien entity. The hidden truths of the Grays and their connection to Judaism and Christianity are "revealed."

The Theosophical concept of the "Harmonic Convergence" set up, is explained and added to the list of crimes committed by the controlled Christians. The natural catastrophes are their fault also. The second Holocaust begins. In a matter of a few years of continued resistance and even militant resistance by "Christian professing" people who know just enough about prophecy without knowing their Savior, fight back and become dangerous to themselves and others. This leads to another "Final solution". The first Holocaust is perhaps justified on the same alien implant basis. Hitler then becomes a Hero of mankind instead of the mass murderer.

In the midst of all of this we have the two witnesses who are explaining by the Word of God just what is going on and why. We also have the Antichrist and False prophet who came on the scene. Both are said to have an assumed 31/2 years of ministry or power. You have two seeds and two ways of looking at these events and people. One will see the two witness as the Antichrist and False Prophet, and the Antichrist and False Prophet will be seen as the two witnesses representing possibly Tao. The Ying and the Yang. One who looks like the traditional Anglo-Saxon Jesus is the False Prophet who directs the worlds attention and worship to the Antichrist Adolf Hitler who now reveals himself and the whole world marvels. (This could not happen until the principles of reincarnation, Karma and ascension to an Avatar are taught and made to be understood by the common man). Israel and Egypt are horrified. It fortunately results in a national repentance and acceptance of the real Jesus Christ.

By now the real mark of the beast, whether a challenge of commitment or a literal mark is openly implemented and it creates the division of one camp from the other. The two wittiness reach the end of their ministry and are killed. Three days later there is a resurrection and ascension in the sight of everyone. It is explained away as the Antichrist and the False prophet being tossed into the lake of fire or as the New Agers would say taken to another dimension where they can work out their karma and be in a happier place.

Immediately after this, a phony Judgment by the false prophet takes place. This will somehow include a bringing down and capturing of real angels who along with many earthbound Christians who will be judged and killed. This will be a fake "White Throne" Judgment. Any theological discrepancies will be quickly and easily explained away by the sudden shock and impact of so many changes and the "proof" of this intergalactic war.

Then the real rapture hits. Suddenly all of God's people are gone. This is explained as the second removal of those who would not accept the New Age. This event would be explained as the Biblical separation of the sheep and goats, and wheat and tares mentioned by Jesus.

At the second coming of Christ, it is recorded that Jesus Himself puts a new name upon the foreheads of His own that no one else knows. All that are left take this mark thinking they have just entered this thousand year rein of the Christ and instead they have taken the real mark of the beast! As the Armies gather to finish off Israel and get to the center of the earth following an occult tradition of the axis pole, the Holy of Holies in Jerusalem, The real Christ returns and with nothing but a word from His mouth the Armies are destroyed.

I have simplified this greatly, as there are many details and probably a million questions about particulars. But it is not my point to assume all of the details and wrap this up in a neat little package. I can't do that, no one can. This is only an educated guess. If this pattern begins to happen I am sure God will reveal more needed details as we need it. This is just a generalization of how events may happen that include "aliens" and the ancient myths and prophecies from all religions and the occult. This would be the coming together of all things in an opposite direction than that of God's. It will only be by having God's Spirit in you that you will even be able to tell who is who.

Consider this Mockery.

God revealed Himself to the Jew first. Law, Jews, Burnt offering. It was through the Law that the Jews came into the presence of God by a burnt offering. When Hitler came the first time He destroyed the Law, took the Jew and made him the burnt offering.

Christians= Faith by Grace. With Jesus fulfilling the Law, a Christians way into the presence of God is by Faith in God's grace. If Hitler is to come back a second time, he destroys faith by explaining away everything in "natural" terms through technology and "Aliens". He then takes the Christian and kills him by "Grace" which will be a mercy killing. With an understanding of being innocently infected by an "Alien" entity that causes us to resist the New Age which in turn causes the natural catastrophes, we are killed for the benefit of mankind and ourselves. With the embedded belief in reincarnation, this would not be a final act of death, as we would simply come back again and be free of this "Alien implant"

Strange, imaginative, maybe even scary? Perhaps, but this might be the end of the New Age Rainbow and the inclusion of UFO's and Aliens in an End-Time scenario.

Part Five

The New Age/Alien Agenda = The Nazi Goals

In this last chapter we have seen the plans and agenda of the New Agers and the messages of the Aliens as being the same. Is it really a continuation of the Nazi agenda? This last section will include quotes from Hitler himself. These are documented in the appendix.

Guidance by "Invisible Forces" and the use of Magic

"... it is less a question of human insight than the play and workings of forces which can perhaps be recognized from the first, but cannot forever be guided."
quote from Mein Kampf

"But in his estate shall he honor the God of forces: and a god whom his fathers knew not."
Dan11:38

The Occult and Secret Societies

"The hierarchical organization and initiation through symbolic rites, that is to say, without bothering the brain but by working on the imagination through magic and symbols of a cult, all this is the dangerous element, and the element I have taken over."

Occult based Science

"There is a Nordic and National-Socialist Science which is apposed to Judaeo- Christian Liberal Science"

Dangers and Greatness ahead:

"Our Revolution is a new stage or, rather, the final stage in an evolution which will end by abolishing history...You know nothing about me; my party comrades have no conception of the dreams which haunt me...the world has reached a turning point; we are now at a critical moment in time...The planet will undergo an upheaval which you uninitiated people cannot understand...What is happening is something more than the advent of a new religion."

Create the New Man

"Anyone who interprets National Socialism merely as a political movement knows almost nothing about it. It is more than religion; it is the determination to create a new man."

"Creation is not yet completed. Man has reached a definite stage of metamorphosis. The ancient human species is already in a state of decline, just managing to survive. Humanity accomplishes a step up once every seven hundred years, and the ultimate aim is the coming of the Sons of God. All creative forces will be concentrated in a new species. The two varieties will evolve rapidly in different directions. One will disappear, and the other will flourish. It will be infinitely superior to modern man. Do you understand the profound meaning of our National- Socialist movement?"

" I will tell you a secret...I am founding an Order. It is from there that the second stage will emerge- the stage of the Man-God, when Man will be the measure and center of the world. The Man-God, that splendid Being, will be an object of worship...But there are other stages about which I am not permitted to speak..."

Globalism with a Caste system

"I had to encourage "national" feelings for reasons of expediency; but I was already aware that the "nation" idea could only have a temporary value. The day will come when even here in Germany what is known as "nationalism" will practically have ceased to exist. What will take it"s place in the world will be a universal society of masters and overlords."

"What will the social order of the future look like? Comrades, I will tell you: there will be class of overlords, and after them the rank and file of Party members in hierarchical order, and then the great mass of anonymous followers, servants and workers in perpetuity, and beneath them, again all the conquered foreign races, the modern slaves. And over and above all these there will reign a new and exalted nobility of whom I cannot speak...But of all these plans the ordinary militant members will know nothing..."

Who or What did Hitler see

"The New Man is living amongst us! He is there! What more do you want? I will tell you a secret: I have seen the New Man. He is intrepid and cruel! I was afraid in his presence!"

Did Hitler understand Nazism would become a religion?

"I will become a religious figure"

One last word from Der Fuhrer.

In the book "*The Sign*" by Robert Van Kampen he quotes from a movie made by the personal aid to Hitler, the last person to see him alive. If true, we have a prophetic last word spoken by Der Fuhrer. Hitler"s last words to his aid was, " **to break up and scatter to the West**". In response to this statement, the aid replied to Hitler, "For whom should we fight now for?" With that, Hitler said in a monotone voice, **"For the coming man"**. With that Hitler closed the door to his bunker and shot himself with his own gun, his wife swallowing a capsule of cyanide along his side.

We can now see that this same message and beliefs of Hitler and the Nazis are the same as the Aliens as well as the New Age globalist beliefs and agenda. In this we see the full account of the Lying Sign and Lying Wonder. The UFO and its message.

UFO Conclusion

I will let this be the end of the first part of this book. We have covered the entire subject of the clouds of heaven, what they are, how they work and where they travel to. We have seen the plan of non human rebels in alliance with human agents, who imitate these clouds with the nut and bolt UFO. Their desire is to rob the glory from God and replace His very presence with their own as Aliens. We have learned that the way these rebels accomplish their goals was to give one man and his group the forbidden physics to produce the technology of a man made UFO, the sign and lying wonder. Aided by an elite group of wealthy globalists this rebel alliance will deceive the whole world to unite in a God rejecting One World government/religion. We have seen the dangerous act against America and the important role She will play in this. We have understood this New Age spiritual movement as the spirit of Antichrist. This plan breaches time and space to deceive if it were possible, the very elect.

Next we will take a Biblical look at Aliens. Who they are, where they come from, what they are doing with abductions and how they fit into this plan beyond time and space. Their story is somewhat separate from the UFO story with a different set of goals. And yet their story will dovetail into the material you have already learned about the UFO. We will conclude this section with a coming two phase Invasion. One is clandestine spanning time and space, while the other will culminate in a literal full scale Invasion of Earth from below not above!

Section Two: The Aliens

In this next section we will take a complete look at scriptures which speak about human and non-human entities and their involvement with mankind. The most broad biological term for Alien is:

> *"A plant or an animal that occurs in or is natural- ized in a region to which it is not native."*
> **New World Dictionary**

On that basis these non human entities may truly be Aliens. However, from a Biblical perspective, we do have to consider the many scriptures which describe beings as angels and fallen angels of various orders. To the person outside of faith this term might seem like a religious one based on ignorance and superstition. I ask that you look past the term with all of the stereotypical misconceptions, and consider these as real beings. If you can do this you might see an amazing line up and explanation for much that is being experienced in our time. For those standing in faith, you might have to set aside some preconceived misunderstandings that have followed the Church since medieval times. With an open mind let's allow the Bible to interpret itself by itself about such creatures.

Within the UFO community there are three main types of Aliens that have claimed to be encountered throughout the whole world. They are the little Grays, the Hybrid and the Nordic. There are mentions of other non human variations that are snake like reptilians and others that are insect-like. We will discuss them in brief but our focus will be on the thee main types. In these three I hope to reveal a story of who they are and where they come from. We will discover their agenda which explains other mysteries and reveals their true purpose and goals.

A truly loving God would not leave His people without sound answers to explain such strange creatures and horrific events. This might seem like a pretty lofty claim but I promise you by diligently digging into the Bible I have found scriptures that reveal all of these truths.

Chapter Ten
The Grays: Aliens or the Biblical Nachash?

Part One

Gray Guys Everywhere

Today you can't turn on your TV, open a magazine or travel to the corner store with out seeing this image hawking some product. A trip to Roswell becomes a Mecca of every type of merchandise imaginable. The recent popularization of this image is not one solely created by Madison Avenue Marketing or Hollywood film makers.

Skeptics would have you believe that the reason this is the image seen by alleged abductees is because of this recent promotion and popularity. If we had no prior traces in history or recorded images that match this one, anyone would have to agree with their conclusions. However, that is not the case if you investigate the facts.

History Abounds With Their Image

This image has been recorded throughout history in various forms for as long as man has been around. We have cave drawings in Australia, artwork from Ancient Sumaria to South America. The mystical culture of the Etruscan's depicting their ghostly images on pottery. Even a medieval stained glass window from a European Church reveals a "higher wisdom" given to man by what looks like a typical Gray. Medieval legends and myths of "fairies" who carry off babies or the "wee people" who take strangers away that wander off at night into a forest, or the Incubus and Succubus "spirits" that can walk through walls and come in the night to have sexual relations with humans may not be unfounded.

These all have a similar scenario to that of modern abductions. Even the late Carl Sagan researched the well-documented case of Anne Jeffries in 1645. She was found outside in a "fit" as records describe. This "fit" was more of a comatose state and she eventually came out of it. After this she was said to have received a clairvoyant and healing ability. Her memory of what happened to her before she fell into this fit is what is even more interesting. She recalled a half dozen little men that "paralyzed" her and took her to a castle in the sky. There she was seduced and then returned where she was found. Now it would be absurd to say that anything from that time could be confirmed. However, the fact is that a well-documented case of abduction was recorded in this early time, before T.V. and Hollywood.

More recently and still before their known popularity this image was recorded as the "spirit being" Alester Crowely came into contact with in Cairo, Egypt in 1904. This contact produced his *"Book of the Law"* which enhanced his Occult Society "The Ordo Templi Orientus".

As I was in the process of writing this book I was following up on some strange relics exhibited at the Detroit Institute of Arts in my hometown. In a display of very old puppets, I was surprised to see a puppet of a Gray included in the collection. He had the typical large head and big black eyes, his frame thin and stick like. The oddest thing was the title and date. "Future Ghost 1920" Future Ghost indeed, it seems almost prophetic. The inspiration certainly did not come from Hollywood in 1920!

The image of this "Gray" became reintroduced in the early 60's after the highly publicized abduction case of Barney and Betty Hill. In their account Barney saw the Grays in company of an officer he identified as a Nazi! Betty told of the "star map" she was shown of where they came from. Almost twenty years later this map was matched with recent knowledge of mapping as a part of the Orion system.

Part Two

Grays: A General Description

They vary in height from 3 1/2 to 4 1/2 feet tall. They have a grey elastic reptilian like skin. They have an underdeveloped slit for a mouth, small holes for the ears and nose if any at all. They're four or six digital fingers and toes are webbed. They have no internal organs as we have and no digestive or respiratory system. They do apparently have a circulatory system of a gray substance that when opened smells like ozone, with a large pump like organ connected. They have no hair, sex organs or anus. Their large dark slanted almond shaped eyes appear solid black because of a black filament like a filter over their eyes. Their heads are disproportionately larger than their tiny thin frames. The extreme size of their head is said to encase two brains.

With this, they are supposed to be much more intelligent than humans. They speak only by telepathic means, and have the ability to "freeze or suspend" a person motionless during an abduction experience. Perhaps this ability is done in the same manner as a dolphin which stuns fish using a form of a sonic blast. Supposedly they reproduce by cloning and transferring their consciousness into the new body, much like putting on a new suit. They lack body fluids and need human or bovine (cattle) blood and glandular fluids to survive.

Recently it has been discovered that bovine blood can be used as plasma for humans in cases of emergency. They ingest this through their skin by soaking in vats of the fluids. They expel the waste through their skin, which results in a sulfurous smell. When undernourished, they have a greenish color to their skin. These "Grays" also have variations in the taller more insect-like leaders. They are now said to have a collective "hive" conscience and organizational structure similar to an insect colony.

Part Three

What they say about themselves:

They claim to be from "Zeta Rectili", a star system in the belt of Orion. They say they have created mankind, through enhancing existing primates with DNA restructuring and have interacted

173

with us throughout our history. The most disturbing claim they say, is that they created the world's religions and one in particular, Jesus Christ to teach the world peace. They believe in a universal consciousness energy in an eastern or Theosophical idea of God not as a person but rather a force to be utilized. They claim that their home world went through some cataclysmic changes that our own earth will soon be going through. They also claim that their hybridization of the human race is a mutual necessity for survival of both races. There is a need for mankind to be "upgraded" to a higher level to survive the coming earth changes. In this they justify their actions of abductions. They warn abductees that we have to rethink our world view in this manner to "harmonize" with these coming changes.

Their Connection to Us:

The "Grays" are the primary group responsible for abductions and perhaps the cattle slaughters. One of several versions of the story is that shortly after the Roswell crash and alleged recovery of a UFO in 1947 or in April of 1964 at Holloman AFB, a treaty was signed with the United States Government and the Grays. Included in the treaty was an exchange. The U.S. would receive alien technology in trade for the allowance of underground bases to be built and the tolerance of "controlled" abductions of our citizens for the extraction of needed genetic material for their experiments. Men and women have claimed that sperm and eggs have been removed, even fetuses. Another common theme is that these Grays have implanted abductees with a "learning" process of certain duties for some unspecified purpose or event in the near future. Many believe this to be a massive evacuation of a portion of the population before these alleged cataclysmic events happen. Some recent reports have claimed that the Grays have not kept to their agreement with the Government. These reports state that they have abducted over the agreed amount of people and killing of cattle.

An alleged "incident" happened, with exchange of gunfire, with the result of three human military security forces killed at the Deluce underground complex. Since this event an uneasy co-existence is maintained with our government regretfully realizing that they are powerless to stop the Grays from doing whatever they want.

How much of this actually happened or if any of this actually happened I do not know. Someone however, wants us to believe this and has provided enough documentation to suggest it as fact.

Part Four

Investigators are divided about Grays

Much of the compilation of information about these Grays has been through independent professional investigators. Most of these people have a background with education and credentials that should be seriously considered.

Within the investigative community there are several camps about "Grays". Some believe they are dangerous and attend only to their own desires and agenda. They believe the Grays to be chronic liars. They display no emotion and comprehend human emotions only on an observable level. They look at humans much the same way as a farmer may look at his cows. They see humans as inferior beings. They are quite capable of killing humans for the desired fluids as sustenance. In Third World nations there have even been human mutilations reported much in the same manner as many cattle have been found.

One such researcher, who has been warning people about the Grays' agenda, is John Leer. He is the son of Bill Leer the founder of the Leer Jet Corporation. A former pilot for the CIA he first got interested in UFO's from hearing rumors while working within the intelligence community. He has used his position of influence and connections to investigate the UFO phenomena. As a part of his investigative findings, Lear states that the Grays are using us for food as well as genetic experimentation! Within the UFO community, he once had a creditable reputation. Because of his outspokenness in these rather odd sounding matters, he is looked upon now as rather obscure and extreme. In a correspondence with him he advised me he no longer was involved with the investigation of this subject. Between the lines he advised me to also do the same. He speaks cautiously but respectfully of another well-known UFO investigator, Bill Moore. Leer speculates that he might be working for the government to assist in covering up major reports and misinform the public. Bill Moore states that John Leer has gone to great lengths to seek out the most outrageous claims and proclaim them as fact, using his reputation and position as credibility. In doing this Moore says the whole subject and serious research is discredited by Leers actions.

These suspicions and entangled problems are typical within the UFO community. It is enough to make anyone's head spin in frustration and confusion at times. Most investigators are very protective of their information and sources, suspicious of other investigators and usually have their own agendas. Many have grouped themselves into camps according to beliefs and accuse each other of being Government agents or kooks. I am confident that in my quest for understanding, I have the Bible as a guideline that I can follow. It is absolute and can sift through the many conflicting and confusing personalities and ideas to reveal what really is going on!

Another camp within the UFO community believes that the Grays are here to help out mankind. Some are even abductees who prefer to be called experiencers. They believe that in spite of being forcibly taken and experimented on, the Grays have a higher ultimate goal in helping mankind. This kind of "end justifies the means" outlook is reminiscent of another time in history when many atrocities were overlooked for the sake of a "higher" goal. Some abductees believe that they have been chosen to mediate this message of warning and hope for mankind. I make no value judgment upon any of these people. I believe in my limited exposure to abductees, that most are sincere, normal people from a cross section of life. Usually they have more to lose, than to gain by public exposure of their experience. Some have become well known and outspoken as almost evangelists for the "New Age" agenda of the Grays and their prophetic warnings and messages. One abductee even wrote a book for children to dispel their fear of Aliens and explain their friendly agenda. As I have said I make no moral judgment upon those people who carry the message of the Grays. They may be very moral decent people who are sincere in their efforts. The only problem is that they are sincerely wrong and perhaps, unknowingly, leading many others down a wrong path. To qualify my claims let me go to the only source of stability and soundness concerning these matters; The Bible.

Part Five

What the Bible Says About the Grays?

"Now the serpent was more subtle than any beast of the field which the LORD God had made ".

Gen 3:1

To begin our understanding we have to go all the way back to the Garden of Eden. By going back to the original Hebrew words with a 21st century perspective a different way of looking at the Serpent comes into view!

Are we to believe that the initiator of the entire fall of mankind was a snake or a temporarily demonized one? **Nachash**, the Hebrew word for serpent means snake from its hiss. Its root word means to enchant or to prognosticate. The emphasis is on the action of the snake as being like a snake not necessarily that it is a snake.

Dr. Henery M. Morris states in his book, *The Genesis Record,* that some (scholars) maintain that **Nachash** originally meant "upright shining creature". This would give a whole new perspective to just what the "serpent" really is. In Genesis 3:1, He is said to be subtler than all the other creatures created by God. Subtle means "intelligence applied in a crafty or manipulative manner". This certainly is not talking about the reptile we know as a snake.

> **"And the LORD God said unto the serpent, Because thou hast done this, thou art cursed above all cattle, and above every beast of the field; upon thy belly shalt thou go, and dust shalt thou eat all the days of thy life:"**
>
> **Gen 3:14**

In Gen 3 we get the illustration that because the serpent deceived Adam and Eve he would be made to crawl on his belly and eat dust for the rest of his life. Again by going back to the original language and redefining these words in light of 21st century knowledge, the story takes another very realistic twist.

The Hebrew, *"al gachown yalak"* for upon the belly and life can actually mean, "from above a reptile (as a superior form) from the issue of the fetus as its source yet being outside the belly, you will continue on in your material life." Only in modern times could this scripture be understood for what it might imply. A superior reptilian form that carries on life outside of normal reproduction can be by the means of cloning! A seraphim is an order of angelic being, the root word Seraph in Sanskrit means reptile. Even Doctors Young and Strong in their Concordance of the Bible concur with these word definitions without drawing these rather strange conclusions!

Dr. Spiros Zodhiates Th.D. comments in his Hebrew-Greek Bible about the word **"cursed"** in Gen3:

> *This word has been interpreted as meaning to bind (with a spell) to hem in with obstacles, to render powerless, to resist. Thus the first curses in Gen3:14,17, "Thou art cursed above all cattle, and Cursed is the ground for thy sake" means, You are banned from all the other animals and condemned be the soil [i.e., it's fertility to men is banned] on your account.*

In light of this possible meaning to the scriptures just who or what is this Nachash?

1. The serpent is an upright shining creature. The Grays appear to shine in the dark.

2. The serpent is more intelligent than man in a crafty manipulative way. The Grays have two brains in their oversized head and are liars.

3. The serpent has been restricted from reproduction of both man and animals. The Grays have no sexual organs.

4. The serpent would reproduce as a superior reptilian form but as outside the normal reproductive manner. The Grays say they no longer reproduce sexually but transfer their minds from their damaged bodies into a clone of themselves to continue on.

5. The serpent would eat "dust" to sustain in this form. Former Investigator John Leer claims that they eat the genetic make-up of mankind. The Biblical use of **aphar** for dust is the same word used for what mankind was created from.

6. The Book of Enoch states that the fallen angels are, "withered and the silence of their mouths perpetual" Grays are said to only speak telepathically and with a thin frail frame they look withered.

This is truly an amazing line up of characteristics that perfectly fit a description of the Grays and the serpent of the Bible! Because they are one in the same!

Recent Promotional Campaign:

The sudden common knowledge of "Grays" to the public is more than a coincidence. Grays are in many novelty shops on tee shirts, they sell pop and candy on Saturday mourning T.V.. Documentaries are filled with their images both good and evil. They are the theme of video and role-playing games. It is more than just a passing fad. There is in a sense, a promotion of building an acceptance to the idea of such creatures in the public mind, good or evil. More than a social trend, there may be ulterior motives for this promotion.

Different Conditions Produced Different State of Existence

Before we look at the Hybrid, we need to understand another historical event which explains many of today's actions by the **Nachash.** Their same actions have been recorded in the Bible as happening on a global scale in our past. What most people of faith in the Bible fail to understand is that there is a big difference in fallen angels and the invisible spirits we call demons. The **Nachash** or Gray is a very physical being while the "demon" is a disembodied spirit. The Great Flood of Noah will explain everything we need to know and why there is a difference. We have already viewed the technology of this time. Now we shall look at the genetic hybridization and manipulation of the human race.

Chapter Eleven
Fallen Angels of Genesis 6 and the Great Flood

" But as the days of Noah were, so shall also the coming of the Son of man be."

Matt 24:37

History Repeats Itself:

The above statement made by Jesus was a warning not only of the suddenness of His return but also of the events that would lead to His return. In this it would be very important to understand what the world was like before the flood and what events took place. Why? The old saying goes, "Those that fail to understand history are doomed to repeat it." Many peculiar events took place that caused the Great Flood. The flood was a drastic action taken by God because He was left with no other alternative. These same peculiar events for slightly different reasons would take place again and cause God to take another drastic action.

Today as we begin a new century we are on the verge of new technologies that challenge our moral and ethical senses. Cloning, Gene Splicing and the integrating of machine with biological components are no longer the topics of science fiction, they are today's dilemma. For as much good that can be offered, there is also a potential horror of abuse, the same we experienced before! So where will it go from here?

With an increasing amount of sightings of UFO's and alleged cases of Abductions with genetic experiments as part of the experience, something peculiar is happening...AGAIN. In order to understand these events we must contrast them with the events and the world that existed before the flood. Let's first take a look and understand what the physical world was like. It was very different from what we know today.

Part One

The Old World:

The Physical Conditions

Many scientists that believe in the cosmology given in the Scriptures say that a thick canopy of water vapor existed over the entire earth. The weight of this canopy gave an atmospheric pressure much higher than that of today. There was a constant stable climate of approximately 72 degrees Fahrenheit, with no rain or winds. Any precipitation was a mist or dew that formed on the early morning ground. The sunlight would appear as a diffused glow, as this thick canopy would block out radiation from the suns harmful rays. A "greenhouse" effect would be the result in a sub-tropic condition of rich lush vegetation on the one huge continent. (Gen 10:25) This environment was better enhanced to maintain and prolong life as well as congenial in comfort.

Recently in biomedical research, it has been shown that both high pressures and the absence of mutation producing radiation contribute significantly to longevity of life. In addition, the human genetic system and its bloodstream had a purity very unlike our degenerated state of today. This was the result of very few accumulated mutant genes, and primeval absence of disease-producing organisms. (Which was a part of the result of sin and its increase not yet fully developed or experienced?)

From this understanding of the environment and the human biological response to it, it is not unreasonable to see how Cain, Able or Seth married their sisters. Genetically they would be pure enough to inter breed without harm. It also explains the longevity of life, the average life span being around 900 years. It was only after the flood and the bursting of this water vapor canopy that allowed the rays to penetrate the earth, that man's life-span reduced gradually until the time of King David, when the average age was about 76 years as it somewhat remains today. This environment was truly Eden - like.

Spiritual Conditions

At about the same time just before the flood, there were two prophets of God, Enoch and Noah. While there was no written word of God at the time, there was knowledge of God. Part of this pre-flood knowledge was an understanding of the heavens.

Comets, Eclipses, Constellations were all placed as a pictorial representation of the things of God or as He said, "to determine the times and seasons". This was not the modern day practice of Astrology. Oral traditions of the oracles of God were probably what was claimed and preached by these two men. The flood generation would have been only one life span from Adam and Eve. This would make the oral teaching relatively recent news. One of the first prophecies of the Bible was probably a long awaited promise even for the Antediluvians. In Geneses 3:15 the first prophecy stated:

"And I will put enmity between thee and the woman, and between thy seed and her seed; it shall bruise thy head, and thou shalt bruise his heel."
Gen 3:15

In the Hebrew "bruise his heel" means to "set back". In this sense Satan's seed would cause Jesus to be set back or to die. In this however, and what Satan never understood was the fact that this act would also be his undoing. As the woman's seed would crush the serpent's head. This was the result of the resurrection and the beginning of the end for Satan. This would happen through the woman's (Eve's) lineage. This was the first prophecy that from this seed of the woman, God himself would come down to destroy the work of Satan and restore all things first spiritually, then physically. This is where a great deception and a very unusual intervention came into play.

Genesis 6 Controversy:

Probably no other text of Scripture has ever been so controversial than that of Genesis the 6th Chapter. There is so much to cover that I don't even desire to address the controversy here. In the appendix of this book I will briefly address the other thoughts on Genesis 6 as well as a breakdown.

I would suggest reading *Alien Encounters* by Chuck Missler *and The Omega Conspiracy* by IDE Thomas. Both of these books cover the Genesis 6 account extensively. Their work is so good it doesn't need to be repeated here. I strongly suggest both as excellent sources of the Flood account and Fallen Angels with their return. Both are well documented and draw from many sources.

The importance of understanding that the "Sons of God" are Angelic beings and that Genesis 6 is a description of the hybridization of the human race cannot be over stressed. A more recent liberal interpretation removes anything supernatural from happening and greatly distorts scripture to attempt to prove it. Amazingly many conservative denominations have embraced this unsound idea. Angelic intervention is the only interpretation that follows true word etymology and contextual use. It is the only one that has a logical flow to explain many other parts to this one story. It is the only one that is in keeping with the nature and character of God as the loving patient God. Please refer to the appendix for my short explanation of the controversy.

Part two

A Strong Delusion Past

The Biblical Account

Based upon the original languages, I have paraphrased Genesis 6 to its more specific meanings. In this much more could be said about these events.

"And it came to pass as when mankind began to be plentiful upon the surface of the earth, and female descendants were born unto them, that the fallen angels revealed themselves as messengers and determined who had moral goodness, and took them as wives; the ones who were tested and judged to be excellent. My vital spirit in man shall determine with understanding and not remain concealed from the ancient times past to judge with understanding. For that he is also a created mortal body, yet shall his days be a hundred and twenty years. There were (giants) fallen ones, mighty tyrants in the earth, and also after that, when the fallen angels had sexual intercourse with the female descendants of mankind, and they bore children to them, the same became mighty ones, strong and tyrannical, famous warriors which were concealed from times past, eternal yet men who were weakened and made mortal. And God saw that the wickedness was great in the earth and that every imagination, purpose and desire of his being was only evil everyday...The earth also was marred and ruined to decay before and behold, it was pulled down to ruin; for all the blood relations had been polluted in

**their own pathways upon the earth and God said to
Noah, "The end of flesh is come before me: for the
earth is filled with violence through them. And I will
destroy them from the earth."**

Gen 6:1-5, 11-13. (UJWV)

This gives us a vivid image of what really happened and one quite
different than the image most people have. Traditionally most of
us thought of evil and wickedness running wild and random as
a total state of anarchy. I believe that in reality it was not so
obvious. Evil is far more dangerous when it is made to look good
and has science and logic added. This evil is not just merely
committing acts of random violence. It includes man opposing
the principles of faith in God as part of his social order into self-
reliance and trust in "messengers" that had a new message and
a new deal for mankind. This was a deception on a mass level
never repeated until the end of times. The world before the flood
became what many today desire to rebuild as the "New Age
Utopia". As recorded in most cultural memories it was a "Golden
Age of the god's".

Only the Bible tells us a different side to this same time as a
horror. Now these "messengers" did not come to mankind looking
like gray aliens. According to other scriptures they left their
eternal position and body to mate. I am sure they came looking
like a bunch of Kevin Sabo's or Fabio's or other desirable men.
The woman would be flattered to believe they were "chosen" to
produce the promised seed. These were not evil, ungodly women.
The ones selected were the most likely candidates for the seed to
come through. Satan not knowing the specifics would imitate the
fulfillment of the first prophecy in Genesis 3 with a slight twisting
of the truth to contaminate them all! These were morally chaste
and perhaps religious people. However they made one mistake,
they had unbelief of God's true ways and His two prophets who
warned of the deception. Enoch and Noah's warnings were not
listened to, as the flatteries of these handsome men were desired
more.

A common mistake in thinking is, "if the Angels sinned why
was mankind punished also?" Satan cannot exercise any more
power over man than what we give him. His power of influence
is always by permission. This is why "aliens" though superior to
us, do not just take us over today. They need our permission.
They must make us desirous of what they are and have to offer.
The old excuse, "The devil made me do it," does not work. That
was the excuse Adam gave God; "the woman you gave me made

me..." and Eve's excuse, "the serpent deceived me". Man is held accountable for his own actions and in this Genesis account man stands without excuse.

God sent two prophets to warn mankind, but man refused, preferring to believe a lie rather than the truth. This preference was motivated by their own lusts for an easy comfortable and pliable way to do and have everything their way and put God's permission upon it. This gave them a false hope and a false belief system that rapidly engulfed all of mankind. This system slowly and subtly led man from unbelief in God's ways to a progression conformed into Satan's desire that created a hell on earth. Such is the ways of the subtleties of sin and its progression upon a person, a family, a nation or an entire world. What gave mankind the desire and openness to re-evaluate everything they thought they knew and accept a different path? ...Technology. The marvel of new ways to build, travel and other aids to ease daily living gave credibility to their message. It is only logical to understand that if fallen angels intermixed and lived with humans they would also desire the standard of living with its comforts and ease that they were accustomed to in their eternal state of living. That would mean they would bring with them the understanding and application of the physics of their realm to incorporate it into this realm. They would in turn teach and bring to man this same superior level of knowledge. Their offspring would grasp and understand things much quicker than normal humans, creating a pressure for all peoples to be a part of this new brain trust or lag behind as mere mortals. In this competitive manner, inclusion of the entire human race would take a very short time. It would be a matter of survival.

From God's point of view, this was a horror. Someone just gave his little child a loaded gun to play with. Abuse would be the only possible outcome in this distorted universe and our fallen state. The sense of morality from disobedience to God would continue to grow along with the technology. By this statement, I am not saying that the technology is bad in itself. It is man's inability to utilize it properly that is in error. Especially when it comes packaged with a rebel philosophy opposed to God, it always leads to decadence. Although the Bible does not mention some of these specifics other historical literature does.

Other Historical Accounts
The Book of Enoch

Although not recognized as canonical literature, the Apostle Jude in the Bible has quoted the Ethiopic version called Enoch 1. There are several distinct writing styles and there was uncertainty of authorship for the whole book. This (in part) prevented it from becoming a part of the Bible. The book however, was recognized for its historical content in the time of Jesus and was accepted as such and quoted. In it we find the mention of one type of fallen angels called "Watchers" (this term is used by Daniel) who **"scattered over the earth the secrets of heaven"**. We are told that God was angry that they disclosed certain secrets of heaven to their offspring, things men were striving to learn, and which God did not intend to reveal to fallen man. Along with these secrets, other acts began to take place that even shocked the citizens of earth. **"They began to devour one another, and drink the blood."**

The Book of Jubilee

The book of Jubilee is another book, which failed the canonical test of the Bible but is recognized for it's historical content. This book describes the same interbreeding of Angelic and Human entities. It gives a date of this event as being as some interpret 3,543 B.C.. It also says that this happened in the time of Jared, the fifth from Adam in lineage.

The Zadokite document

This minor document was discovered almost fifty years ago in the attic of an old synagogue in Cairo. It's thought to be related to the Dead Sea Scrolls. It reads:*" **Because they walked in the stubbornness of their hearts, the watchers of heaven fell, yea, they were caught thereby because they kept not the commandments of God. So too their sons whose bodies were as mountains."**

Josephus: Antiquity of the Jews

The Jewish historian Josephus, in his most famous work "Antiquities of the Jews" (1st century A.D.) record's the pre-flood events with the idea of angel/human relationships. He tells of their offspring as having superhuman strength, and were known for their extreme wickedness. He also adds, **"For the tradition is that these men did what resembled the acts of those**

men the Grecians called the Giants". He also describes Noah's witness against the self-reliant unbelieving offspring and their cruelty.

Myths and Legends Also Abound:

There are also worldwide myths and legends from almost all cultures with this same theme. Greek, Roman and Nordic Mythology record this "Golden age of god's and their raping or lusting after human women. Their offspring such as Hercules and many other Titans become the "Hero's of old" just as the Bible records that they would be, "men of renown". The ancient Sumerians, Incas, Teutons, South Sea Islanders even Koreans have traditions to their origins as being from "gods" who descended from the heavens and intermarried producing their particular ancestors.

Many distorted "monsters" and beasts are equally a part of this time. Mythological monsters and dragons of Roman, Greek, Nordic and Asian Mythology may be a memory of real beings.The Bible mentions that the bloodlines or pathways of the animals were changed. Could this be an indication of genetic manipulation? Are these mythical beasts and monsters the trace memories of real creatures? Could many of the monstrous dinosaur fossil remains be the result of genetic manipulation? If they are not, then what is? The Bible states this alteration as a historical fact. To imagine man and T. Rex or Raptors existing together would truly be a hell on earth just as the Bible has declared. But we have always been told man and dinosaur never existed together! In Texas, the famous Pulluxie riverbed has human and dinosaur prints along and overlapping each other. There were claims that the footprints were carved in by someone as a hoax. An average sized man could comfortably fit right into this so called non-human impression. To end the controversy, Dr. Carl Baugh videotaped himself and a crew of workers removing the rock from areas of the riverbed. Underneath the removed rock were human and dinosaur prints in stride just where they left off. The Bible gives us a detailed description of an animal that could be nothing else but one of the gentile plant eating types. God stated that He made him and mankind was there also.

> **"Look now at the behemoth, which I made along with you; he eats grass like an ox. See now, his strength is in his hips, and his power is in his stomach muscles. He moves his tail like a cedar; the sin-**

ews of his thighs are tightly knit. His bones are like beams of bronze, his ribs like bars of iron..."
Job 40:15 (NKJ)

Again we have myths, legends, Archeological evidence and the Bible describing the same things. Some of the most interesting Myths come from India. In the Mahabharata and other ancient Sanskrit texts, there are mentioned "gods" producing children from earth women who inherited supernatural skills and learning from their fathers. In some texts there are mentions of combat with flying Vimnas, (description similar to a UFO) missiles and explosions with after effects of nuclear blasts! The Bible concurs with some of this violence and being pulled down to ruin (pollution or fallout). Again not fairy tales but trace memories of real events.

Another theme that seems to run in most of the other cultural myths of this "golden Age" is the benign nature of some of the giants or offspring. Some were even called "Heros" but their actions indicate that they have the same sin nature as that of man and acted. Many cultures claim their origin from this union. Only the Bible records this as an invasion of creation, and an unredeemable situation resulting in drastic action.

Part Three

Angels that Sinned: Crossing Over the Line

"For if God spared not the angels that sinned, but cast them down to hell, and delivered them into chains of darkness, to be reserved unto judgment; And spared not the old world, but saved Noah, the eighth person, a preacher of righteousness, bringing in the Flood upon the world of the ungodly;"
2 Peter 2:4,5,

Those who do not want to face what is being said here try to separate vs 4 from 5 as separate events. It is assumed that the angels that sinned were a pre-Adamic event. Although this supposed event is not mentioned anywhere in the Bible, it is assumed to be the joining of Satan in some unmentioned prior rebellion at some unknown past time before man's creation. Satan's fall started in the Garden of Eden as the overseer of God's creation. (Ezk28) The fall is a continual process carried out all the way through mankind's history of linear time. This is the fall! You cannot separate vs 4 from 5. In context a contrast of punishment and deliverance is being shown. The first example is those being judged and punished. The second example is those who are spared and delivered. In proper context, judgment and deliverance are exemplified by using two historical examples, Noah's flood and Sodom and Gomorrah. There is no doubt who Peter thought the sons of God were in the Genesis 6 account - The angels that sinned!

Left Their Proper Place:

> **"And the angels which kept not their first estate, but left their own habitation, he hath reserved in everlasting chains under darkness unto the judgment of the great day."**
>
> **Jude 6**

While Jude in context here does not tie this event with the flood situation it is because this was common knowledge in his time and not debated or disputed. These angels that "left their estate and habitation experience the same specific and unusual punishment mentioned by Peter. This punishment is what ties the two together as the same group and event. You cannot assume that it is a different event because you do not like the implications of what is being said. There is no mention of any other event in the Bible. This is not some vague mention of any pre-Adamic "fall". This is clearly an event of spirit celestial beings transforming into earthly terrestrial forms. The original language bears this out.

Let's look at the word "estate" and "habitation". Estate in the Greek, is **arche**; it means "first ruling place or position, i.e. original position". This same word is used in Ephesians 6:12 as principalities, "a government position or rank within the demonic/angelic realm". "Habitation" in the Greek is **oiketerion**, this is "a house or dwelling place" and in context meaning figuratively the "body". This same Greek word is used in 2 Corinthians 5:4 as "tabernacle", and in context is referring to the "body". Clearly and logically look at this text paraphrased,

> **"And the angels which kept not their original position, but left their own bodies, he hath reserved in everlasting chains under darkness unto judgment of the great day."**
>
> **Jude 6**

There is no way out of the understanding here; Angels left their eternal position in heaven, and their celestial bodies (1 Co 15:40) because they did this they were placed in chains of darkness. These same chains of darkness are placed on the "angels that sinned" mentioned by Peter during the flood. One in the same!

Evidence in Fossil Remains

The Caveman Myth: A Judgment From God Not Ascension of Man.

Imagine if scientists from the future came upon a city in our day as an archeological dig. In this city they found its residents dead in their homes while in the midst of daily routines. This would clearly indicate that some catastrophe must have happened to kill these residents where they stood while in their daily routine. To think otherwise would be rather foolish. Yet this is just what the public is expected to believe by "modern scientist-priests" today in regard to "CAVEMEN".

Cavemen: a term used by scientists to describe an assumed civilization of early human beings that dwelled in caves. If evolution were true then the remains of a sub-human species living in primitive structures like caves would be just what you would expect to find. However there are some major problems with what we do find that are inconsistent with this whole idea! Why is it that we find the bodily remains of these people in their caves as though they died there while in their daily life? We find no bedrock cemeteries with Fred and Wilma headstones or markers showing generations with a social structure. Consistent with "caveman" diggings is the dead bodies lying within the caves. Makeshift burials are found with bodies but these are within the structure of the caves along with the dead bodies of others unburied in a daily routine of living! This is more of an indication of some kind of world wide catastrophic event that resulted in the deaths of all within these caves.

One problem today is that most scientists are trained that evolution is a fact and not just a theory. Most do not believe in any accounts contained in the Bible as having any accurate historical reality. In their unbelief they reject the obvious evidence as described in the scriptures and draw a wild fictional history of pre-dawn man and his "ascension" to that of "Modern man" today. The fact is the Bible gives us an account of two major catastrophes in our history. One was the Great Flood that encompassed the entire world. The Bible records that this event took 40 days and

40 nights to accomplish the final resulting worldwide flood. In that time, it is only common sense to realize that the peoples of the Earth would seek high ground and seek the only natural protection available, CAVES! In this environment, they would bury their dead in makeshift graves, hunt, eat whatever they could catch with whatever primitive weapons they could form and perhaps try to record upon the walls events as they happened. Children would also draw cave pictures to help calm them from the terror around them. Eventually there they died in the caves while struggling to survive.

Even the myth that these were primitive forerunners to modern man does not hold up. Recently scientists admitted that Neanderthal man walked upright, having the same posture as modern man. It has also been admitted that the Neanderthal man's cranial capacity is actually slightly larger than that of "modern Man". His bone structure also indicates muscle and sinew that would make him far stronger than that of modern man. Recent DNA tests have shown this being to be a completely different species than that of man! The Bible mentions a time when there was a "different species" of non-humans that existed on the earth! Did you also know that Cro-Magnon an early Caucasian had a larger brain capacity than that of a modern Caucasian man. There have also been skeletal remains of the other races that were more advanced than that of modern man. The Mullions, a Semitic race was discovered living as an entire civilization that suddenly died. Their fossil remains being the largest ever found in one dig. Their cranial capacity also was larger than that of a modern Semitic man. The Boskop man, were also fossil remains of a Negroid race who had a larger brain capacity than that of a modern Negroid man. How are these inconsistencies explained? They aren't! They are completely ignored or overtly suppressed from the general public. If evolution by the process of natural selection were the truth, then we would expect the superior life forms to survive and overtake the weaker ones.

Our fossil remains indicate just the opposite. This is exactly what the Bible indicates happened, a judgment from God upon the "son's of God" and their offspring, the "mighty men of renown". We have their fossil remains, these inconsistencies are never addressed, they are just sort of swept under the carpet of ignorance. Even the most ardent skeptic cannot ignore the evidence that is overwhelming. What we find is what is declared in the Bible, remains of a different species of human and altered human remains!

Part Four

Judgment for the Sons of God and Their Offspring, the Mighty Men of Renown

> **"...and cast them down to hell, and delivered them into chains of darkness, to be reserved unto judgment.**
>
> **2 Peter 2:4**

> **"...he hath reserved in everlasting chains under darkness unto the day of judgment."**
>
> **Jude 6**

It is important to realize just exactly what the punishment was that was placed upon the angels that sinned and their offspring. It is in this understanding of the sentence imposed that we discover the disembodied spirits that play havoc on earth today and just how the reappearance of the "sons of God" take place, which is slightly different in the last days as is was before the flood. On the surface from both scriptures one would imagine prisoners chained in heavy iron shackles to a wall in some dark pit forever! I must admit this was my personal image until I looked at all the words in the original Greek.

Peter said these angels were **"delivered"** ***Paradidomi*** the Greek word used here for delivered according to Thayer's can mean "to deliver up to another to keep or use". This idea is consistent with Peter and Jude's use of ***teros,*** for "reserved". This is the idea that they are put under watch or guarding not from escaping but in the sense of withholding for a personal end, and also in the sense to fulfill prophecy or a command. Next is real interesting in that the term **"chains of darkness"** is referring possibly to much more than what first appears. ***Zophos*** for "darkness" means "a dark shroud (a wrap around enclosure) like a cloud". Strong's includes the idea of a "ghost". Jude uses the word **Desmond** for "chains". This includes a figurative meaning, (aside from a meaning of a binding of any type) as "an impediment or disability". In Mark 7:35 this same word is used as string: ***"the string of his tongue was loosed"*** **Desmond** was the word used here to describe the impediment or **"string"** that was loosed to heal the dumb man who could not speak. Jude also uses the word ***Hupo***, for "under". This addition reinforces this idea of an impediment; so the meaning is, as an inferior position or condition. Peter uses the word ***Seria*** for chains. No, this is not proof of a different event.

It is another example of the amazing harmony of the Scriptures. This word further defines these chains in function. This overlap of the same event gives us a whole picture of one event. **Seria** as developed from its root and derivatives **Suro** and **Airo** can convey the idea of a preference or choice to be trailed or dragged down and to be taken up or away. This going up and down is described in the gospel of Luke.

> **"Jesus asked him saying, What is thy name? And he said Legion: because many devils were entered into him. And they besought him that he would not command them to go down into the deep."**
> **Luke 8:29**

Many times the deep, depth, waters, sea and pit are all describing a subterranean portion of sheol or hell. In this text the word "abussos" for "depth" means "bottomless depth". The implication here is that this is where they were supposed to go, into the bottomless pit. In this sense, these spirits are in a continual "chain" or cycle of going up and down from the pit. Through various occult practices they are loosed to roam the surface of the earth as a ghost or invisible demon spirit, then occasionally being cast back to the pit under the authority of the name Jesus only to ascend and roam again.

In adding all this up so far; we have the angels that sinned, and their offspring that are given over to be reserved for fulfilling prophecy, which we shall see is their judgment and leads to their eventual total destruction. They are put into a lesser form in a dark shroud like cloud - a ghost. This chain is also a cycle of going up and down from the pit (Tartaros the lowest level of Hades) to the surface world.

What we have when we add this altogether is a ghost or a disembodied spirit! These invisible covert spirits that pretend to be deceased loved ones, or haunting ghosts, avatars, angels, and all of the channeled spirit guides of the entire empowerment of the New Age movement. They are now pretending to be the good guys so as to gain credibility and acceptability when they reappear as the "Nordics" or Angels or Pleadians, however manner you want to perceive them, they are still demons from hell.

Poetic Justice

I have to admit it is just like God to give to these rebels a form of poetic justice. They crossed over to our realm motivated by the sensual lusts of this dimension. They desire to have a physical form like us and yet maintain and exploit their angelic powers over mankind to "Lord" over us. As a result, God takes away both terrestrial and celestial bodies from them. By placing their consciousness in a lesser form as a ghost or shadow, having no form or substance causing them to roam as a "wandering star" yet able to see and desire without the senses. This would be a living hell for ones motivated by lusts. The eye is always seeing but the heart never fulfilled. Roaming the earth they seek to occupy humans to vicariously experience the sensual pleasures until they will once again be set free... and they will be set free again.

Part Five

Disembodied Spirits are Different than Fallen Angels

This state is not the normal condition of spiritual entities as assumed or believed my many today. In their normal state, they are ministering spirits but they do possess a celestial body. It may be hard for some to realize but these bodies must be subject to some limitations of material reality even in the eternal realm. We are aware that they engage each other in conflict, (Dan 10 :12,13, Rev 12:7) they can eat and can have a physical interaction with humans. (Gen 19:3) There can be a reasonable implication that if angels engage in warfare and struggles of combat, they may suffer some form of damage or setbacks. If you think not, then explain how or why combat would accomplish anything. Resistance or victory must at least experience some kind of short-term results from this heavenly warfare. If there can be a physical set back in combat, yet the angels are eternal, an ability to transfer their souls into a cloned body of themselves may be the logical answer? This process may be alluded to in Gen 3 about the serpent. He was to carry on in a superior reptilian form, as from the fetus yet outside the belly. This cloning process could be some of the "secrets of heaven" made known to fallen man. It is this ability by the ones that sinned and their offspring that is prevented by this special judgment. In this lesser disembodied state they are only semi-inter-active and "trapped" in a ghost-like state.

These two states, the natural angelic form and the ghost-like form are quite different from each other. There is a danger in assuming that all spiritual entities are not physical entities. This danger does not allow you to see the enemy in his full deceptive abilities. It is this misconception that is very popular within the modern Church today. The unfortunate result is in the refusal to see just how much physical activity is really taking place by spiritual forces in our midst.

Part Six

Final Comment on the Flood

The sons of God were supernatural beings, angelic rebels that tried to usurp God and His creation. The mighty men of renown were anomalous offspring of human/angels, a world population of creatures never meant to be. Not objects of wonder and desire as recorded by secular myth and legends but a horror destined for total destruction. The Giants were a part of this great rebellion and reappear after the flood. We will mention more on them in the Hollow Earth section.

The world before the flood was a technological wonder but also a spiritual horror with only faint traces left and understood today. All of man's legends and myths from every culture are but a faint memory of this time. The Biblical perspective and the real scientific evidence of these same events were overturned and undermined and all but forgotten. These liberal re-interpretations of scripture and the unbelieving miss-interpretation of material evidence cannot continue to blind the eyes of the Church. Misunderstanding of this important section of mankind's history has ill equipped the Church with no rhyme or reason to refute the current claims of modern popular Theosophical views, or the false enticement of new technologies that promise we will be like gods. As time progresses, there are more thinking and praying Christians coming to the same conclusions and quoting the same scriptures. In time these people will become the voice of stability and reason for a shaken up doubting and unbelieving world.

We now have an understanding of the difference between fallen angels and the disembodied spirits called demons. We see that the invisible demons are in this ghost like state as punishment. They will not continue in this state as we have to understand that part of their judgment includes a prophesied resurrection to their total destruction in the last days. This we shall look at next.

195

Chapter Twelve
A Satanic Resurrection: The Real Army of Darkness

A Reprieve for the Angels That Sinned and Their Offspring.

The Resurrection for Total Annihilation.

This is a story of death and resurrection of non-human entities. By many different texts of scripture describing the same event, this composite makes a story. The current natural state of the angels that sinned and their hybrid offspring is that of a disembodied ghost or spirit. This state of existence is the result of their part death and special judgment in the Great flood. They do not want to stay in this existence. They are given a special reprieve but one that will result to their total annihilation as indicated by this next text.

Part One

Supernatural Intervention

In the 26th chapter of Isaiah, a series of promises and judgments are given for God's people and the nations around them. Included in this is the mention of the **rapha**, which are the "ghosts of the Giants". Their fate is set and they will not be a part of the resurrection. But then they are "visited". This word signifies something of an intervention or alteration of a natural process. This same word is used when Sarah was visited in her old age and conceived Isaac. Gen 21:1. Something supernatural is going on here. Let's look at the text.

> **"Oh Lord our God, other lords beside thee have had dominion over us: (better rendered married unto us) but by thee only will we make mention of thy name. They are dead, they shall not live; they are deceased, (rapha) they shall not rise: therefore**

thou visited and destroyed them, and made their memory to perish. "

Isaiah 26:13,14

As it is with many prophetic scriptures, this jumps from the present condition, an action taking place and then the eventual demise with even their memory erased. This obviously has not yet happened, but it is spoken in the past tense. Understanding events from God's perspective, it has already happened. For us in a linear time frame it is still a future event.

The word **Paqad** for "visited", has a very wide meaning, the most common use is that of "drawing or mustering up an army". The second one as mentioned is the "supernatural intervention of the natural course of events". I believe the meaning here is twofold. It is a divine intervention of a normal process to allow for a resurrection of these giants, the angels that sinned and their offspring for the express purpose to be mustered up as an army to their final destruction. There is also the strong emphasis that this action is under control and part of God's plan. Other scriptures can confirm this two-fold definition.

This same event is mentioned by the Apostle Peter,

"For Christ also once suffered for sins, the just for the unjust, that He might bring us to God, being put to death in the flesh, but quickened in the Spirit: By which He went and Preached unto the spirits in prison; which sometimes were disobedient, when the longsuffering of God waited in the days of Noah, while the ark was a preparing, wherein few, that is eight souls were saved by water."

1Peter 3:18-20

The word for preached, does not mean that Jesus went and proclaimed the gospel to anyone. This word without a definer simply means he made a proclamation about something. Also the spirits in prison were not departed human souls but spirit beings. When the word is used without a modifier, it refers only to spirit beings. This event then could be the visitation and the proclamation mentioned in Isaiah 26. After the fulfillment of the law and His death as a sacrifice, Jesus could announce to the spirits who tried to prevent His incarnation, a new set of conditions and terms that He would deal with them on. They would be set loose, (resurrected as an army) but only to fulfill

God's will for the judgment of total annihilation so that even their memory would be erased.

Part Two

Resurrection Begins with a Subterranean Encounter

> **"Hell from beneath is moved for thee to meet thee at thy coming: it stirreth up the dead for thee, even all the chief ones of the earth; it hath raised up from their thrones all the kings of the nations. All they shall speak and say unto thee, Art thou also become weak as we? art thou become like unto us? Thy pomp is brought down to the grave, and the noise of thy viols: the worm is spread under thee, and the worms cover thee."**
>
> **Isa 14:9-11 (KJV)**

This appointed time is mentioned in Isaiah 14:9 as a "satanic resurrection" This is the time after the life and first mission of the Antichrist was accomplished. This text of scripture is very obscure in its surface understanding but look at what happens by using other correct variables in this text. By a more specific language use, this suggests a life once used up and descending into hell. It also suggests that the Antichrist would also have two different and separate appearances just like that of Christ's, it would be in a same but opposite pattern. (Posted on my website echoesofenoch.org, I have a complete breakdown at how this is rendered)

As I stated in the Flying Saucer section, *The Sign* by Robert Van Kampen, expounds with excellent documentation this very thought with Hitler as a conclusion. On page 212, He says,

> **"The parallels between Hitler and what the Scriptures reveal about Antichrist are almost too obvious to point out."**

In reference to Hitler's second coming he states, **" In the end times Hitler's dream will become Satan's reality"**

Now let's see this scripture using the other possible variables from the original languages:

"Hell from beneath is excited for you, to meet you at your coming: it wakes up the dead for you, even all the chief ones of the earth; it has raised up from their thrones all the Kings of the Nations. All they shall ask you, "Are you also become weak as we? Are you become like us?" Your majesty and glory is brought with you down to the grave, and the clamor of your spent life: The man is spread out into the place of Christ's as a garment."

This rendering is actually describing the same but opposite resurrection power applied to the Antichrist as a satanic version of Christ's resurrection. This mortal possessed man now deceased, completing the first half of his mission, descends into hell and moves into a redemptive role producing the same resurrection results of Christ's! The Bible described Christ after His resurrection as the: **"the firstborn among many brethren."** Rom 8:29(KJV) **"Moving into the place of Christ's"**, as this text of scripture may read out means that the Antichrist would be the firstborn of His own. This text would indicate an order of events duplicating the whole redemptive process. You must also realize though that this is just a cheap imitation of the real power of God. Nevertheless it does produce short termed similar results. Cloning just may be the means of this imitation and related to the "image of the beast".

It was the Nazis through the work of Dr. Joseph Mengela that cloning was first developed! It was also the Nazis that tried to flee as fugitives to the alleged Hollow Earth. As I mentioned before, the desires of the Grays may have been as a loan to the fleeing Nazis. The Hitler/Nazi vehicle may be the human agents necessary for Satan to have permission to interfere into the physical affairs of mankind in the same unprecedented manner as before the flood.

The book of Job further mentions this process as being "repaired".

"Dead things are formed under the waters, and the inhabitants thereof. Hell is naked before him, and destruction hath no covering."

Job 26:5,6

Commentators have suggested that this is a description of the creation of whales or other large marine life forms. I do not believe when digging deeper into the original language this bears out.

"Dead things." - *Rapha* again is used here meaning ghosts, the deceased.

"Are formed" - This is most interesting. *Chuwl* a combined meaning, is "a twisting or whirling manner in a circular or spiraling pattern". Could this be an allusion to a double helix coil as the genetic pattern or model of DNA? It also has the idea of "bringing forth", as in birthing or perverting the process and the pains of birth. In all of this it is not too hard to consider something genetic and manipulative is going on, not by the Creator but by the imitator.

"From under the waters" - where is this happening? Ocean depths or subterranean? This is happening within the waters as opposed to the surface or below the ocean at the opening of the subterranean realm.

"And the inhabitants thereof" - In most all KJV study Bibles, this is footnoted as better rendered as "with the inhabitants thereof." This could be describing the joint effort to resurrect these ghosts through genetic manipulation. With the alliance of the serpent or upright shining creatures, i.e. The grays and the fugitives fleeing God's wrath, the Nazis? mentioned by Amos as they collaborate their efforts as one. In the Hollow Earth section we will realize more about this.

This corresponds with the rest of Job 26:vs 6. It is in this context that clearly the above description is speaking of activity going on in the subterranean realm.

"Hell is naked before him" Can only mean that God sees everything that is happening.

"Destruction has no covering" They believe that they are secretly accomplishing their goals, yet from God's perspective he sees their creative powers as only destruction which is not concealed. This is all part of God's plan. They can run but they cannot hide, they have a destiny to fulfill that they do not believe will happen. Death at the Battle of Armageddon in the Valley of Megiddo in Israel is that destiny!

Part Three

Genetic Mixing is Also within the Last "Beast Empire".

> "And whereas thou saw the feet and toes, part of potters' clay, and part of iron, the kingdom shall be divided; but there shall be in it of the strength of the iron, forasmuch as thou saw the iron mixed with miry clay. And as the toes of the feet were part of iron, and part of clay, so the kingdom shall be partly strong, and partly broken. And whereas thou saw iron mixed with miry clay, they shall mingle themselves with the seed of men: but they shall not cleave one to another, even as iron is not mixed with clay."
>
> **Dan 2:41-43**

In context, this divided kingdom is opposed to each other, yet ultimately serves the same goals. One part is scattered, one part united. Isaiah mentions that Dan and the Philistines have some relationship together in the end time where all this genetic activity takes place. Here we see these two groups, one united (US) one scattered (Nazis) opposed and now united working together within the same structure and performing the same activity. Yes the U.S. via The U.N. is headed in that direction with the New Age Movement as the cement!

The "mixing the seed with men" has been traditionally the understanding that this was the ruling class mixing with the working class in a communistic or socialist form of government. The original language in no way even remotely suggests this idea. The term for "miry clay" literally means "**filth to be swept away from burnt clay of the potter**". I hardly believe that this is the view God has of the working class. This would be the view He might hold to a forbidden seed of fallen angels. "*Seed* or **Zera**" means "progeny , offspring, fruit or sperm". In context, this is describing a mixing off Human genes with the Fallen Angels in a clinical situation (i.e. abductions) rather than the pre-flood method of marriages. "They shall not cleave one to another," is not referring to an unsuccessful mixing but rather the lack of a personal relationship such as marriage. This time it would be clinical, without the personal contact and relationship. This is the exact claim made about Alien Abductions as we will soon see.

In Joel 2:1-11, Rev9:1-11, 16:12-15 and Jude 4-16 there is described a very physical invasion of Earth by non-human entities. For our purpose now we just need to understand that this is where the hybridization process of a resurrection ends. We will end this Alien section on those particulars in detail. For now it is important to continue to understand what the Bible has to offer us with evidence of other fallen angels, their possible origin and what it means to be "cast out" of heaven. This casting out has determined their current condition and their future plans and goals. We need to understand this to see how it correlates to the idea of an Alien presence for they are one in the same.

Chapter Thirteen
Angels Cast Out of Heaven: More Fugitives on the Run

Many Other Fallen Angels

It is important to understand that not all of the fallen angels were involved in the Genesis 6 intermingling of the human race. The Book of Enoch alleges that about 200 of the fallen angels were actually involved. We have discussed their judgment and eventual resurrection to total destruction so what about the rest? What does the Bible tell us about them? There is no outright statement with direct conclusions but there are verses that reveal enough to logically make a connection. This I can show you next.

Part One

Other Alien and Angel Lineups with Scripture

As I have already shown the Biblical serpent has a meaning describing the "Grays". Within the UFO community, a couple of other known "Aliens" are described. One is more like a humanoid reptilian type and the other is a taller Gray variation that looks more like a Mantis type insect. The Bible may actually allude to both types of these "Aliens" as other orders of Angels.

One order of Angelic being is called a "*Seraphim*" The root word from this angelic order is **Saraph.** In the Hindu Sanskrit language **Saraph** means "a reptile". As part of the Angelic host this could be one of their physical forms. Another mention of these entities are from the words of Jesus. In context, Jesus told His disciples after experiencing the victory of exorcizing demons out of people that,

> **"Behold, I give unto you power to tread on serpents and scorpions, and over all the power of the enemy: and nothing shall by any means hurt you."**
>
> **Luke 10:19**

I believe that it is more than a coincidence that in the same breath, Jesus mentions both types of creatures. Certainly in context, Jesus was not talking about the animal and insect life on earth. He was speaking about spirit beings. The word for *Scorpion* in the Greek, **skorpios** (4689) in Hebrew **aqrab** (6137) again we have the word emphasis on the characteristics of a scorpion but not the actual animal. The word derived in Greek from the base *skopos* means to see from concealment, a sentry, scout or WATCHER! These are the same type of angelic beings that left their heavenly positions and heavenly bodies (2 Pe 2:4, Jude 1:6) to cohabit with humans in Genesis 6 before the flood of Noah. Some scholars have claimed that these terms are speaking figuratively of humans acting like these animals. Consistent contextual use however can only suggest heavenly beings, in which case these are simple terms for two different types of angelic creatures.

Part Two

Fugitives Looking for Redemption:

Just before His arrest and coming trial and death, Jesus stated to his disciples,

"Now is the judgment of this world: now shall the prince of this world be cast out."

John 12:31

Jesus was describing an event he knew was about to happen as He went to the cross. As Jesus hung on the cross there was a war going on in the heavens. As it was recorded in the Gospels, at the very moment of death the physical skies became darkened. By this description, it is only logical to assume that the war took place in the second heaven representing outer space.

"And there was war in heaven: Michael and his angels fought against the dragon; and the dragon fought and his angels, and prevailed not; neither was their place found any more in heaven. And the great dragon was cast out, that old serpent, called the Devil, and Satan, which deceives the whole world: he was cast out into the earth, and his angels were cast out with him. And I heard a loud voice saying in heaven, Now is come salvation, and strength, and the kingdom of our God, and the power of his Christ: for the accuser of our brethren is

cast down, which accused them before our God day and night".

Rev 12:7?10 (KJV)

You see, before the cross, Satan and his fallen angels had access to heaven to accuse mankind.(Job 1:6) The death of Jesus on the cross repaired the paradox created in the Garden of Eden. This ended Satan and his followers access to the eternal realm as well as the physical heavens. Being cast down with their fellow disembodied comrades who were physically destroyed by the flood, they are all on the run as fugitives. In the Greek to be cast down literally means on dry land amongst men. This then can only mean that they are limited to existence on this planet Earth! This condition would have been for the last 2,000 years. This entire body of rebels is described by the term Leviathan. Job and Isaiah describe this very thing:

"By his spirit he has garnished the heavens; he hath formed the crooked serpent"

Job 26:13

"*Garnished*" means to "make clean, bright or beautiful". "*Formed*" can mean "to dissolve or wound", "*crooked*" here means "fleeing as a fugitive, or to bolt or suddenly leave". This could read out better like this:

"By his spirit he has made clean, the heavens; his hand has wounded the fleeing serpent."

Job 26:13

This is describing the time of being cast out of the heavens after the cross. Isaiah labels the same serpent as both crooked and piercing and defines both as being Leviathan.

"In that day the Lord with his sore and great and strong sword shall punish leviathan the piercing serpent, even leviathan that crooked serpent; and he shall slay the dragon that is in the sea"

Isaiah 27:1 (KJV)

"Piercing" means "fugitive or the serpent as fleeing "and is the same word used as "*crooked*" in Job 26. "*shall punish*" is the word **Paqad** meaning to intervene supernaturally and/or muster up as an army. The same word is used in Isaiah 26:14, describing the resurrection of the disembodied spirits from the flood! Crooked here is describing a twisted or wresting action, and in context the sense of taking by force. The facts here are that not only is this serpent a fugitive, but he now has the addition of the others who have been mustered up as a forceful army. The word **Paqad** is the connecting link with the serpent now acting with violent force. This text helps to confirm the idea of a fleeing enemy composed of several forms of refugees. But here, it also describes the steps and additions leading to final destruction of the entire rebel alliance called Leviathan. This we will see happens at the final battle on Earth know as Armageddon. With the few scriptures we have looked at so far, there is enough evidence that the various orders of fallen angels have a perfect line up as todays so called alien types most commonly seen. Collectivly they are the Biblical serpent Leviathan which is on the run. To find a way out, Satan imitates in the same but opposite fashion the whole redemptive process that did him in. His hope is to produce the same results for himself and his minions. The important fact is that these "fallen angels" have been cast into the earth. They no longer have access to the eternal realm or outer space; they are earth bound for a season. Judgment is coming and they are fleeing as fugitives desperately trying to find an escape route. They are rebels and they will, with the help of man find a way out... for a time.

Part Three

So Where Did Angels Live in the Heavens?

We know that these non human entities were cast out of the eternal realm. They were also cast on the earth in a very physical form. To be "*cast down*" means, "on dry land amongst men" this strongly suggests a physical as well as spiritual dimension to their existence.

So where did they live? Is it heresy to claim that they actually might have lived on other planets? Satan is described as having certain mobility while still in the heavens during the Old Testament times before Christ.

> **" thou hast walked up and down in the midst of the stones of fire."**
>
> **Ezek 28:14 (KJV)**

So just what are the stones of fire? Could this be in reference to stars and planets? David E. Flynn is a Christian researcher /

scholar. In his book *Cydonia The Secret Chronicles of Mars,* he makes a convincing presentation that Mars and perhaps other planets and star system were once part of an occupied angelic realm. The Bible refers to the second heaven as the realm of outer space which would include planets.

Satan and his fallen followers also had access to the very throne of God in the eternal realm outside of time which is described as the third heaven. (The first being earth's atmosphere)

> **"Now there was a day when the sons of God came to present themselves before the LORD, and Satan came also among them."**
>
> **Job 1:6 (KJV)**

Now this may take away the magical mystical mysteries from many Christian believers' minds, but why should we cling to unrealistic beliefs that have no scriptural support? For too long, (myself included,) we have had this vague undeveloped belief that somehow angels are magical invisible spirits that sit on a cloud with a harp or fly endlessly around a throne singing "Holy, Holy, Holy".

Yes we do get this image from John's view of heaven, but there is nothing to indicate that this is continual. Angels have been created as slightly higher than humans. They are more intelligent. As a sentient being, is it so illogical to believe that they probably have a culture and social order? Even lesser forms of animals have a social structure. In 1 Co 15:40 Paul describes the difference of celestial and terrestrial bodies. In this description it is obvious that the celestial bodies are also very physical. Is it also illogical to believe that Angels could actually live within God's kingdom or dimension on very real material planets? I think as we are presented with more half truths and outright lies against our faith in a personal God, this concept is much more preferable than the unrealistic and vague traditional ideas which are very child like. Angels even describe themselves as fellow servants of God. This similar position could also indicate a similar physical existence in their realm. "Mana" is described as angel food in the Bible which also suggests the physical nature of these heavenly beings.

The scriptures line up with the claims made by the Aliens as to where they come from. The Grays claim planets in the Orion system as their homeland. The Nordics claim their home is in the constellation of the Pleiades. It is interesting and again more

Jim Wilhelmsen

than a coincidence that the Scriptures mention both these places in the same text.

In context, God is making rhetorical statements to Job about His own power and knowledge of creation with order, boundaries and limits. Within these scriptures is a mother load of information about our cosmology. One section says,

"Can you bind the cluster of the Pleiades, or loose the belt of Orion?"

Job 38:31 (NKJ)

Is it just a coincidence that both places are mentioned? On the surface this rendering would indicate the question could you bring together the loosely tied constellation of the Pleiades or loose the belt of Orion? This simple statement makes sense because of the actual physical characteristics of each constellation. But can it say more in a Biblical symbolic sense? Let me play the mystic and show you how it might read out as an encrypted message.

The first statement, *"bind"* can mean "to bring together in a conspiratorial sense", *"cluster"* can be better rendered by it's root word "as a quick lacing together", the *"Pleiades"* name means "a stored golden ornament". So it could say,

"Can you plot together the quick lacing of the stored golden ornament. "

The second statement describes loose, to mean, to unbind as to set free and also to open, as in a doorway. Belt can mean as something drawn or tied up. It also has the idea of this being in some kind of a procession. The name Orion can mean fools or arrogant. Therefore you could have,

"or set free the tied up procession of the arrogant fools?"

We already know about the Grays so I will begin with the latter statement first. The Grays being associated with Orion, were to continue on in life in a restricted form without sexual reproductive organs and sensory organs that are "withered" as Enoch stated. Jude and Peter stated that the ones that sinned before the flood were reserved in chains as an impediment and cycle of going up and down. Both of these groups are tied up or restricted in a procession of time. I would also suppose from God's view their overall rebellion would make them arrogant fools.

208

So is God also asking in rhetorical fashion,

"Can you change the condition of the Grays situation?"

Remember they are the ones that say they are from Orion!

I have to get ahead of myself a bit here. We will learn further in this section about the Nordics. I believe I can show you through some prophetic scripture that they are the end of the genetic rainbow, a created shell for the serpent to hide in. (Isa 14:29). "*Gold*" is always symbolic as "divine or godlike or God himself". *Ornament* suggests the outward "shell or earth suite one might wear as an ornament". The *quick lacing* suggests an "intermixing in a rushed situation as in a means of escape".

So again is God saying rhetorically?

"Can you conspire to put together a quick hybridization of the reserved shell of the Nordic?"

By injecting very common symbolic Biblical terms and viewing this text from this genetic perspective, the outcome is truly amazing. I truly felt inspired by God to understand this however I must admit myself it's a bit on the mystical side. This type of Biblical interpretive method called a "sod" is rare but in keeping with typical Hebrew interpretation of the scriptures. So nevertheless there it is. If unconvinced now perhaps when you see the many other scriptures that cross-reference themselves with this thought you will see a constant pattern that cannot be mere coincidence.

Within these few scriptures, the association of star systems with certain "Aliens" as fallen angels might be alluded to in the scriptures as well as the various types that have been seen.

It may not be so unreasonable to believe that these entities at one time lived in those locations either in the eternal dimension or our fallen one. In either case there is every implication that they are here now with a great need to escape. This escape explains the Hybrid who is only a transitional stage. To understand this transition, we have to include Cattle Mutilations and Alien Abductions as a part of a process. We will review these next.

Chapter Fourteen
The Hybrid: A Bridge between Two Entities: The Escape Route

Part One

A Transition Revealed

> **"...to pluck from the serpent's soil, an extrusion of offspring, shining ones to cover with obscurity the serpent."**
>   **Isaiah 14:29 (UJWV)**

We will look at the above scripture in depth later. For now from this verse, it can be noted that the serpent will create a shell to hide in. This explains the transition from a non human form to a human one. This was Satan's desire as he stated in Isaiah 14:13

"I will exalt my throne above the stars of God"

The Hebrew word for *"throne"* is **Kis-say**. It means a "canopied or covered throne". The root, means to "cloth or cover". Jesus described a building made not of hands, he meant the human body as the temple of God and not a building. The throne in the holy of holies was symbolic of the inner heart of man of the same temple, one where God would dwell. In the same symbolic manner this throne could be the bodily form.

Satan's desire is to elevate above the angelic order to a higher form. The resurrected form of God's children is one above the angelic host. This is assumed because we will be joint heirs with God Himself. (Rom8:17) His desire requires something in the genetic makeup of mankind to produce this effect.

Unlike the physical death suffered the last time they crossed over into our form, this time they do not want to be subject to a physical death in this new earth suit. They want more this time. According to Joel 2:8 they will do it.

"And when they fall upon the sword, they will not be wounded."

Part two

Genetic Development Required:

Angels and Demons learn and develop just as we do. They are not God, even though they come from an eternal dimension, they are not all knowing. They need to develop technology to imitate the Power of God.

"Unto whom it was revealed, that not unto them-selves, but unto us they do minister the things, which are now reported unto you by them that have preached the gospel unto you with the Holy Ghost sent down from heaven: which things the angels desire to look into."

1Peter 1:12,

In context here, the whole resurrection, salvation and redemptive process is something the angels desire to study. Many times when angels are mentioned it is without distinction of being good or bad. In context we are not really told but I would suggest that the rebel angels would desire to study to duplicate the same actions for themselves. In the first step to create and further develop the hybrid we need to understand what is going on with cattle mutilations.

Part three

Cattle Mutilations: A "Mining" for Resources; Food and Construction Elements

A "Hushed Up" Event

The average person removed from the area of the western United States, hasn't even a clue as to how large and widespread this unusual occurrence really was and still is. It means that the ability to cover up and side step the issue was, on the most part successful. By 1976 there had been almost 2,000 cases in the United States. There have been scattered cases throughout the world with a concentration in Puerto Rico of about 300 cases.

Ten years later there is well over 10,000 cases reported in the United States alone, as of this writing, I have not got the current amounts but they have risen steadily.

You may have vague recollections of these events back in the early seventies; cattle were found dead and "butchered" by possible Satanists as the news reporters stated. The actual facts that you never heard on any public news would suggest a completely different story. It isn't that they were lying, they just failed to disclose all the details and facts even after analyzed by trained experts. For many of you that are not too familiar with cattle mutilations, particular details may be very surprising to you.

A Typical Scenario

The typical mutilation did not consist of a bloody carcass, torn or ripped flesh with animal or human footprints leading to or from the body. What was found in all cases were no prints of any kind leading to or from the body. Not even the slightest trace of blood in or around the body. The blood was removed entirely without the collapse of the veins. This suggests the removal of the blood as being pumped out while the animal is still alive in a manner unknown, especially in the field removed from the use of sophisticated equipment. One eye, an ear, the tongue removed all at the same point, in a cookie cutter pattern, the lips, udders (if female) sex organs, anus cored out to the intestinal tract, also glandular and body fluids gone. The removal was done with such laser-like precision that the cuts were divided between cells. There was a cauterization along all of the cuts, suggesting a heat source such as a laser cut. We are talking about this as being in the late sixties, early seventies. Known technology was not present for such results back then.

Another interesting thing is that this was done on firstborn male and female animals. Typical UFO sightings and or black unmarked helicopters were sighted before or after these events in some cases.

Humans too!

Human mutilations have also been found. Details are never released to the public and only through the persistent efforts by investigators were some details revealed and similarities noted with the cattle deaths. Most documented incidents (perhaps a dozen) have come from South America. It has been speculated that during flap sightings of UFOs, many disappearances and unsolved crimes that include mutilation in those areas may produce more identifiable cases. Some investigation has started in this way, but with much resistance by the unbelief of local officials for such outlandish sounding claims.

A Connection Should Be Made!

If the "Grays" need blood and body fluids as food, and we find this is exactly what has been taken, the connection should be obvious. Also what they lack in sensory and sexual reproductive organs are what is taken. No one has actually seen "Grays" slaughtering cattle. Very few cases involve UFO sightings. There are more black unmarked helicopters sighted than UFOs. Regardless you have one Entity lacking the very thing that disappears from the slaughtering. This is obviously circumstantial evidence worth investigating.

It is interesting to note that in cases of emergencies, bovine (cow) blood can be used for human transfusions. This strongly suggests a mining of genetic resources in progress

Part Four

A Strange Harvest Indeed: Living Idols under Construction

At a time when I was first researching this topic of Mutilations, I read the book, " *An Alien Harvest*" by the nation's leading investigator of mutilations, Linda Moulton Howe. I woke up in the middle of the night to a voice,

> **"Eyes have they, but they see not, ears have they but they hear not."**

I knew that voice, it was my heavenly Dad pressing me forward in to understanding His Word. I raced for my Bible, I knew that was in scripture somewhere and felt the urgency to look it up right then at four in the mourning.

> **"The idols of the heathen are silver and gold, the work of men's hands. They have mouths, but they speak not; eyes have they, but they see not. They have ears, but they hear not; neither is their any breath in their mouths. They that make them are**

like unto them: so is every one that trusteth in
them."
Psalms 135:15-18

Following the same pattern, of the same but opposite, I realized
that something more was under construction. In the past man
created idols and worshiped them as gods. Their faith and beliefs
were just as dead and empty as what they worshiped. So what
if you made a living idol? In a legalistic manner, according to the
Scriptures, your faith and belief would be as alive as the living
idol as well as those who worshiped it. Faith is not necessary, as
you have the real thing in front of your five senses. Even if it is a
lie! I remembered another scripture in Revelations.

The Hybrid Transformed Will Become the Image of Desire

**"And deceived them that dwell on the earth by the
means of those miracles which he had power to do
in the sight of the beast; saying to them that dwell
on the earth, that they should make an image to
the beast, which had the wound by the sword, and
did live. And he had power to give life (breath) unto
the image of the beast, that the image should both
speak, and cause that as many as would not worship the image of the beast should be killed."**
Rev 13:14,15

The term "image of the beast" is a collective noun. It is speaking
of an entire group. There is an entire army under construction;
exactly what Daniel and Joel saw. This is the same army being
drawn up to total destruction. These cattle mutilations are not
ritualistic or religious "black art" sacrifices, they are mining
resources for food and developed genetic technology, a method
of self redemption and a place to hide.

This shell is the Nordic, the tall Blond or Red haired Caucasian
once called the Aryan. This Aryan image was once proclaimed by
Adolf Hitler as the ultimate genetic goal for mankind to achieve!
One which he also desired as an object of worship!

*"Anyone who interprets National Socialism mere-
ly as a political movement knows almost nothing*

about it. It is more than religion; it is the determination to create a new man."

Adolf Hitler"

" I will tell you a secret...I am founding an Order. It is from there that the second stage will emerge- the stage of the Man-God, when Man will be the measure and center of the world. The Man-God, that splendid Being, will be an object of worship...But there are other stages about which I am not permitted to speak..."

Heinrich Himmler

Church History has been consistent in recording Caucasian images for angels. This same image is recorded by many ancient civilizations as heavenly gods who gave them a sudden boost in knowledge and Theosophical spiritual views. I believe this group is being set up to be reintroduced into our society as the "good guy" angel/aliens here to lead mankind into a "New Age".

Like it or not this image has been subtly introduced in several ways as a desired one. Whether the Aryan, Angel or friendly Nordic Alien, this image has been made desirable by many for different reasons. The cattle mutilations are only the first step to create this image. Humans are needed for a variety of genetic needs also. We shall look at this next. There is much to cover so the entire next chapter is devoted to this Phenomenon called Alien Abduction.

Chapter Fifteen
What the Bible says about Alien Abductions

Part One

General Background

A New One on All of Us!

While explaining my work in ministry, I usually get a response of laughter that turns into blank stares of perplexity when people realize I'm not joking with them about Alien Abductions. Unfortunately this subject is looked upon as a Jerry Springer freak show topic and the stuff for supermarket tabloids. I realize that most of the laughter is not from a lack of compassion, as it is more from a lack of information. This is a new one on all of us. While the News media mocks and pokes fun at the subject creating this lunatic fringe image, there is another side to this phenomenon. Many professionals in fields that have crossed paths with this strange phenomenon are taking the subject seriously.

Abductions are Taken Seriously

In the summer of 1992 at MIT Cambridge, Ma, The Abduction Study Conference was held. On the board and in attendance were many Doctorates of various professional fields of study and practice, including a Nobel Prize winning Psychiatrist Dr. John E. Mack. These professionals from a wide variety of fields found themselves involved with the abduction phenomena. Some have been from the medical profession who have removed foreign objects or recorded sudden known pregnancies that were no longer the case with no evidence of a natural termination. Most have been mental health professionals who have recorded cognitive and regressive stories of abductions at the hands of similar non-human entities. Others have been the many researchers and investigators of the UFO phenomena. They also have creditable backgrounds with testimonies and records of cases involving the abduction phenomena.

A 690 page book was published from their results of scrutinizing over 300 of the most credible documented cases. What was particularly important to me was the fact that most of the cases selected were ones in which the abductees had cognitive memory of their experiences. Their findings were both objective and thorough as anyone could possibly be at this present time. Without their knowledge, many of their findings agree with what the Scriptures also declare about this phenomenon. Some findings were even conflicting with many of their own personal beliefs but objectively reported anyway. The Conference truly reflected the finest in objective examination of a very misunderstood problem.

Typical Abduction Scenario

Abductions are most common in two situations. They are either in the late night hours intruding upon a person asleep in their bed, or in an isolated remote area at night, either driving on a road, camping or simply taking a quiet walk. The typical bedroom intrusion abduction in most cases includes a form of forewarning such as a ringing or humming noise that is more internal than external. A sudden bright light or beam of light maybe projected into a room. There can be a sudden waking from sleep to a presence in the room with the inability to move. Sometimes there is a sensation of floating through a wall or out a window into a bright light or craft. Being strapped onto a bare metallic examination table with attached equipment and surrounded by small reptilian gray "aliens" with oversized heads and bulbous black eyes. Also the taller insect-like "leaders" are seen.

Many times abductions are during a UFO sighting in a remote area at night. The only thing remembered was seeing an object and resuming their actions but with a loss of time up to several hours. Sometimes cars have been miles from where they were at the time of the sighting. Sometimes clothes have been replaced improperly. People have found themselves in different places than where they had the sighting and not remembering how they got there. The medical examinations are the predominate theme to abductions. These examinations include extraction of semen and eggs. Dr. David M. Jacobs gave testimony that

"...women report that rather than an egg being collected; they know something has been implanted in them. At the end of the procedure, they might be told that they are now pregnant...the women have

> **engaged in absolutely no sexual relations at the time of the pregnancy ...What is far more frequently is that the women feel that they are no longer pregnant after one to eleven weeks...fetal extractions appear to be far more common than once thought and there is reason to believe that the majority of female abductees might have had these procedures... They appear to be the central focus of the abduction phenomenon and is possible that they are the reason for the UFO phenomenon in general"**
>
> **...Dr. Jacobs**

Also included is the insertion of objects into the sinus cavity, hands and feet or scoop marks where skin and tissue have been removed. In most cases the memories of these events are erased only to surface later as bad dreams. Also, sudden memory flashes that are almost immediately repressed by the conscious mind in fear are experienced. The sporadic and incomplete regaining of these memories cannot be discredited as mass hysteria produced by Hollywood or Jerry Springer. This scenario is typical of thousands worldwide and may not include all events but the typical abduction includes many. The patterns are consistent regardless of what part of the world it may have happened. These many reports cannot be so easily dismissed. Something very real is happening to many people.

Part Two

Evidence and Witness Testimonies

The first demand by most everyone is, "Where's the proof?" The proof is there, but it is a matter of perception. There are thousands of cases. They all have these similarities and patterns of the above particular sequence of events. The claims are much more than mass hysteria or mere coincidence. To claim this is hysteria, created by the media, is demeaning to those who have had the experience. It is also inconsistent to an earlier history of similar cases documented long before the media even existed.

A Case in 1645

The late Carl Sagan researched the well-documented case of Anne Jeffries in 1645. She was found outside in a "fit" as records describe. This "fit" was more of a comatose state and she eventually came out of it. After this she was said to have received a clairvoyant and healing ability. Her memory of what happened to her before she fell into this fit is what is even more interesting. She recalled half dozen little men that "paralyzed" her and took her to a castle in the sky. There she was seduced and then returned where she was found. Now it would be absurd to say that anything from that time could be confirmed. However, the fact is that a well-documented case of abduction was recorded in this early time, before T.V. and Hollywood.

Skeptical Arrogance

To disregard the many similar testimonies from so many ordinary people is both illogical and willful ignorance on behalf of the accusing skeptic. In many cases the abductee has more to lose than to gain by going public. When skeptics go further to accuse and discredit the individuals as being uneducated, ill informed or unstable, in an effort to support their own unbelief, these actions are gross vane arrogance! Who has given these skeptics the standard or rule to measure others testimonies and experiences. What gives them some "enlightened insight" or edge on the knowledge of the subject? Where is the proof of their enlightened edge? These many testimonies are proof and should not be treated so lightly or so easily discredited by the vanity of skeptics!

Hard Evidence

Smaller amounts of people have reported their abductors as tall, blond haired, blue-eyed Humanoids called the Nordics. Medical examinations and experiments by this group are said to be far less traumatic and painful.

One such abductee who has learned to accept and even embrace his captors is David E. Caywood of Dearborn, Michigan. One of the well-known cases, it is probably one of the best examples with unexplained evidence left behind. A claimed abductee since a child, he prefers to be called an experiencer. He describes his Nordic abductors fondly and accepts their Theosophical beliefs. I talked with David and he is a very friendly, polite and intelligent man. He was very helpful in contacting other abductees for some of my own research. I do not agree with his world view and feelings toward his captors. I believe he is wrong about his captors and is being deceived by them. Nevertheless, he carries within him evidence of something unexplained. A recent MRI scan in 1996 revealed an anomalous object at the base of his brain stem. Doctors have stated that such an object if planted in that location should have killed him. They cannot explain its existence or purpose. They do not have the ability to remove it because it would kill him. Other silicone, crystalline and metallic objects have been removed from other abductees. They are kept as evidence. On examination they are composed of known earthly elements. Because of this, skeptics treat it as nothing but a hoax or a "normal" foreign object. If (as I believe) these implants were terrestrial in origin, we would expect them to be identifiable. Because the objects have nothing unknown, does not make them any less real. Most are silicone based and perhaps an electronic coded surveillance chip. Others contain combinations of metallic alloys that are obviously synthetically produced. This is the smoking gun but it is still a matter of perception.

I personally believe that abductions are much more common and include a large part of the population since the late 40's. It is amazing how the human mind will tolerate and accept the unbelievable when there is no other alternative. Who would ever believe normal people could have this experience? And how do many of these normal people carry on afterwards? Many might keep up such a good front so that no one would ever know.

It Happened to a Normal Guy.

The father of my childhood sweetheart is just such a case. In 1966, Ed, (Not his real name) a typical suburban husband and father of three children worked as a Detective for a major department store. He was about as far removed as a person could be from the idea of aliens and flying saucers. One night he woke up to hear the screaming of his daughter in her room. As he opened up the door to the upstairs hallway, the whole area was filled with a strange bright blue light emitted from her bedroom. He ran to the daughter's room where the source of this light was emitted from and opened the door. There crouched upon her bed was his terrified daughter pointing out the bedroom window screaming:

> *" There, over there, they are right out there next to the big tree!"*

As he gazed out the window there was a large, glowing, metallic object hovering behind the tree shining a bright bluish light at the house. Suddenly it just disappeared out of sight, traveling at an amazing speed.

After this event, Ed never shared this with anyone, even to this day. He sort of just passed it on without further pondering. Ed was an assertive, take-charge kind of guy. His job required this of him. Perhaps, because he could not reference this to any normal experience, as well as the helplessness of not being able to do anything about it, he just closed it out of his mind completely. One thing he did realize was that if this got out to anyone, his job and life could be greatly affected.

Only after running into my old childhood friend 30 years later, did she share this event with me as she became aware of my research. On the outside you would have never known that this man could have ever had such a horrible experience. He never let this go beyond his own family. I asked my friend to ask her Dad what he thought about all of this now. With much more recent information and understanding, I was curious about what he might have to say. His only comment was, "I guess they were aliens." He was still reluctant to even say anything more after all this time, even to his own daughter. For over thirty years he has carefully kept this amazing story bottled up inside. How many other very normal people have had similar experiences that they have just bottled up and never mentioned?

Confiding in the Pastor

As a Pastor not afraid of the supernatural, I have had many people open up to me with very extreme supernatural experiences of many different types. Two members of my congregation told me of "dreams" they had as children of "pumpkin headed people" that used to come into their room or little gray "stick men". The latter experience happened to a woman who remembered her experiences as childhood "nightmares".

One night as she thought she woke up from one of her dreams, she found herself floating above her bed with a bright light shining from her window. It was only a dream wasn't it? She questioned the memories of her dreams as perhaps being more because of identifying the stick men from a documentary she saw on TV about Abductions. The documentary triggered off further memories of floating and she became concerned. There may be much more to many of these childhood dreams than what is given credit for.

The man who saw the pumpkin-headed people also attributed them to childhood dreams. He is 52 and was a child long before the popular image of the Gray was known or published. His description along with the rest of the details followed the same typical patterns.

These are but a very few of many incidents never before published or made known to the public. Every investigator and researcher involved has their own files full of similar incidents. Something is going on. It is tangible and very real on the physical plane and not just illusions by Satan or mixed up magnetic brain wave patterns as some ridiculous claims have stated.

Christians included:

When I first ventured into this area of abductions, I assumed that Christians would be impervious to such attacks. I was wrong. My own counseling experience confirms that these patterns exist for Christians as well as non-Christians. While living in Roswell NM, I had three cases from my own church at the same time. One case was a woman who, while in her twenties became "pregnant" while her husband was on an overseas short term work trip. She had no relations during his absence and was horrified by the whole situation. In a matter of three months the pregnancy was terminated without any action on her part. She began to question her sanity and thought it was all in her mind. While this dilemma was going on she had bad dreams of small demonic looking creatures at the foot of her bed as she lay motionless and helpless to get away.

Another woman, a daughter of a Missionary Pastor, told me of her teenage experience. She had pain in her pubic area and her parents took her to a doctor. The doctor asked her when she lost her virginity, shocked; she said never, I am a virgin! He told her, "Dear, you have all the indications internally, that you have been pregnant, and I need to know when this happened. How traumatic this was for her to experience such an accusation. Years of guilt and uncertainty as to what happened remained upon her for the next two decades. In the same manner until the day I met her, she experienced many bad dreams and paranormal experiences with ghostlike apparitions in her room at night. Her father although a Minister who loved and served God with years of dedication was "open " to the Alien /UFO ideas popular at the time and was active in the UFO community while living in Roswell. He investigated and wrote articles for a local UFO publication.

The last case is the most dramatic. A woman in her mid thirties told me the story that happened several years prior to our meeting where she became pregnant while her husbands was overseas on an extended missions trip. She was shocked because she had no relations with anyone and was a faithful wife and follower of Jesus Christ. In the same sudden fashion, she was no longer pregnant three months later. This time unlike the other cases, she had conclusive proof that she had been pregnant and it wasn't just her imagination. She had an MRI showing a severed placenta and a torn egg sack. She was going to provide me with this evidence. Upon hearing this story, another "famous" researcher tried to talk me into giving him the information. A controversy evolved and suddenly I found resistance from my own church and Pastor. Our Pastor claimed he was "freaked out" about this whole subject and stated to me, "I only want what is real". I agreed with him and was not getting this whole picture, that this was his way of telling me that he did not believe that any of this was real! My own Pastor became instrumental in stopping the woman from having any further involvement with me. The evidence was stopped from ever being presented. I was soon afterward excluded from any involvement with church activities. I was never confronted about leaving but was shunned to the point I had no other choice than to leave. His unbelief and resistance to providing the truth will someday be something he will have to account for.

The happy end to these stories was the fact that each person received answers and a closure with sound Biblical answers to the trauma they faced in their lives. With a short amount of counseling, they all received total termination to any supernatural visitations and experiences by standing on the authority and use of the name of Jesus to stop these entities from intruding into their lives any further.. The Missionary/Pastor also had his miss-understandings about UFOs and Aliens corrected by our developed friendship and sharing from the scriptures. He has since gone on to be with the Lord but in his passing he was able to repent and adjust his past involvement in the UFO community into something positive.

Alien Abductions are a Real Problem

Until a few years ago, only those directly involved in the UFO investigating community have addressed this problem seriously. Because of this only route, the people who have gone through this horrible experience are in many cases led away from former Christian beliefs into a variety of different philosophies.

From my perspective as a Christian Minister, this could be like jumping out of the frying pan into the fire itself. You see, some of these philosophies and practices are generated by the same entities involved in the abductions! In this sandwich of a bad experience and then miss-guidance of counseling, the results are that Abductees are actually encouraged to continue on a path leading to acceptance and further abduction experiences. Instead of trying to escape this danger and deception they become a willing zealot to their agenda!

Much of the false concepts are reinforced by the fact that many after the abduction experience have supernatural experiences of psychic premonitions, Out of body experiences, healings and other paranormal activity.

Taking a Fresh Look from the Bible

In this kind of review you must go back to the original languages used and look at many words and contextual usage in light of 21st century technology. As you do this a whole new understanding is revealed. It is not that the Bible translators mistranslated many of the original words. Hebrew and Greek have many variations for the same word. Without understanding current technology that was being described in a future prophetic sense the translators used the only other correct alternative words that for them, made any sense. In this understanding, certain Bible words are not mistranslated; it is just that their true meaning could not have been fully understood until such technology or events would reveal them. In this sense, it is like a time capsule. It is released on a need to know basis, dependant upon the increased knowledge and events existing at the proper time that would bring out the full potential or word usage and meaning.

This is just what the prophet Daniel was told about the visions he received, as he was to record them in the Bible.

> **"But thou, O Daniel, shut up the words, and seal the book, even to the time of the end: many shall run to and fro, and knowledge shall be increased... And he said, "Go thy way, Daniel: for the words are closed up and sealed till the time of the end."**
> **Dan 12:4,9**

We are at that end. This is the time that these secrets are revealed. This is that time of knowledge increasing at such a rapid rate never before recorded in our known history.

Part Three
The Scriptures Allude to Abductions

Sneaking in Darkness

Some scriptures allude to abductions stealthily searching for something in man. In Rev 9:4,5 locusts ascend out of the bottomless pit when it was opened by an angel with a "key". For five months the Locusts function is to "sting men" but not kill them. Biblical time does not have to be literal. At this time I have no clue as to what this period might be...yet. The word for *Locusts*, in context has a pattern of a symbolic meaning, "as nations". The word for the "*stings*" that they give, only to those who have not the seal of God in their foreheads, has an etymology that suggests the sting as "a touchstone". It was a stone used to test the quality of silver and gold by scratching it upon the stone. I believe this is also in reference to the abductions going on right now. The abductions might also be alluded to in Joel 2 as this same invading army of Rev 9. In this description,

> **"they shall climb up upon the houses; they shall enter in at the windows like a thief."**
>
> **Joel 2:9**

They need something from the genetic makeup of mankind. They extract this stealthily in the night. These creatures seem to only operate in the darkness of night in clandestine, sneaky ways. Also, in this text, Joel describes an army that is not your normal earthly one. Here is another rendering, going back to the original languages, using other proper variables of word use.

> **"A day of ignorance and concealment, a day of practiced magic and the lowering of high things, as the dawn spreads out upon the mountains, a huge abundant congregated mighty people come into existence that has never been before and shall never be after... and when they fall upon the sword, they shall not be wounded."**
>
> **Joel 2:1, 2, 8.**

Abductions are Creating "Earth suits"

The abductions are for the mixing of the serpents' seed with mankind to create the image proclaimed by Hitler as the "Master

225

Race" Now with a repackaged Theosophy they are presented as Good Angel/Aliens.

The prophet Isaiah at a time when the Philistines were gloating about a great victory gave this prophetic warning.

> **"Rejoice not thou whole Palestina, because the rod of him that smote thee is broken: for out of the serpents root shall come forth a cockatrice, and his fruit shall be a fiery flying serpent."**
> **Isaiah 14:29**

Now once again on the surface this does not appear to be saying much that makes sense. By once again, going back to variables in the original language with a 21st century outlook, a different picture may be illustrated for us and much more relevant for today. This could be a possible rendering:

> **"Rejoice not all of you Philistines, because the tribe of Israel (Dan) that punished you is broken off, to pluck from the serpents soil, an extrusion of offspring, shining ones to cover with obscurity the serpent."**
> **(UJWV)**

The Philistines were the last group of people to have the remaining "seed" of the Giants or **Nephilim** remain in their gene pool. They were the race of giants that existed in various tribes that God told the Israelites to completely destroy. These were the same ones present before the flood and part of the reason for it.

This amazing verse when re-examined, is telling us that from their interbred stock containing this seed of the serpent and the genetic stock of the serpent would come an extrusion of offspring. I have been told that gene splicing could be described as a process of "extruding" the desired DNA from its source! From this scripture we have a progression of generational development. From the serpent, or Gray, we have a spliced hybrid a result of Gray/Human splicing. From sexual encounters of this hybrid with members of the human race who bear the genetic trace of the Nephilim, the modern day decedents of the Philistines, a refined human-like "shell" is created for the Grays, and the disembodied spirits to slip into like a suit. It light of this text, it would be important to know who the Philistines were.

"Earth Suits" in the Image of the Philistines

So Who were the Philistines?

In Gen 10:14 they are referred to as descendants of Ham who were black. This was true in the third millennium B.C. They were the original settlers, being peaceful agriculturalists of Hamatic descent. They were uprooted by a belligerent maritime "sea people" who invaded and conquered the land from Capthor. (Crete). These guys acted much like the later Vikings, and perhaps are one in the same. Amos 9:7 refers to the Philistines from Caphtor.

The Capthorim in Isaiah's time had long since been called the Philistines who occupied Philistia. They were the Aryans, Indo-Europeans. On the temple of Rameses III in Medinet, a relief shows them to be tall Hellenic-looking people. The name Philistine means "migratory". Japheth, the eldest son of Noah was said to be the first descendent of the White or Caucasian Race. It was said that God would enlarge Japheth and he would dwell in the tents of Shem and Canaan would be his servant. This shows a people on the move with a genetic tenancy to invent, conquer and dominate. Being the firstborn of the human race they would hold "Legal" birthright of any inheritance. I say this only in the sense of Satan being a legal adversary trying to stake a claim, he would naturally use the firstborn in a legal sense, as well as a biological one for certain genetic traits. Especially when the promised spiritual redemption and "chosen" came from the descendants of Shem.

I believe an army is under construction. The warrior traits of Cain and the physical attributes, as the root of the serpent are what they desire. This strain would be stronger in the firstborn of the human race. This is why there is both legal and biological preference placed upon the whites.

Evidence Concurs With Scripture.

At the 1997 MUFON meeting in Grand Rapids, I had a chance to talk with Dr. David Jacobs and Budd Hopkins. These two men are acclaimed to be among the top "experts" on Alien Abductions. I asked them a leading question of just who was being abducted. In a tongue in cheek manner they replied almost in harmony,

"The question is, who isn't being abducted."

227

They truly believe that this phenomenon is much larger than could be imagined. I tend to agree with them based on what I believe the Word of God tells me about it. I then asked if there was any particular group or race that seemed to experience this act more than others.

> ***"Well, members of all the races have been abducted,"***

(in an almost embarrassed manner as if not wanting to be miss-understood,) they continued to confess that,

> ***"however there is a disproportionate amount of whites that seem to be abducted, and we don't know why really".***

I figured he would say that, as a matter of fact I was counting on it. It tells me that their findings concur with what the Bible tells me.

Part Four

Help from the Antichrist

We also get this same theme alluded to at the hand of the Antichrist. Again this is not so easily seen on the surface but by using proper Biblical symbolism and a more detailed meaning from the original languages from this genetic perspective this scripture can read out to make the same claim.

> **"But in his estate shall he honor the God of forces (the invisible forces Hitler always spoke of ?): and a god whom his fathers new not shall he honor with gold and silver, and with precious stones, and pleasant things, Thus shall he do in the most strong holds with a strange god, whom he shall acknowledge and increase with glory: and he shall cause Them to rule over many and shall divide the land for gain."**
>
> **Daniel 11:38,39**

The previous scripture above this one declares the he does not believe in any god and has placed himself in a position in his own heart as god. Now here it appears that he does acknowledge some god. In the original language, "*honor*" means "to pay tribute, to increase or make fat". *"God of forces"* is in the sense of "a defense or guardian". He increases or fortifies a position of defense. A god his fathers knew not, means to have an intimate personal relationship or contact with? He shall increase with gold, silver and precious stones and pleasant things (or things desired).

This text sounds almost outrageous at first appearance. Remember the building of idols as described in Psalms. Many have looked at this passage with the idea of economic help as these elements are the standard for economy. (Or used to be). Back to the original language we could be looking at building elements in a completely different manner.

> **"He will abundantly supply the shining of gold, pieces of silvering, and rare stony ground, and things desired."**

This is the literal meaning. It does not seem to make sense at first glance but here, we must use some standard biblical symbolism.

Elements of Construction

Gold is "deity or God" the *"shining of Gold"* would be the light reflecting from it. Jesus is described as the radiance of His (The Father's) glory and the image of His person. Heb 1:3 therefore the *"reflection of God"*. He is also called the "firstborn of many brethren". Born-again believers in Christ are described as taking on the "image of Christ" by the power of His spirit. 1Col 3:10, 2Co3:18 and John1:12. There is something that produces the reflection of God within mankind that is being extracted and spliced with this "demon seed". This perhaps is either reproducing something to look like humans or something to give an appearance of a resurrected body. Of what exactly I am not sure at this time. But be assured, there is something being taken and spliced. It is for the purpose of imitating the "reflection of God".

Silver is symbolic of "redemption". **Silvering** is a coating or plating process, therefore, "a redemptive covering". Cattle was used in the Old Testament as a sacrifice for a "redemptive covering" for sins.(Firstborn preferred). The first stages of development is to produce a hybrid with sensory organs from animals that in turn can reproduce with humans producing the end product, the Nordic or a humanoid with a DNA signature of the serpent.

Precious stones are actually *"rare stoney ground"*. Rare stony ground is described as the state of the human heart unregenerate by the Holy Spirit. What the Bible refers to as being "born again" is when a melding of His Holy Spirit and our human spirit come together. **Ezk36:26,27** "Rare stony places" suggests the "unsaved", or at least a certain type of an unsaved individual. As previously mentioned in Isaiah 14, the Caucasian from the Philistine linage could be this type of "rare stony ground".

Precious things is better rendered, "things desired". Now let's put this together and see how it sounds.

> " **He will abundantly supply the reflection of God, a redemptive covering, rare Stony ground and things desired."**
>
> **(UJWV)**

He supplies, something genetic reflecting the image of God from abductions, a redemptive covering from Cattle Mutilations, genetic material from the unredeemed or serpents seed And other needs such as underground bases, permission to exercise power in the affairs of men and... food.). The coincidence of this interpretation is uncanny. It speaks to us today about what is going on right under our own noses! This could be how Daniel "shut up and sealed" the words of prophecy into the text, not to be understood until such events would reveal the hidden meaning behind the word usage.

Fallen Angels Genetically Crossover to Becomes the Nordic Good Guy Aliens

Notice also in the text, he acknowledges a strange god. This means he takes an intense study and understanding of an (It was strange to fine this as one of the meanings) ALIEN GOD! Perhaps studying the physics and technology of their culture as what happened before the flood could be included in this intense study.

He will increase them with glory. We have already seen that they have a glory throughout history and quite a promotional campaign going on right now. He will cause them to rule over many. This cross-references with Rev 13:13,14. The image of the beast is to be worshiped. Power is given them over the people of the earth. This will not be imposed like in the movie *Independence day*, it will be compelled and desired. Perhaps by presenting themselves as the Nordics who they will claim are actually the angels of the Bible who have done all the good intervention upon earth throughout our history. They will be adored and power given to them willingly! This too is some time in the near future.

Now in a clandestine manner the army is being built and placed into position like a chess game. There is a trade going on here. He (the antichrist) is supplying these things for a price. Perhaps technology, and a forbidden physics of the eternal dimension. He divides the land or soil. "Adamah" is the word used for "soil". It is a generic word used generally for "land in the physical sense". There is a connection with man to it as *"Adam"* is used for "man" and derived from the same root to be made red or ruddy. He could be dividing "physical land" or figuratively land as in soil as "genetic material" of which man was made from.

Part Five

Your Defense Department At Work:

Notice his estate or position from where he operates is one from a defensive one? In Daniel 9:27 we see an army of idols that comes from the highest level of defense. The Abomination that makes desolate performed in the Second Temple by Antiochus Epiphanies IV who was a foreshadow of the Antichrist as a symbolic type of what is to come. He placed a pig upon the altar in the Holy of Holies, the inner sanctuary. He also placed statues representing false gods on the ramparts of the temple. Ramparts are the highest point of defense for ancient buildings and castles. In this symbolism, Only a lamb without spot was to be sacrificed upon the alter. This was symbolic of Jesus' first mission to be the "Lamb of God". In mockery and I believe prophetic symbolism, The Antichrist as the pig, an unclean animal in the eyes of the Jews was slaughtered in the place of the lamb. The Antichrist would assume the same function and mission. After the sacrifice the "shekinah glory" would emanate from the inner chamber, from outside the reflected light would appear to shine from the ramparts. As a mockery, false idols are placed there instead.

This same pattern was also reproduced in Herod's Temple in 70AD. It was recorded that Titus of Rome placed a statue of Zeus in the Holy of Holies and each Roman legion placed their banners upon the ramparts of the temple walls in mockery to the Jews. This pattern is more than coincidental. This pattern could be symbolic of a day when the highest level of defense from within the innermost sanctity of the country supposed to reflect the glory of God instead produces the risen Antichrist and an "army of Idols" to follow. As we have seen that would be the sides of the North, America and the Pentagon, the highest level of defense! Again No coincidence!

Clues of Coincidence?

It makes me wonder why after World War II did our Defense department changed from within from Operation Paperclip and the Gehlen organization. The outward show was a new building, The Pentagon. The Philistines held their power by a five city fortification called the "Pentapolos". Both are reminiscent of Satan's Pentagram and his five "I willed plan". Coincidental symbolism, or real signs and wonders to give us a clue?

Are we simply carrying over and continuing on with the technology gleaned from Nazi Germany in cloning technology as we did with the space program? Is America part of the divided kingdom of Daniel 2 The alluded alliance mentioned in Job with the Stork that becomes the Ostrich who plays with the Horse and the rider. The one who becomes the harlot who rides upon the beast with the inscription upon her head?

> **"And upon her forehead was a name written, MYS-TERY, BABYLON THE GREAT, THE MOTHER OF HAR-LOTS AND ABOMINATIONS OF THE EARTH."**
> **Rev 17:5**

These coincidences are truly beyond Science-Fiction.

A Need for Grace

I don't want you to think I am casually slamming my country because I am not. We have a negative destiny that will be played out. In spite of that, America and the American people, even most of our military are not the bad guys here! We have all been deceived on a scale like just prior to the Great Flood. I believe only a very small amount of the highest Military officials (MJ 12) actually know they are dealing with former Nazis, fallen angels and the god of this age. The majority are told they are dealing with "Aliens" and their technology. These are not bad men plotting evil against the people of America or the World. They are deceived Patriotic Americans believing that they are serving their country and God.

One such experience happened to me while doing a UFO show. The show was just outside of Wright Patterson AFB in Ohio.

This base has always been the location for processing captured foreign aircraft. I had a table set up and was selling my booklets there. A man approached me and flatly stated that he was an agnostic and did not want to be preached too. I laughed and told him, "OK? What would you like from me". He said he just wanted some information to help someone else.

Then he proceeded to tell me his story. He stated that he used to be an Officer stationed at Wright Patterson AFB. He was a Psychiatrist on staff there and was approached by Military Security agents. He was told he would receive two patients that were under great stress. He was told that everything that transpired in the secessions came under National Security.

He then stated that two officers who were working on back engineering of Alien craft were under great emotional stress. They became aware of some details about their projects that included an actual alien presence within the United States and it was destroying their faith, marriage and disrupting their work abilities. They were both "born again Baptists" and could not seem to reconcile what they were doing. They could not find any answers from their Churches, suitable to match their knowledge of what they were involved in. Only Biblical answers would help and the man confessed to me that he had nothing to offer them that would help. He said he started coming to UFO shows with the hope of finding answers for himself as he never believed in any of this until that incident. When he saw my table he was truly excited. Regardless of his personal beliefs, I could tell he was a kind man who truly cared about people. He bought everything I had and left pleased that he might have some answers for them. It makes me wonder how many more like them are out there. How many need to know what The Bible has to say about it all.

I still believe in America and the integrity of individuals who are deceived and need to know the truth.

Part Six

Abductions Are a Physical and Spiritual Reality

In the Proceedings of the Abduction Study Conference held at MIT in 1991, the admission that an abduction was stopped in progress while singing Christian Hymns and quoting Scripture is recorded. Now why on earth would this have any effect on an "Alien". If we are dealing with natural beings on a natural level, then why does this spiritual dimension exist? As real as I believe abductions are, this is a clear indication that this is a spiritual problem as well as a physical one. We are in fact dealing with the fallen angels of Genesis 6.

No Other Name

I don't think any other piece of evidence is more compelling than that of Joe Jordan's personal testimony and experience. Joe is a State section director of Mutual U F O Network or MUFON. in Florida where he resides. He works in the design department for Sea Ray Boats as well. In Joe's own words:

> *"As a field investigator interviews were done with some of our local experiencers. While working on a couple of very strange cases, the girlfriend I had at the time became very concerned for my well-being. She said that working in this realm , I could possibly encounter an evil force. I needed protection. I told her in my New Age thinking that evil was just a per-ception, hers being probably different from mine, and I had protection, I had some powerful crystals that I carried. She said I needed real protection, not some rocks. I said, what are you offering? She asked if I would look at something in the Bible with her. I said, Oh no. That has nothing to do with the field I work in. She asked if I had not always said I was the most open minded and objective person be-ing an investigator. She got me. We looked at what the Bible had to say and it was like I was hit with a bolt of lightning. For the first time it made real sense to me. I had been brought up in the church but had never seen it shown to me as it was now. I wanted what the Bible had to offer. I knew what I had to do to have it. I made a profession of faith and was baptized in my parents church.*
>
> *There was an interview we had done with an alien abduction experiencer 6 months before I gave my life to Christ. It meant little to me then but in my new faith this was important. This was the case of a man who stopped an abduction in progress and Included this interesting fact: "In fear, not being a religious man he cried out," Jesus, Jesus help me". This was unheard of to us. We had not read or heard anything about anyone stopping an experience. I*

contacted some of the leading abduction research-ers in the country to ask about what they thought of this case. They each asked to go off the record after I shared this man's experience with them. I said that was fine, just help me out. They said they also had come across cases like this. I asked them why we had not received any information from them or heard about this. They replied that they didn't know what to make of it. They also confessed, that they were afraid to go there because it might affect their credibility in the UFO realm. I told them I was going to take this information and get it out because I had nothing to lose, I wasn't writing books or lecturing, I worked for living. They said, Please do. We can't. Knowing that this case was not one of a kind, I set up to find other testimonies like it Over the next couple of years."

Joe now has a very productive ministry, The CE 4 Research Group, which effectively assists victims of Alien Abductions. As a part of his ministry, he speaks to Churches around the country bringing some of the "experiencers" with him to testify of their victory over this problem.

Today CE4 Research has more than 100 cases that he has worked with showing that the name and authority of Jesus Christ stops these alien abductions

Dr. Chris Ward of Logos Ministries also in Florida has several degrees as an Ordained Minister. He has almost thirty years in front line ministry dealing with Demonic possession and exorcism. Recently using the same spiritual process he has always used on spirit beings, he has included abduction cases to his ministry with great success.

As an additional update; Joe Jordan, Dave Ruffino of Delusion Resistance and myself have combined our abduction counseling ministries to form the Alien Abduction Crises Centers of America. or AACCOA. We are creating a nation wide network of help for abductees to be channeled into a local church by local counselors offering friendship and support after their initial help through our free service. To my knowledge the above mentioned people are the only ones from a Christian Pastoral background that provide this Biblical based alternative help to abduction victims on the whole planet. We recently have gone international as we now have added connections with South Africa and others to follow.

It is time other researchers with the same information in their files came forward. This kind of evidence proclaims the reality of the spiritual side of abductions. Fear of what others will think and holding back important information only delays in revealing the real truth. This is a spiritual battle we all need to fight!

> **"For we wrestle not against flesh and blood, but against principalities, against powers, against the rulers of the darkness of this world, against spiritual wickedness in high places."**
>
> **Eph 6:11**

The amazing evidence that the mere mention of the name Jesus or quoting scripture from the Bible and singing Christian hymns is effective against "Aliens" speaks loudly that this is a spiritual problem. The various expressions are not to be taken as a formula for it is the individuals faith and trust in that one name that holds this kind of power. This again concurs with what the Bible has to say.

> **"Wherefore God also hath highly exalted Him, and given Him a name which is above every name: That at the name of Jesus every knee should bow, of things in heaven, and things in earth, and things under the earth; And that every tongue should confess that Jesus Christ is Lord, to the glory of God the Father."**
>
> **Philippians 2:11**

That text is pretty self explanatory and needs no further commentary. Our final look at abductions will be the destinations.

Destinations Are Subterranean Not Extraterrestrial!

I believe most abduction cases are true. The problem is hypnotic regression. In the process it is hard to distinguish fact from imagination or possible demonic input. As the subconscious is brought out to the forefront, the imagination is a part of this. But how can you tell one from the other? You can't. From a Christian point of view, it is important to be in control of your own mind at all times. Passive forms of "letting go" gives possible control of your mind to other entities...this process is forbidden in the Bible for our own safety. Hypnosis places you in a mental place of no control!

Thirty one out of the three hundred cases from the Abduction Study Conference at M.I.T., included the observation of a destination. The most familiar destination is into a mother ship. The abductees leave the small ship to find themselves in a "hangar" of a larger one. Some see an otherworldly environment. (But this does not include any transition of leaving earth into space, or entering the alien world from space).

Ten cases involve the actual transition, but all of them go into a subterranean world. In some cases the ship dives under the sea, enters a cavern or a dark tunnel hewn out of rock. In all the cases, they eventually see the otherworldly landscape. Two distinct types are seen; one the landscape is sparse with sickly vegetation, usually more like a desert, with signs of devastation. Typically, it is dark or dim with a small reddish sun, if any at all. A futuristic city may thrive in the midst. The second landscape is one of a bright, but uniformly lit or diffused light, no sun, no horizon visible, with a lush, moist, heavily vegetated landscape also holding a futuristic city, but obviously subterranean.

Both scenes are explained by the captors that their planet suffered some kind of disaster, and have a problem with reproduction. This, they say, is why they take eggs and sperm from us. These same beings warn us that the same catastrophes are ahead for earth. Some experience a religious or mystical ceremony underscoring the preciousness of life. Transportation time between earth and the other world is at most a couple of hours. In spite of this evidence, these researchers insist on believing that these journeys are extraterrestrial. Evidence is overwhelmingly in favor of the fact that if true, they are never seen leaving or entering another world from space. They are always traveling in dark tunnels leading to a subterranean other world, and the travel time is negligible.

Probably the thought never crossed their minds that they never left earth because scientist-priests says it is impossible for our earth to be hollow. So, they go to another world that is hollow. If these stories hold any truth, as I believe they do, they are going to a real literal Hell in Sheol or Nod, not another planet! I believe the integrity of this conference was very well done. Their own results support an inner earth destination and origin and not the E.T. agenda most want to believe. Because the idea of a hollow earth is directly related to the "Aliens" and their agenda we will see what the Bible has to say about such a thing next.

Chapter Sixteen
A Hollow Earth?

Modern Science says no!

Modern Science will tell you that it is impossible for the earth to be "Hollow". This same Modern Science will tell you man came from a monkey and there are no such things as UFOs. The "official" position of the Church (Holy Roman version) at one time was that; the earth was flat. The emerging sciences began to realize that this was wrong. Today in the minds of too many people, the Bible has lost its validity because men were wrong! It is funny that the Bible declared the earth was round long before there was a "Modern Science" or The Church! (Holy Roman type).

> **"It is He who sits above the circle of the earth, and its inhabitants are like grasshoppers, who stretches out the heavens like a curtain, and spreads them out like a tent to dwell in."**
>
> **Isaiah 40:22**

The Bible has always remained true; it is man's own interpretation or rather the lack of proper interpretive procedures that are flawed!

Part One

Unclear Thinking about a Hollow Earth

Most Christians profess belief in a literal "Hell". When pressed to define where it is, most will point to the ground or define this never-never land in another dimension on some spiritual plane. A vague unclear concept of hell has been taught for centuries. The result is another great miss-conception within much of traditional Christianity concerning the separation of spirit and flesh.

The actual evidence scientifically is no more conclusive about a Hollow Earth than it is about Evolution or UFOs. There is valid scientific proof that hollow planets and moons may be the norm and not even an exception. The actual fact is that we (at least the public) know very little about the inner condition of the earth.

The point is that in spite of any claims made by science, it has not been proven that the earth is solid.

I believe because science has been able to produce many conveniences of technology, Scientists have moved into the place of being what I call Scientist - Priests. They tell us what to believe both spiritually and in the physical natural realm and we are to unquestionably accept it. This was what people once did with the Priests of the Holy Roman Empire. All we have done is focused the same behavior from Organized Religion to Organized Science which for many has become their unquestionable religion. I believe the Church is embarrassed by the staunch position of Scientists Priests who proclaim with ridicule the very thought of a hollow earth.

Legends Abound:

Legends abound throughout many cultures about the origin of the first people who inhabited the earth. Some describe a race appearing from inside the earth. For example Indian folklore tells of "white tribes that live in the earth" appearing occasionally from caves. A series of Cave drawings from India shows a group of people emerging from a hollow void beneath the earth. According to local legends these were the first human beings that left a subterranean world to begin populating the surface world.

Native American legends from the Mandan, Sioux and Tuscarawas include their tribal origins as coming from inside the earth. Eskimos have the same tribal teachings. The Shawnees claim a civilization of "whites" lived in Florida before they arrived and left their buildings going back into caves in the earth. Incas have a similar folklore of a subterranean white race that travels via caves. From China, Iceland and the South American Aztecs, their writings tell of an inner domain created by the "gods" for the first humans. An Eastern legend describes that the origin of Adam came from inside the earth. A Hindu legend adds that Adam was a king of a group who fled a great cataclysm into the hollow earth and then returned to repopulate afterward. Tibetan monks refer to two underground areas "Shambhala" and "Agatha" as underground dwelling places for ascended masters and others. Orpheus went into the earth to seek out Eurydice of Greek mythology, Apollo's real home was among the Hyperborean inside the earth of Roman Mythology. The Valkyries descended and ascended into an inner domain in Nordic mythology. Even today, the Bon Po sect of Tibet claim to be in contact with underground masters and the "King of the World"; Lord Matreya, in tunnels and caverns in the Himalayan mountains. Names like Agharti, Shambhala, Shangri-La, Thule, Arktos, Valhalla, and Hades all speak of different cultural beliefs in an inner earth. The concept in myth and legend is truly as universal as the Flood.

Part Two

Historical Evidence

Sir Edmund Halley

The first person to write an entire work on a hollow earth was the famous English Astronomer and Mathematician; Sir Edmund Halley (yes, the comet guy) In 1692 he published his theory about a hollow earth. His theory was developed from working with Sir Isaac Newton on earth magnetism fluctuations and the possible causes. His solution, the earth was hollow. He believed there were three concentric cones with a molten lava core, which served as an "inner sun".

John Simms

Many in the beginning of the 19th century had popularized a hollow earth. This idea was taken seriously in our own history in America. John Simms a former Captain and decorated hero in the U.S. Army dedicated his life to undertaking the theory of a hollow earth. He believed there was a civilization that existed there as well, with openings at both poles. He died in 1829 with his dream unrealized but his ideas inspired the expedition of 1838

Charles Wilkes

Simms ideas were responsible for the ill-fated government-backed Expedition of 1838-1840 to the Antarctic led by Charles Wilkes. The Smithsonian Institute was built for the express purpose of holding the findings of this effort. It was supported by President John Quincy Adams and approved by Congress. There were many other explorers in the late 19th and early 20th century that set out explore the Polar Regions.

Admiral Richard Byrd

The most recent and successful exploration was that of Admiral Richard Byrd. Making many flights over both poles and mapping the Antarctic, Byrd became Americas "expert". In his early years (1929) he made a flight with his navigator Lloyd K. Grenlie over the Antarctic discovering a range of high mountain peaks called the "Rockefeller Mountains", named after the sponsor of the expedition.

It is alleged that they made a filming of a second trip that year. The newsreel film was played all over theaters in America describing both trips. In this film it showed photographs of "the land beyond the pole" including Mountains, trees, rivers and a large animal identified as a Woolly Mammoth! But of course today this film no longer exists. Grenlie before his death had confirmed the existence of the movie. In his book, " *World beyond the poles.*" (1959) Author F.A. Giannini presents signed testimonies of witnesses who remember viewing the movie. (I personally remember my Grandfather telling me as a child that he saw this newsreel clip in 1929.)

Many of the last trips made by Byrd started out with enthusiastic claims of being the most important discoveries to be made. Upon returning the Press gave little fanfare and Byrd said nothing. In a Diary claimed to be the "lost Diary" of his Antarctic trip in 1947 there is an entry,

Flight Log, Camp Arctic, Feb 19, 1947

"We are crossing over the small mountain range still proceeding northward...Beyond the mountain range is what appears to be a small river...... There should be no green valley here. Something is definitely wrong and abnormal here...We should be over ice and snow. From the port side there are great forests growing on the mountain side......The instruments are still spinning. The gyroscope is oscillating back and forth...I alter the altitude to 1400 feet and execute a sharp left turn...The light here seems different. I cannot see the sun anymore...We make another left turn and spot what seems to be a large animal of some kind below...it looks like a mammoth-like animal. This is incredible, but there it is... temperature indicator reads 74 degrees...Continue our heading. Navigation instruments seem normal now...Radio is not functioning. The countryside is more level than normal...Ahead we spot what seem like habitations. This is impossible! Aircraft seems light and oddly buoyant. The controls refuse to respond. The engines of our craft have stopped running. The landing process is beginning...I am mak-

ing a hasty last entry in the flight log. I do not know what is going to happen now..."

Hollow earth researchers are divided about the diary. The skepticism is mostly based on the next entry where Byrd describes that his plane was forced landed by a flying disk. There was a swastika-like marking on it. He then encountered tall, blond hair, blue eyed men who spoke English in a broken German-Nordic accent. He was given a tour and a message to the surface warning them about the use of testing nuclear weapons.

Red Flag Warning!

As much as I would like to believe in this lost diary there are some real problems. I have no problem with the content, even though it all might sound wacky to most. My problem is the manner in which he responded to what he was experiencing. Wasn't it already recorded that he made this trip and filmed it in 1929? Then why is he so taken back and surprised in 1947??? Would he not make comments that this was just like or similar to the last trip he had already made? He would have an attitude of, been there, done that slant to his writing. This is too convenient in timing and inconsistent to his past experiences.

I have no doubt that these events occurred; I just doubt that this diary is genuine. When investigating anything that is being covered up or silenced, you have to expect a lot of spurious information added for a variety of reasons. I believe someone well aware of the truth tried to create documentation to prove their case.

But proof may be in the suspicious reactions of our own government (U.S.) to the Nazi colony and Byrd's trip to the Antarctic in 1947 named Operation High-Jump. Admiral Byrd, our only expert on the Antarctic, commands the expedition. The venture was equipped with 13 ships including an aircraft carrier, two sea planes and 4,000 ground troops, the convoy steams to the Antarctic. There were no civilian research ships in the count. All of the ships were typical military support and combat ships common to a military contingency. The public is told that this was a scientific expedition to "test" military equipment in extreme cold conditions; the expedition is outfitted for 8 months. This would not seem unusual except the expedition maneuvered like a military assault. They made a two-point landing converging on an area named "Neu-Schwabenland" which the Nazi's explored and sectioned off, claiming it as theirs. The expedition returns to America a few weeks later after suffering heavy losses of equipment. Washington censures Admiral Byrd to be silent about the failed operation. What actually happened in the Antarctic we may never know. What we find are trace evidence of some kind of cover-up. Another piece of evidence we find is the authentic Diary of Byrd's

In the authentic Diary of Byrd's, his last entry before his death in 1957 tells us something of a truth.

> *"December 25, 1956 these last few years since 1947 have not been so kind. I now make my final entry in this singular diary. In closing I must state that I have faithfully kept this matter secret as directed all these years. It has been completely against my values and moral rights. Now I seem to sense a long night coming on and this secret will not die with me, but as truth shall, it shall triumph. It is the only hope for all mankind. I have seen and it has quickened my spirit and set me free. I have done my duty towards the monstrous military industrial complex. Now the long night of the Arctic ends, the brilliant sunshine of truth shall come again, and those who are of darkness shall fail in flight. For I have seen that land beyond the poles, the center of the great unknown."*

It was then signed with his signature Richard E. Byrd, United States Navy. This entry indicates that he was silenced from what he experienced and knew. In any conspiracies and cover-ups you will not find hard evidence, only the results of suspicious actions and reactions, along with traces and bits of evidence that create more questions than answers.

Part Three

Occult Beliefs:

Science Fiction or Fact?

Sir Edward Bulwer-Lytton was known worldwide for his book, *The last days of Pompeii*. He was a high ranking Freemason, a Rosicrucian and a member of the neo-pagan English social order known as the "Golden Dawn". He wrote a book (supposedly fiction) called, *The Coming Race* (1871).

This story tells of highly developed subterranean beings that possess a mysterious power of the Vril-Ya Force. The beings are described as extremely tall Caucasians with superhuman strength. This strength enables them to utilize a strap on device of wings, which enables them to fly. Their life span ranges into centuries. The Vril power is a mental one that is focused into a crystal staff that each person possesses. They view human surface dwellers as one would view cattle or pets. The story claims that they will one day emerge from their underground caverns to reclaim the surface and dominate us. Although presented to the public as fiction, occult initiates believed this to be truth veiled in a fictional story.

One of the secret societies that merged with the Thule society to form the Nazi party was the Vril society. They based their entire society upon this occult "fiction" book. Their desire was to discover and develop this power of the Vril and contact the inner beings to form an alliance. As way out as this might sound, actions were taken seriously to achieve this goal. In modern times it would be the same as the Masons merging with the official Stark Trek fan club to form a powerful political movement.

Not so New Age concept:

H.P. Blavatsky, spiritualist medium and founder of Theosophy stated that the North Pole is the region of Atma, a pure electro-magnetic soul of the earth and spirituality called The Gate, whereas the South Pole is called "The Pit." cosmically and terrestrially. The North pole was considered positive and the South Pole was negative. She wrote about the Aryan "master race" and their subterranean origin from within the earth. The earth then was like a living force with energy and light flowing inward into the North Pole and excreting out of the South Pole. Mankind emerging from the "womb" to live on the surface is compared to a "birthing".

At the turn of the 19th century many intellectuals and German Aristocrats took Blavatsky's Theosophy based upon her main work *Secret Doctrines* to heart. The Thule society was formed based upon Theosophy and the Secret Doctrine. As mentioned this was the intellectual and financial group that later became a part of the Nazi party!

Part Four

A 19ᵗʰ Century Christian Perspective:

H.M. Howell, a Christian Educator, wrote in his book, "The Kosmic Problem Solved," (1895)He claimed that a parallel existed between the ocean currents and the four rivers mentioned in Genesis 2:10-14 as flowing out of Eden. Eden then would be on the concave side of the globe, with the waters welling out through the hole at the South Pole, completing its course back into the earth at the opening in the North Pole. I mention this visionary and inspired man of God because he got it right! We shall now look at what the Word of God tells us about our own world. It is truly Beyond Science Fiction!

Part Five

What Jesus Had to Say About a Hollow Earth:

While speaking to his disciples about stewardship, faith and forgiveness Jesus told an actual, literal story of Lazarus and the rich man. He does not name the rich man but he names the beggar, Lazarus. Whenever Jesus spoke a parable, he never used personal names, therefore this was an actual event being described by Jesus.

> **"There was a certain rich man, which was clothed in fine linen, and fared sumptuously every day: And there was a certain beggar named Lazarus, which was laid at his gate, full of sores, And desiring to be fed with the crumbs which fell from the rich man's table: moreover the dogs came and licked his sores. And it came to pass that he died, and was carried by the angels into Abraham's bosom: the rich man also died, and was buried; And in hell he lift up his eyes, being in torments, and saw Abraham afar off, and Lazarus in his bosom. And he cried and said, Father Abraham, have mercy on me, and send Lazarus, that he may dip the tip of his finger in water, and cool my tongue; for I am tormented in this flame. But Abraham said, Son, remember that you in your lifetime receded your good things, and likewise Lazarus evil things: but now he is comforted, and you are tormented... And beside all this, between us and you there is a great gulf fixed: so that they which**

**would pass from here to you cannot; neither can
they pass to us that would come from there..."**
                                                          Luke 16"19-26

For now, let's look at the geographical details disregarding the
spiritual implications. We have two areas separated by a gulf or
chasm, which is fixed. When we hear of "Abraham's bosom" we
usually think of the upper front body area between the arms.
Another meaning familiar to the ancient culture as described
by Thayer's Concordance is the bosom of a garment. That is
the hollow formed by the upper forepart of a Tunic. This is a
rather loose garment bound by a girdle or sash used for keeping
and carrying things (the fold or pocket). This literal event told
by Jesus describes a two-part pocket, one negative and one
positive separated between each other by a gulf. This was the
Old Testament concept of Hell or Sheol as being a place where all
departed souls went to one or the other place.

Part Six

More Scriptures Support a Hollow Earth

The Bible contains additional scripture to support this idea of a
two chambered hollow earth.

**"The sorrows of death compass me and the pains
of hell got a hold upon me, I found trouble and sor-
row."**
                                                          Psalms 116:3,

The word "*pains*", in Hebrew is **metsar** meaning "something
tight". It comes from the Hebrew root, **qebah** meaning the
"paunch (as a cavity) the first stomach of a cud chewing animal".
(They have more than one stomach!) In the etymology of the
word for "pain" we get the understanding of the two-chambered
hollow earth. In addition, words such as the sea, abyss, pit and
the deep interchangeably mean the same place within the earth.
When the flood came the fountains of the "deep" burst forth to
the surface. Where did they burst? Subterranean! That would
also mean that H.M. Howell was right about the parallel of the
ocean currents and the four rivers from Eden.

After the cross, before the resurrection, Jesus went to both chambers of a hollow earth:

The New Testament understanding is that before the death and resurrection of Jesus, all who died in faith could not leave this fallen dimension until a way back had been accomplished.

After the death and resurrection of Jesus, He descended to declare a further judgment upon the angels that sinned in Taratus and set the captives free in paradise.

> **"Now this, "He ascended" what does it mean but that He also first descended into the lower parts of the earth?"**
>
> **Eph 4:9**

This population depletion of paradise is described in Matthew 27:52,53,

> **"...and the graves were opened and many bodies of the saints which slept arose. And came out of the graves after His resurrection and went into the holy city and appeared unto many."**

After this time the upper half of Sheol was left empty. Now, upon death of those born of the Spirit they go directly to be with the Lord in the heavenly dimension.(2Co 5:8)

We have already discussed the other half of the decent of Jesus. In the Lower chamber Jesus declared a further judgment to the fallen angels and their offspring. For our sake, here it is important to see that Jesus went to both chambers right after His death before His resurrection. Understanding this by the Bibles own statements draws some other rather interesting conclusions!

Part Seven

Where is the Garden of Eden?

If Abraham's bosom is paradise then just what is paradise? Jesus told the thief next to Him on the cross that, ***"today you shall be with me in Paradise."*** After the cross he did not ascend to heaven, He went into the bowels of the earth, to Abraham's bosom where Lazarus went which was paradise. It is very important to understand this connection. Because many further implications are made by this. This is a domain within the earth itself. It was called Abraham's bosom and Paradise. There is no other Paradise mentioned anywhere else. This is the only Paradise mentioned. Let's look at why is this important.

> **"...to him that overcomes will I give to eat of the TREE OF LIFE which is in the midst of the PARADISE of God."**
>
> **Rev 2:7**

We know that the tree of life is in the Garden of Eden! There is only one Tree of Life. That would mean that Eden and Paradise are one in the same and so is Abraham's bosom. Where are they? Inside a HOLLOW EARTH!

The Garden of Eden then is not on the surface in some invisible never- never land or forgotten ethereal place, but subterranean. The many cultural myths of man ascending from an inner earth are but a trace memory of what the Bible concurs!

Part Eight

Holes At The Poles?

Does the Bible mention anything like this?

> **"The waters are hid as with a stone, and the face of the deep is frozen"**
>
> **Job 38:30.**

This is very interesting indeed. The waters "hid" are the internal waters of the deep or abyss. Like a stone on top the excess flood waters frozen now covers the face or opening of the abyss. This ice covering is what we call the Arctic and Antarctic circles. Frozen like a rock to cover the openings of the inner earth and the waters "hid" within. This was only a resulted effect after the flood.

> **"He gathered the waters of the sea together as an heap: he laid up the depth in storehouses."**
>
> **Job26:10**

> **"He hath compassed the waters with bounds until the day and night come to an end."**
>
> **Ps 33:7**

He hath compassed literally means; He inscribed a circle over the face of the waters. Before the flood there was a complete easy access in and out.

> **"For this they are willingly ignorant of, that by the Word of God the heavens were of old, and the earth standing out of the water and in the water: Whereby the world that then was, being overflowed with water perished: But the heavens and the earth, which are now, by the same word are kept in store, reserved unto fire against the day of judgment and perdition of ungodly men."**
>
> **2Peter 3:5-7**

The Greek word for "*earth*" means in its general term, "arable land". The Greek word, **sunistao**, for "*standing*" is better rendered, "united together". In this sense submerge land or flooded land is not what is mentioned here but rather surface land out of the waters, and surface land in the waters (subterranean). With this understanding we can see that the arable land was united together out of the water and in the water. But the flood changed this. Verse 6 states that the world (ordered arraignment) before was destroyed in the flood.

Now the face or openings at the poles are covered over by the frozen flood waters and the inner and outer realms separated from each other. One chamber, is empty of population it's opening is sealed off until the end of time. The other chamber thrives with a population. The only inhabitants there are rebels. Be they Fallen angels in Tartarus (a lower level in Hades) or departed souls of the damned (upper level of Hades) or east of Eden in the land of Nod - humans!

Could this be a possible scriptural reference to Neu-Schwabenland and The Nazi Colonization of the Antarctic after the War?

This lower chamber will be breached at sometime in our history. A possible rendering of Job26:8 states,

> **" He binds up the waters as a thicket (a fortress) before broken into a hidden opening underneath.**
>
> **Job 26:8"**

We have two poles, one is covered over until the end of time, and the other is "broken into. This could correspond with another scripture of someone who would "dig into hell" Both combined could be telling us of the Nazi expedition and possible colonization of the Antarctic

Part Nine

Subterranean Human Life!

This story gets just keeps getting stranger as we go along, yet the scriptures confirm such strangeness! Now let's look at a commandment God told Israel to abide by.

> **"Thou shalt not make unto thee any graven image, or any likeness of anything that is in heaven above, or that is in the earth beneath, or that IS IN THE WATER UNDER THE EARTH."**
> **Exodus 20:4**

> **" Woe to the inhabitants of the earth and of the sea!...**
> **Rev 12:12**

As we understand that Eden is an inner earth domain there is a further implication of another group of people that are actually down there. We need to reexamine another well known text of scripture to find out from this new realization just where did Cain go?

Sentenced IN The Earth!

Let's take a look at the dialog between God and Cain right after he killed Abel.

> **"And now art thou cursed FROM the earth, which hath opened up her mouth to receive thy brothers blood from thy hand. When thou tillest the ground, it shall not henceforth yield unto thee her strength; a fugitive and a vagabond shalt thou be IN THE EARTH. And Cain said unto the Lord, my punishment is greater than I can bear. Behold, thou hast driven me this day FROM THE FACE (surface) OF THE EARTH; and I shall be a fugitive and a vagabond IN THE EARTH; and it shall come to pass, that every one that finds me shall slay me.**

And the Lord said unto him, Therefore whosoever slayeth Cain, vengeance shall be taken on him seven fold, and the Lord set a mark upon Cain, lest any finding him should kill him. And Cain went out from the presence of the Lord, and dwelt in the land of Nod, EAST OF EDEN."

Gen 4:11-16.

It is interesting to note that in the many translations of the Bible, only the older English versions the King James and the American Standard, use the translation "in the earth". All of the more recent translations simply say "on the earth". Quite a big liberal speculation placed upon God's Word because of the assumption that the earth is solid and therefore could not contain life inside. The only other translation I am aware of that agrees with the older versions is the Torah. This is the Old Testament translated into the English by the Jews themselves!

Regardless of this compromise of interpretation, from prior scriptures, the Bible clearly establishes that Eden or Paradise and Hell are two separate chambers inside the earth. With that firmly established, (at least according to the Bible itself) the only word that could be used in context is "IN" !

Cain was removed from the surface of the earth into a subterranean realm. He was given a "mark" that he would not be killed by others. This Hebrew word **owth** means "an identifying mark in the sense of an agreement". When translated into the Greek, the word used is **semion,** in the sense of a "supernatural sign" of some type.

Could Cain's Descendants Be a Part of the Giants of Gen 6?

This mark may be their size, for fear of being killed they might have been given height. The "Giants" of Gen 6, it is stated, were there when this hybridization of the Earth took place and also after that. In the sentence structure of this context, the "Giants" may not be the name of the offspring; they are just there with the fallen angels as a part of what is going on before the flood. In a conversation I had with Bible Scholar Mike Heiser, he agreed that the contextual use of Giants in Genesis 6 indicated a separate group.

When Cain killed Abel it was in the "process of time" this actually means in the last days. This would be referring to a time just prior to the great flood. This could mean Cain, before he became a murderer, could have produced a mixed or diluted strain of his descendants, who remained on the surface and still had some redemptive value. This would be indicated by God's statement to Cain when He said.

" Then the LORD said to Cain, "Why are you angry? Why is your face downcast? If you do what is right, will you not be accepted? But if you do not do what is right, sin is crouching at your door; it desires to have you, but you must master it."

Gen 4:6-7(NIV)

Cain could have been accepted but he was warned that sin was like a crouched animal waiting to pounce on him and consume him. He may have had a natural weakness that destined him to this. The Hebrew is strong here for the word *"desire"* and can mean "a total consumption".

The rest of the judgment against Cain includes; "the soil not yielding her strength". This may not mean an agricultural problem, but rather a genetic defect of some type. Soil, seed land and fruit have always, in the Scriptures been used to refer to the literal geographical elements, spiritual conditions or physical bloodline. Something in Cain changed him from everyone else and separation was necessary.

Cain's bloodline may be the seed of the serpent mentioned in Gen 3. Cain was a bad guy. The Bible says so. I John 3:12 **"Not as Cain, who was of that wicked one,"** In context here, this statement about Cain's relation can mean more than a spiritual fact that he was of the wicked one because he committed murder. It might also imply that he was actually from the wicked one in a physical sense as well. It was in his blood.

The "Giant" lineage is traceable after the flood by the same Hebrew word used for *"Giant"* as the "sons of Anak". Certain tribes had this intermixing. These were the only ones of the Old Testament which God said to destroy completely. Only the Philistine lineage remained to contain this "seed." This was the same lineage Goliath came from, he was a big white guy with a bad attitude! The word "Giant" has another meaning as "a tyrant or bully" and can mean much more than physical stature. The Physical stature though, is clearly defined in the OT. Num 13:33, Deu2:11, 20, 3:11,13 Jsh 12:4, 13:12,15:8,17:15 and18:16.

Nazi Relatives? Cain's Descendants! The Real Kings of the East!

If Nod is east of Eden and Eden is inside the earth...that means that Nod is inside the earth too! All of these scriptures present a serious implication of who the Kings of the East (mentioned in Rev 19:12) really are and their real identity and location.

The ideas of H.M. Howell's ocean currents actually being the "rivers" flowing out of Eden, gives us a whole new way to look at this text in Revelations.

> **"And the sixth angel poured out his vial upon the great river Euphrates; and the water thereof was dried up, that the way of the kings of the east might be prepared." Rev 16:12 (KJV)**

The Name *"Euphrates"* from the Greek to the Hebrew describes the river flowing out of Eden. **Perath** the Hebrew name means "to break forth or to be plentiful". *"Water"* here can have a specific meaning as the waters reserved or stored up from the flood waters. This would be the ice caps covering the polar holes. *"Dried up"* has a slant to the meaning as to "evaporate or melt". Adding this together, it could be that one of the ocean currents is modified or changed, creating a warming that melts the reserved flood waters of the Antarctic, allowing the Kings of the East to be released in mass from an inner earth. Did this in fact already happen?

In Rev 9, it is described that the **"pit or abyss is opened."** Locust then ascend out of the pit. These are the same locusts mentioned by Joel in the second chapter as an invading army. There is a consistent symbolic use of locust as meaning nations outside of God's kingdom in a spiritual sense but also including a physical one too. While there is much controversy about the text of these scriptures, few believe in a total literal interpretation. Many believe in a symbolic political idea. The fact remains that this is not conclusive in any way. The slant I present by the original language and word use is another viable option and might just further explain an inner earth alliance and coming invasion.

As strange as this all sounds the Bible stands true upon itself. The worldwide legends of "white" tribes and ascended "masters" may not be myth at all but the continual encounters with a race from within. The search by Hitler and the Nazis for blood relations from an inner earth may have a thread of truth. If Hitler came to his own to proclaim Satan's seed, in the same but opposite pattern, it could mean that the modern day Philistines may be of the Germanic lineage.

Now not to condemn anyone by their race or national bloodline, I must say that I am a Caucasian of Germanic descent and I love the Lord! God has made a provision for salvation that is no longer based on anything but faith. In Isaiah 14 there is an end time prophecy that indicates a genetic tampering involving the Philistines and a tribe used to punish them continually, this would be the tribe of Dan. This genetic tampering started with Nazi Germany and has continued in America. In a separate booklet, *Two Seeds* I address this whole issue extensively. In the back of this book you can purchase one.

The implication from Cain's sentence is that there are human beings living in a subterranean realm! They are still a part of the rebel alliance. Cain's descendants are mentioned only to six generations. If an inner earth has the same environment that the surface once had before the flood, human life spans would average 900 years. This thought runs parallel to many occult beliefs of a time difference or longevity of life as stated in the Bulwer-Lytton's *Coming Race*. This being the case, we would be heading into the last generational period of Cain's descendants!

Chuck Missler, *in his book, "Alien Encounters"* points out a very interesting hidden message encrypted within the scriptures. All names in the Bible have a second meaning. The Names within the linage of Seth from Adam to Noah spells out the entire plan of redemption! From these ten names a message reads out

> **"Man appointed mortal sorrow, The blessed God shall come down teaching. His death shall bring the despairing rest or comfort!"**

What are the mathematical chances that this was coincidental? In the same way we can line up the names of the six-generation lineage of Cain. It reads out:

> **" Strike out to possess, disciplined fugitive, smitten of God, Who is of God, Powerful."**

This is the description of Cain striking out at his brother to take what he felt was his. He was disciplined by being sentenced to be a fugitive in the earth, also "smitten or stricken with a defect but yet given power. This power was ordained from God Himself to fulfill His purpose.

It is recorded that Cain's decedents were the first to raise animals for food, create the arts and music, the first to build cities and the first to work in metals making implements of war. Could the mythical power of the Vril-ya be a part of this power? Whatever their power is, it is part of God's overall plan to fulfill His will.

Were Cain's descendants living safely in a hollow earth while the flood destroyed the surface? Remember, Noah's and his family's bloodline was untainted with this seed of the serpent. Knowing this, the seed could not have been carried over after the flood. All the rest of life was destroyed on the SURFACE! This might be the only logical explanation as to how the "Giants" reappear after the flood. In time, using the cavernous systems from around the world, they could resurface and intermingle with humans through several tribes that were destroyed.

Could there be an element of truth to the weird Aryan Nazi myths? Is there a diluted strain of surface dwellers and a subterranean pure strain possessing a supernatural power living in a hollow earth? Not an Aryan Master race but the seed of the serpent? Cultural Legends and occult myths, as well as the Bible may all speak of this reality. Again it seems, only the Bible tells us a different story. This is not a place of desire but a place of rebels in a real literal Hell!

Part Ten

Conclusion of the Matter:

I hope I have shown that the Bible teaches that there is a hollow earth. Just what the particular physics are is not mentioned beyond holes at the poles. A circular cave system throughout the earth to "protect" or seal off the inner chamber is alluded to in Job 41:15.

The understanding of subterranean life both human and spirit beings existing in a hollow earth makes sense as you add up the myths and legends in contrast to what the Bible actually has to say. You cannot discount the many accounts from abductees or the suspicious actions of governments, which hint of conspiracy. What sounds so foreign to the normal mind is the result of conditioning by scientist-priests.

Also, a special warning to the many believers in a Hollow Earth and others who have a wide variety of beliefs that include a hopeful expectation of "friendly" inner beings ready to "enlighten" us surface dwellers. Nowhere in the Scriptures will you find any suggestion or hint that anything in the Earth at this present time since the resurrection of Christ is good! There are only rebels of the one true God who live there or escaped there. They have no good intention toward mankind; they have their own agenda. Part of this agenda is a prophesied invasion of the surface. Next we need to take a look at the end of the Genetic Rainbow: The Nordic.

Chapter Seventeen
The Nordics:
The End of the Genetic Rainbow

"And no marvel; for Satan himself is transformed into an Angel of light. Therefore it is no great thing if his ministers also be transformed as the ministers of righteousness; whose end shall be according to their works."

Apostle Paul, 2 Co 11: 14-15

" The New Man is living among us!...He is intrepid and cruel! I was afraid in his presence!"

...Adolf Hitler

The Master Race becomes Friendly Aliens

In this section I hope to give evidence that a familiar Nazi agenda is still being propagated. The only thing that has changed through time is the outer dressing. By their own words and actions, they stake their own claim. This claim however, is all a matter of perception, depending on which camp you sit in.

Part One

General Description:

The Name Nordics was derived by the UFO community for there well-defined features from the Germanic, Celtic and Anglo-Saxon variations of the Caucasian race. They are all tall, Blond or Red Hair with Blue eyes. They average in height from 6' to 6 1/2' tall with some reported to be as tall as 8'. They are all trim, muscular and very handsome men or beautiful women just as depicted in the picture above. Consistent to the reports throughout the world in regards to Nordics is the near perfect physical appearance. No one has ever reported plain or physically deficient members in their company. Just what one may expect if you had a choice in the matter through controlled genetics.

Part Two

What They Say About Themselves:

The Nordics seem to have a history that includes a change of address. In the early 50's, contactees claimed these Nordics came from Saturn, Venus and Jupiter. As our space program developed satellites that probed our solar system and explained the hostile conditions on these planets they suddenly changed their location to a star system in the Pleiades. This change is explained away by some within the UFO community as simply being other Nordics.

The Nordics explain that they have had a long time war and hostilities with the Grays. They say they have a non-interference policy with Earth and will only intervene when other parts of the universe are affected by our actions. Their role is as "guardians" of the cosmos and neutral in regards to mankind. When in contact with humans they encourage the individuals to learn and study truths from all sources and help to unite mankind. They proclaim the same Theosophical views of God as an energy force like the Grays, but also include the recycling of humans, telling some that they are related, being incarnate souls from their world.

In the 50's they warned about the use of Nuclear weapons. Now they warn of the same catastrophes that the Grays warn of and another World War. Unlike the Grays they show emotion and appear to have a concern for mankind.

Part Three

What is Said About Them From the UFO Community:

It is generally accepted within the UFO community that these are the good guys. Much of this is derived from the fact that abductions are not as traumatic and do not include the medical experiments. They have warmth in their eyes and appear concerned for the individual and mankind. They are polite and considerate to the individuals taken and consider their feelings, answering questions and giving reassurance that they will be all right.

Many times they have been seen in the company of the Grays. However, it is explained that these are other Nordics created by, or controlled by the Grays as prisoners. Nordics are seen in Great Britain and the rest of Europe more often than in the United States. Some researchers have even compared their involvement with mankind to that of the Angels in the Bible. The Grays are more predominate in the U.S. but it wasn't always so.

Part Four

Early Encounters: Contactees and "Space Brothers"

In the study of the Nordics one must also study the Contactees who first expounded on these "Aliens". In their study we begin to see a real connection.

In the early 50's, normal tall 6'-6'5" Nordics were seen by what was then called "Contactees" in the U.S. The differences from abductions are that Contactees experienced daylight visits as well as in the night. Their encounters are, in most cases, fully remembered without the experience of "lost time" and memory masking.

The image most people get of a contactee is that of some eccentric individual with a weird message. As we begin to study the background of some of the more famous early contactees, you will see this is a myth.

George Adamski

You cannot mention Contactees without mentioning George Adamski. He achieved national fame when he began to have visits from the "Space Brothers" who wanted him to be their spokesman. They told him they were from Venus. They stressed the importance of ceasing nuclear testing and living in peace and harmony. Their message of peace was in a Theosophical view.

Once he overheard the space brothers speaking to each other in fluent German. Being from Poland, he spoke some German, and easily recognized it as such. When he questioned the brothers they answered that they spoke all the languages of earth, although they didn't give an example.

He also took sharp clear pictures of their spacecraft. Skeptics claimed the photos looked like a manufactured Chicken Brooder. Further investigation discovered that the brooder was manufactured after Adamski's photos. The owner was inspired by the photos and fashioned the brooder to look like Adamski's pictures! What is never mentioned is the fact that Adamski's saucers are identical to the alleged captured Nazi blueprints. His images are also consistent with other popular sightings of the time.

Followers of his, at the time were surprised that Adamski had mobility and opportunity afforded to him, comparable to what a Government official would enjoy. It was discovered that Adamski had pre-war connections with American Fascist leader of the "Silver Shirts" William Dudley Pelley. The American Nazi group began their operations in 1932. Pelley was interned during the War. After the war Pelley started an occult group "Soulcraft" and published a racist magazine called *Valor*. He wrote a book in 1950, *Starguests*. Adamski and Pelley were involved together in the I AM cult group whose roots go back to the early days of Theosophy and include beliefs in the hollow earth, alien contact and of course Theosophy.

To the general public, he was very eccentric, to say the least, and did much to discredit the seriousness of UFO research. In spite of his way out manner, some real truths and experiences might be in his midst. Adamski may be a part of a consistent patter to confuse and discredit real truths. By having accurate information disseminated through created unreliable sources such as Adamski, truths are made unbelievable. Then, by giving false information to established legitimate sources a lie is made acceptable. Adamski could have been one good example of this kind of ploy. With a Nazi/Occult connection to his past, he helped lay a foundation for the Nordic "space brother" and their message of warning and hope. In Adamski's book "Flying Saucers have Landed." Adamski states that in one encounter a small brown Asian looking man was with his Nordic brothers. He has an illustration in his book that the barefoot robed man left in the sand from the bottom of his tattooed foot. There in detail was the typical scarred impressions that the Bon Po sect of Tibetian monks wore as part of their religious traditions!

Jack Parsons

Another early contactee with Nordics includes Scientist, Jack Parsons who met the so-called Venusian saucer in the desert in 1946. He is the creator of solid rocket propellant fuel and went on to become one of the founders of the Jet Propulsion Laboratory in Houston and the Aerojet Corporation. To remind you, the

President of this Corporation was none other than former Nazi SS General Walter Dornburger.

Jack was a member and leader of the Agape lodge. This was the American chapter of Aleister Crowley's Occult group, Ordo Templi Orientis, based in England. Aleister Crowley was a world-renowned occultist and Satan worshiper. Prior to the war, Crowley met Adolph Hitler and continued correspondence with him. It has been said that Crowley was everything from a Nazi spy to a double agent working for the allies. There is unclear evidence for both rumors but every indication is that he was involved in spying.

One of Jack Parsons early United States contacts with the Agape Lodge was a man code-named as "Frater H." He had a close association with Jack Parsons and led him to believe that he had come into contact with the same higher powers that Crowley himself came into contact with, in Cairo in 1904. This association of Parsons to Frater H later proved to assist in his downfall. They shared a joint banking account of which Frater H. took the money and wound up marrying Parson's girlfriend. By 1952 Parsons now referred to himself as Belarion Armiluss Al Dajjal Antichrist.

In his home laboratory he dropped a vial of fulminate of mercury and died in the resulting explosion. Jack Parsons was a man with a professional life filled with great achievements. He was hardly the stereotypical contactee as depicted by supermarket tabloids. Yet his personal and spiritual life was filled with the occult, deception and yet another possible Nazi connection. He also paved the way for the Nordic type Alien.

L. Ron Hubbard a.k.a. Frater H.!

Frater H., the man most responsible for leading Parsons into this madness was himself a claimed contactee of the Nordics. His real name is none other than the well-known L.Ron Hubbard, Science-fiction writer, Author of *Dianetics* and Founder of the Church of Scientology. His sphere of influence today in America is renowned. Many movie stars, intellectuals and social elite are ardent followers of his "Church". Within the fast growing Church of Scientology is the doctrine of Aliens as Ascended masters. Their philosophy is just another variation of Theosophy.

Recently his "Church" is suffering persecution in Germany. I believe because of all people, the German people have heard this line before and recognize it for what it really is!

Daniel Fry

Another contactee, Daniel Fry saw his first encounter with early "Nordics" in 1950. He was an employee of Aerojet. This small handful of people did much to influence the perception and image of the Nordic type occupant as the friendly alien.

Other Early Contacts:

People were experiencing all during the 50's and early 60's sightings without "lost time" or regressive memory techniques. In 1957, Everett Clark of Dante, Tennessee reported German speaking saucer people who landed in a field outside his house. Apparently, they were trying to quiet or catch his dog. This event was later considered a hoax. He was charged in a crime of fraud, which indirectly involved trying to cash in on the incident. However, the day before, Reinhold Schmidt, outside Kearney Nebraska, claimed he was taken aboard a Flying saucer. He could still speak some German, taught by his parents. The crew spoke German and behaved like German soldiers. Mr. Clark would have no way of knowing about this other event. It probably really happened but by deceitfully using the situation for personal gain, he discredits the whole matter. The saucer was described by both to resemble the Haunibu type Nazi design saucer. See photo's below.

Left: Adamski's Photo of a Venusian Saucer **Center:** Alleged Nazi Print **Right:** Typical 50's- 70's UFO's

First Documented Modern Abduction.

In 1961, the first "modern" abduction case with lost time, retrieved by hypnosis, was recorded from events experienced by Betty and Barney Hill. In one of the recorded sessions, Barney states in an almost panicked voice that he sees a "Captain" with the little Grays. Asked how he knew he was a Captain, Barney states, because of his hat and uniform. He then stutters and exclaims with fear as if suddenly recognizing the uniform, "He's a Nazi!" Later, this is explained by many, avoiding the implications, that while in a hypnotic, suggestive state the individuals own imagination can interpret some parts and fill in the blanks to complete the story. I personally believe this to be true. It is for that and several other factors; I see hypnosis as an unreliable information source. In this context, however it is too consistent with other stories to entirely dismiss as imagination and is worth mentioning.

Part Five

Recent Nordic Contacts

The more recent contacts with "Nordics" have stated that they are now from the Pleiades. Their recent chosen contactee and spokesman is a Swiss farmer by the name of Billy Meir. The information given through Meir along with his many photographs and movies have stirred up much controversy. Many skeptics and believing investigators have scrutinized all of this. It is claimed that while some investigators tried to reproduce the Meir photos, Meir got them mixed up with his own. Some photos have been debunked and his credibility on the most part has not withstood the controversy with most serious investigators.

From Gary Kinder's book about Billy Meir, *Light Years,* Atlantic Monthly Press 1987, he points out that whatever you might think about Billy Meir, one puzzle remains. A Swiss farmer with a fifth or sixth grade education described in his writings, technology and an understanding of the cosmos beyond his means. These concepts were dictated from a "Nordic" named "Semjase". He included descriptions about a Tychyon propulsion system, healing methods, celestial mechanics and advanced medical equipment. At the time of his writings, in the early 70's, much of this information was a theoretical concept known only by a handful of experts working in specific research and development programs.

In a pattern that is the same but opposite of the Bible's spreading of the Gospel, the Apostles Peter and John while expounding on the teachings from the Scriptures with profound insight were a marvel as they were perceived as not being learned or very sophisticated. Billy Meir may indeed be a "chosen" one to proclaim the wonders of this New Age deception. The Pleiadians proclaim that another World War is inevitable. The only way to prevent it is a spiritual change from within. Of course, the gospel they proclaim is a Theosophical one. Their idea of a change is that each individual becomes their own god from within. The spiritual emphasis of their message has many drawing a comparison to angels. This concept however is in direct opposition to what the Bible declares, And we are further warned that contrary messages of this type are from a messenger of deception, an Angel of light. 2 Co 11:14,15, Gal 1:8

The Intergalactic Angelic War set up

As I have already stated, the popular consensus with most UFO investigators is that these are the "good guys". They have compared their intervention with mankind to that of angels, noting that historical representation depicts them usually as fair-haired beautiful Caucasians. Also noted is their enemy a serpentine, reptilian creature.(Grays) Now we are beginning to see the set up for good alien/bad alien.

John Carpenter well-known investigator quotes Revelations 11 in his video tape, *Centuries of Contact,* MSW/LCSW 1997. He describes this war in heaven as being with Michael the archangel (depicted as a blond hair, blue eyed, handsome man), and the dragon (a reptile). The similarities are unquestionable. From a variety of occult sources, channeling and hypnosis (by the means of contacting other entities through a person) this state of war is described by the "Pleaidians" but not mentioned by the "Grays". With this comparison, we have the "heavenly war" of the Bible, transformed into a sci-fi interstellar struggle. Good Angel/Alien against Bad Demon/Alien with man in the middle forced to choose sides and highly motivated to unite as one on earth.

Part Six

A History of Intervention
Universal Accounts of "White" Spirits, Gods, and Masters from Heaven

It is more than just a coincidence that throughout history many cultures have had encounters with a White Spirit or White masters from the skies. Their visits have coincided with a sudden boost of advancement in their societies. The following is a list of some of the historical and or mythological events of inter-reaction with man and white gods from the heavens.

1. **Ancient Sumeria** - The "Anunnaki" meaning, "Those who from heaven to earth came." Described as white gods from the skies. They were attributed to giving the written language, sciences and building technology. Word etymology is shared with the Biblical Annakim. (Numbers 13:33) These were the sons of Anak, the same giants and genetic link to the "fallen ones" of Genesis 6. Big, bad, white guys with a bad attitude! The

Anunnaki of Sumerian mythology are said to have come from heaven, but now live underground. The similarity is more than a coincidence.

2. **Mesopotamia** - "Ahura Mazda", meaning "spirits of knowledge" were described as "white spirits" that flew in a shiny disk. Ahura Mazda appeared to Zoroaster, who was told he was the one true God. (Always depicted wearing the German Knights cross) Part of their religious practices included human sacrifice.

3. **India** –– "Asura", has the meaning as the "white gods of the wind". They gave understanding of ancient knowledge. "Vishinu" the third deity of the top godhead is to come back on a white horse. Ancient Vedas describe a pre-flood world, filled with aircraft called "Vimnas" engaged in aerial combat, missile launches, and descriptions of nuclear war with fallout and radioactivity.

4. **South America** - "Viracochas" are interpreted as the "White Masters from the skies". They were described as bearded white gods who came from the sky and promised to return. They gave astronomy, building skills, the calendar and culture to the Incas. They were said to have built the ancient ruins of Tiahuanacu in one day with a magic trumpet. They are depicted as riding in a vehicle in a reclined position holding controls of some type. Part of their acquired culture also included ritual human sacrifice.

5. **Mexico** - Quetzalcoatl, meaning "white feathered serpent god whom came from the skies". He is said to have come from a seven star system. Coincidentally the Pleiades are a seven star system. He gave them a calendar as accurate as our atomic clock, knowledge of celestial mechanics and astronomy beyond their means. He left by sea back to his earthly home Tula. "Tula" according to Aztec legends was a place of the sun, which was now frozen over, and the sun disappeared. "Tula" is a variation of Thule, the mythical Aryan capital of the inner earth whose opening is claimed to be in the Antarctic! He promised to return. The Aztecs mistook Cortez as fulfilling the return, which proved to be their downfall. Religious human sacrifice was also a common practice in their culture.

6. **America** - The Hopi Indians encountered the "Bahana". "Bahana" means, "white brother from the skies". The "Bahana" gave them spiritual understandings of a theosophical nature.

There seems to be quite a lot of involvement for a policy of non-intervention! Much of this intervention would appear to have little to do with the rest of the cosmos. What about the prime directive Captain?

Part Seven

A Celestial Trademark Sign?

An interesting connection to these cultures that claim contact with various white gods, brothers and masters, is the common use of the Swastika. Only the Assyrian and Egyptian cultures do not use this symbol. However they do use the German Knights Cross-. These icons are primarily used as a "good luck" and fortune symbol. Is this just mere coincidence? The consistency is just too amazing to discount as chance! Could this symbol be the "white gods" own icon. Are the encountered peoples reproducing them to signify their own good fortune and "luck" for the benefits they have received from their encounters? Certainly not doctrine or anything conclusive, but the supposition does have merit.

Stories Behind the Symbol

From their own tales, pieces may come together.

The Pleiades, is a seven star cluster which is part of the constellation of Taurus, the Bull. The bull has always been symbolic of Baal, Baalim or Baalzebub. These deities were forbidden in both Old and New Testaments as objects of worship and identified as Satanic in nature and accompanied by human sacrifice.

The Dippers, Other seven star systems are the big and little dippers. In occult circles they are called the "plough". In this sense the instrument of planting.

Theosophy as taught by Madame Blavatsky says that at the center of the North Pole is the location of pure "Atma". "Atma" she claim,s is an energy conscious soul, which she also calls "the gate". This in part is where New Agers of today get the idea of "Gia" or "Mother Earth" as a living creature. This gate or axis has other cultural legends as common as the flood story. In all the stories, the common theme is a center location for an opening to other worlds, dimensions and realms. To true Nazi initiates, the Axis powers meant more than others could even begin to understand.

The Swastika: the Symbol of Gravity?

The symbol of the swastika according to Blavatski depicts the flowing in or out of this "Atma power". The left-handed swastika is presumed to be the clockwise rotation and depicts the flowing in of the Atma power at the North Pole. It prophetically describes the Aryan exodus from the inner earth via the North Pole.

The right-handed swastika (the one the Nazis used) is presumed to be the counter-clockwise rotation which depicts the flowing out of the Atma power from the opening at the South Pole referred to as the "Pit". This reverse sign is also the "Wheel of the Black Sun".(The SS or storm troopers are also from the "Order of the Black Sun" hence the black uniforms). This also prophetically depicts the Aryan return to an inner earth via the South Pole or the "Pit". This "pit" may be the same pit mentioned in the Bible in Revelations 17!

This centripetal and centrifugal motion is said to preserve harmony and keeps the universe in steady unceasing motion, including the earth on its axis. The swastika displays this action. This "Atma" power that holds this action together in the physical realm is what we call "gravity"! In this sense the swastika displays the power of gravity! The four winds as gravity and the harnessing of a power only dreamed of.

Adolf Hitler understood this meaning behind the swastika. The final decision to make the arms of the swastika show the right-handed counterclockwise movement was not based as the myth goes, revealing a negative evil meaning opposed to the other cultural uses of the clockwise swastika. In most of the cultures, the arms go either way. Even the early use by the Nazi party, used both movements. Hitler made a final decision based on what he determined to be observed from looking at the skies from the Aryan capital of Thule from before the flood in his "golden age of the god-men".

Taking into account of a shifting of the earths axis with a change in the pole star from Draconis to the present day Polaris we get these images:

Left, Seasonal positions of Ursa Minor around Draconis 6,000years ago.

Right, Present seasonal positions of Ursa Minor around Polaris

Right-handed Swastika Knights Cross

By the visual actions of the clockwise and counter-clockwise revolving of the little and big dippers you can see both icons that were used by the Nazis.

Interwoven within the "Nordics" own statements are the connections to Theosophy and the Nazi agenda. This almost prophetic symbolism runs true to the pattern of the same but opposite satanic pattern after the workings of God. This was also the occult symbolism of the Nazi's never understood by the rest of the world. The consistency is uncanny and probably more than just mere coincidence.

The Swastika: The Symbol of the Sons of God?

It is possible that the symbol of the swastika was an icon of the "sons of god" and their offspring before the flood. It represents the symbol of the power and secrets given to man by these fallen angels, the power and control of gravity! Helena Blavatski states in *The Secret Doctrine* that the Aryan was given this sun wheel sign as their symbol of personal identity. The return and popularization of this ancient symbol in recent times could indicate the prophetic return of the sons of god in the form of the Nordic. It was once the symbol of Theosophy and on the cover of Secret Doctrine. Since WWII both were removed.

Will the Real Nordics Please Stand Up?

By their own words, they have finally decided that they are from the Pleiades. The Pleiades is a seven star system symbolic of Baalam or Lucifer. They consistently proclaim Theosophy as their world-view, both spiritual and natural. Sometimes they speak German. They, like the Grays, don't always tell the truth. (i.e. their origin). Their symbols, if any, have been winged serpents or stylized swastikas. Their actions of noninvolvement include the creation of myths and legends throughout history and in all cultures. Supernatural evidence is left behind by the planting of knowledge and technology beyond the culture's own capabilities. The theology proclaimed to the ancients is that of Theosophy in various forms but consistent. Not one aspect is in harmony with the cosmology and world-view as described in the Bible. This kind of inconsistency is warned of in the Bible.

> **"But though we, or an angel from heaven, preach any other gospel unto you than that which we have preached unto you, let him be accursed."**
>
> **Gal 1:8**

According to the Bible, and their own words, appearance and actions it is not so hard to surmise just who these Nordics are. There may be several origins to these guys.

1. The German speaking normal 6' to 61/2' Nordics (commonly seen in the 50's) are probably the Nazi soldiers in developed German disks that were based in the new fortress of defense in the Antarctic.

2. The tall 8' Nordics are probably the subterranean decedents of Cain. They were sentenced to wander in the land of Nod east of Eden. These "talls" are the real kings of the east (Rev 16:12) and part of the return of the giants of Gen 6! They are also part of the wandering error sent to deceive mankind who does not believe the truth. (2 Thessalonians 2:11- "*delusion*" means "wandering error"). The same ones with the power of the "Vril" who Hitler believed were genetic relations which he sought an alliance with.

3. The prophetic scriptures in Dan 2:43, Isaiah 14:9+29, 26:14, Gen 6:4, Job 26:5 and Rev 13:15 describe a genetic hybridization and resurrection of the fallen angels and their offspring who are now disembodied spirits. They will once again appear like flesh and blood humans to again deceive mankind. The fallen angels in reptilian form will also receive a "shell" to crossover and hide in as mentioned in Isaiah 14:29. Their purpose mentioned by Jude is to disrupt the affairs of men and lead us into a deception.

> **"For there are certain men crept in unawares, who were before of old ordained to this condemnation,.."**
>
> **Jude 1:4**

Although described as men, Jude further defines them with non human definitions.

Part Eight

A Future Nordic Intervention?

It is claimed that George Washington had a vision of America in three parts. The first two accurately described the conflict and outcome of the Revolutionary War and the Civil War. The third and last part is yet to happen. In 1818, this vision was first published in the *National Tribune*. There were no documented disputes to the article when it was published. However, there was a lack of verifiable evidence to the source. The best of researchers can only find a third party source which amounts to nothing more than a rumor. In spite of the lack of source evidence, this vision has been widely accepted by many. It was considered reliable enough to be quoted by Gary Allen and Larry Abraham in their well known book, *None Dare call it Conspiracy.* Other patriotic literature has published this vision extensively. Do not let the cries of skeptics or the lack of evidence keep you from understanding the importance of this vision. True or not, the story is widely published and commonly accepted by many. This makes the third part of this prophecy a seed planted into the American mind regardless of any disputes of authenticity. As Hitler wrote in Mine Kamph,

> **"Truth is not what is; truth is what people believe it to be"**

Here is the third part of this prophecy as given by an angelic visitor to George Washington before our independence.

> **.. " Again I heard the mysterious voice saying, "Son of the Republic, Look and learn." At this, the dark, shadowy Angel placed a trumpet to his mouth and blew three distinct blasts; and taking water from the ocean, he sprinkles it upon Europe, Asia and Africa. Then my eyes beheld a fearful scene; from each of these countries arose thick, black clouds that were joined into one. And throughout this mass gleamed a dark red light by which I saw hoards of armed men, who, moving with the cloud, marched by land and sailed by sea to America, which country was enveloped in the volume of cloud. And I dimly**

saw these vast armies devastate the whole country and burn villages, towns and cities that I beheld spring up. As my ears listened to the thundering of cannon, clashing of swords, and the shouts and cries of millions in mortal combat, I again heard the mysterious voice saying, "Son of the Republic, look and learn". When the voice ceased, the dark, shadowy Angel placed his trumpet once more to his mouth and blew a long fearful blast. Instantly, a light as of a thousand suns shone down from above me, and pierced and broke into fragments the dark cloud, which enveloped America. At the same moment the Angel upon whose head still shown the word "Union", and who still bore our national flag in one hand and the sword in the other, descended from heaven attended by LEGIONS OF WHITE SPIRITS. These immediately joined the inhabitants of America who I perceived were neigh overcome, but who immediately taking courage again, closed up their broken ranks and renewed the battle. Again amid the fearful noise of conflict, I heard the mysterious voice saying, "Son of the Republic, look and learn." As the voice ceased, the Angel for the last time dipped water from the ocean and sprinkled it upon America, the dark clouds rolled back, together with the armies it had brought, leaving the inhabitants of the land victorious."

I believe the speculative point is well made here for the future assistance and intervention by these same "white spirits". In light of September 11th, 2001 this is not so far fetched. In our pursuit of terrorists we may incur the wrath of the rest of the world some day. We have to do what we must to defend ourselves. But we may just be innocent pawns playing into the hands of those desiring a global state. If we are ever faced with this scenario the question will be, "Who are these white spirits?" Some will see them as deliverers and bearers of a "New Age" for mankind. Others will see them as the wandering error, the image of the beast, deceivers from before the flood...the return of the sons of god. It will someday come down to whether you believe in the Bible or not.

Salvation From the Skies?

The above scenario, may be the way the Nordic is reintroduced into the world. Hitler's dream and vision of the Aryan as the "new man" and the object of worship might be realized in this repackaged presentation. No longer a message of blood and race but one of philosophy and spirituality. The Aryan becomes the friendly deliverer from the stars. He assumes the ancient perceptive role as the angels of old, the legends of the white spirits and the hope for mankind.

It is no small wonder that New Agers seek contact with their "guardian angels" and "spirit guides", with a form of worship and adoration directed toward them. Even the Catholic Church with their Saint and Angel worship crosses over the line. The Scriptures are quite clear in that:

> **"For there is one God, and one mediator between God and men, the man Christ Jesus;"**
> **1 Tim 2:5**

Our entire history is filled with the sudden appearance of heavenly messengers and white spirits from the skies. The undeniable evidence of their reality is found in what knowledge and technology was left to impact the encountered cultures. Their messages and spiritual truths are in direct conflict with the Bible. The many warnings in the Bible of sudden appearances in the skies bearing this contrary message should raise the brow of any unbeliever or skeptic. These are the signs of the return of these "sons of god" What many are experiencing today is reflective of the time just before the flood. This evidence should be taken seriously when investigating anything regarding UFO's Aliens and their agenda. Someday man may be forced by events to ask not so much who the Nordics are, but in contrast to them, Who is Jesus Christ. Your personal answer will have eternal consequences.

> **"And for this cause God shall send them strong delusion,** (a wandering error) **that they should believe a lie: That they all might be damned who believed not the truth,** (manifested truth, Jesus) **but had pleasure in unrighteousness.** (hopeful expectation in a wrong way)
> **II Th 2:11-12**

If you will not believe the truth of the Bible, you will believe the coming big lie!

Chapter Eighteen
Invasion Earth! In Two Waves.

Part One

First Wave; A Clandestine Invasion

The invasion like the movie *Independence Day* is most feared and envisioned, however in order to have something like this happen against God's creation they would have to have permission by our invitation. Therefore the first phase of this invasion is a set up for massive deception. A propaganda and promotional campaign to make evil look good and good look evil. The description in Joel 2 is one that is a clandestine invasion. This is a view from eternity that looks like a swarm descending upon an unsuspecting earth. This includes all time and space!

This is a paraphrase based upon the various options from the original languages. It reveals much more than the generalized definitions.

> "A day of ignorance and concealment, a day of practiced magic and the lowering of high things, as the dawn spreads out upon the mountains, a huge abundant congregated mighty people come into existence that has never been before and shall never be after. A fire (or judgment) consumes before them and behind them a sword blade kindles, The land is as the garden of Eden before them and behind them a desolate wilderness. Yes and nothing shall escape them. The appearance of them is as the appearance of horses and as horseman so shall they run. Like the noise of chariots on top of mountains, so shall they leap like the noise of a flame of fire that devours the stubble, as a strong people set in battle array. Before their face the people shall be much pained, all faces shall gather a flushed anxiety. They shall climb the wall like men of war and they shall march every one on his

273

way, and they shall not break ranks, Neither shall one thrust another, they shall walk everyone in his path and when they FALL UPON THE SWORD, THEY SHALL NOT BE WOUNDED. They shall run to and fro in the city, they shall run upon the wall, they shall climb up upon the houses, they shall enter in at the windows like a thief (abductions?) The earth shall quake before them the heavens shall tremble, the sun and the moon shall be dark and the stars shall withdraw their shining."

Joel 2:1-11.

In a figurative sense from an eternal view they are like a swarm of locusts descending upon its prey, (i.e. a field of crops) destroying everything in its path entering in at all times in all places. I believe this invading army includes many types of plots and plans that transcend time. It is an attack described from the eternal viewpoint. This attack will go unnoticed and undetected from our linear perspective. What will be noticed is the secret societies that keep and maintain the globalist agenda. Like an unseen hand they will direct history and dictate its will. This will be so effective, most refuse to believe it is possible! Like chess pieces placed in the proper time and place with the careful implantation of corrupt ideas, events and anomalies spread throughout all of time, a strategy for a checkmate awaits at the end times. This is an invasion of human like creatures that are no more related to the human race than an insect. It is by these resurrected sons of god and their offspring that this great deception is put upon the world that places mankind at awe with a desire to worship the dragon who gives the beast his power. Rev 13:4

I believe Jude warns us of this event. Whether Jude actually understood the whole process or just the principle without knowing of the mechanics we do not know but this text in his letter would indicate that he understood these were not earthly humans. This is the description of the clandestine invasion!

"For there are certain men crept in unawares, WHO WERE BEFORE OF OLD ordained to this condemna-tion, ungodly men turning the grace of God, and our Lord Jesus Christ,, Likewise also these filthy dream-ers defile the flesh, despise dominion, and speak evil of dignities...But these speak evil of those things which they know not: but what they know natu-rally, as brute beasts, in those things they corrupt

themselves. Woe unto them for they have gone the way of Cain...These are spots in your feasts of charity, when they feast with you, feeding themselves without fear: CLOUDS are they WITHOUT WATER, carried about of winds: trees whose fruit withers, without fruit, TWICE DEAD, plucked up by the roots; Raging waves of the sea, foaming out of their own shame; WANDERING STARS, to whom is reserved the blackness of darkness forever. And Enoch also, the seventh from Adam, prophesied of these, saying, "Behold the Lord cometh with ten thousands of his saints, To execute judgment..."

Jude 4,8,10,12-14,

Now in context, it is rather hard to see these people as mortal human beings. Let's review the evidence as stated in Jude:

1. who were of old, - Not liking the appearance of what this means, the preferred accepted rendering of today is said to mean, "who were written about of old". and implied from this is the sense that these were not the ones of old(solely based on the assumption that this would be impossible) but rather just written about of old. In the Greek this phrase says what it means, "they are the ones of old that were spoken of".

2. Ordained to this condemnation - In this sense these men mentioned or a part of the old are destined to fulfill this role. Why? Because they are something that should never have been in the first place and unredeemable.

3. Clouds without water- Defines the last statement! This could have a dual meaning. First they are compared to as a cloud without water. A cloud is composed of water vapor. The indication here can only mean that they are something similar only in appearance and not composition. Water is also symbolic of the spirit. This could also be implying that this is a vessel without a spirit.

4. Twice dead- This can be referring to the opposite of the idea of being twice born. To be born once in the flesh and again once in the spirit. The saying goes, "Born once, die twice, Born twice die once." To be dead twice in this sense is to be dead spiritually and to have already been dead once before the flood! The men of old, men of renown.

5. Wandering stars - This is a term for fallen angles. In the broadest sense the term can mean any messenger. But again in this context the same judgment imposed upon the "angels that sinned" is mentioned here also, the blackness of eternal darkness forever.

The rendering of the term "strong delusion" of 2 Thessalonians 2:11 is more accurately defined as "Wandering error". The same wandering error sent by God for all to believe who will not believe in Him. This suggests that GOD is still in control! Even in something as horrible as this! The text here reviews and uses every term for these beings called the men of renown, of which a judgment was given and a destiny to fulfill at the end of time. Clearly these are not mere ungodly human beings that are spoken of here. Jude concludes that these are the same ones that Enoch prophesied against before the flood. This mention overlaps the already mentioned rebels and their offspring. They have sown discord, rebellion and inspired false doctrine and worship. These are the same that paint pictures of UFOs in religious paintings, create legends and myths and plant things to be found at a later date that will astound and amaze the world. If you are the first to utilize time as a weapon, you do not disrupt the past drastically so as to jeopardize your own existence and present state. If you are wise, you subtly place your agents all throughout certain times and places like chess pieces to undermine and plant your desired will. At a future time you can call out all your pieces bringing "all things together" to astound and amaze the entire world, convincing them of your agenda and desires. You could also "pluck up" your enemies "by the roots" by going back and placing an invisible yet powerful restructuring of a fifth column presence within the infrastructure of their governments to be activated at a later time in the future. You would set up "secret societies" as safe houses and points of control stations. **Truly beyond science fiction!**

Satan will explain away faith in a personal God, and transport this invading army of "locusts" throughout time as chess pieces carefully placed to be the great delusion or wandering error.

Part Two

The Amazing 39ᵗʰ Chapter of Job: The whole story in one Chapter

Now as I promised here is a rendering of the entire 39ᵗʰ chapter of Job. This just about capsulated everything I have mentioned already. I can almost imagine many indoctrinated Christians that would become outraged at the liberties I have taken. This chapter took almost a month even using my computer program to go back word for word on every word, trying out variables that are questionably within reason. I was amazed at how this ended up reading. Notes are far too much to publish, but upon request I can furnish them for you.

Job 39ᵗʰ Chapter Paraphrased:

Do you know the appointed time when the wild goats (chief ones, Isa 14:9) **from the fortress will give birth?** (Job 26:5,6)

Can you protect the females (Does) **that are made to bear offspring?**

(Genetic abductions?)

Can you record the amount of months they come to abundant fullness? (Dan 9:27) (As massing themselves together against something) **or understanding the appointed time when they are delivered?** (Joel 2:1-3 Rev 9:1-11)

They cast themselves down, they splice their offspring. (Lowering their existence to sexually reproduce, then gene splice their offspring?) (Dan 2:43)

They cast off their ropes (as twisted and tied together as bindings Isa 26:14) (The same ropes mentioned by Peter and Jude? The impediment?)

Their sons are restored to health (the offspring of the sons of God Gen 6) (also the repair in Job 26:11) **they become numerous and great as with the grain separated from the chaff, they go forth and do not return.** (Image of the Beast, Wandering error or stars. Rev 13:15, 2 Thess 2:11 "go forth" has a meaning in the sense of "sending out false prophets" Jude 4-14)

Who has sent for the wild ass (as fruitful [in the sense of a wild seed] i.e. Cain's descendants) **to spread him lose** (Isa 14:11) **or who has understood the riddle, opening the doorway to loosen the bands of the wild ass.** (Dan 8:23 the Antichrist) **Whose descendants have I made a dark empty dwelling in a salted land** (Cain's descendants in a sparse land) **as his permanent dwelling.** (2 Pe 2:4 Jude 1-6) **He** (God) **mockingly laughs and plays with the multitude accidently lighting on the floor.** (Floor in the sense of the lowest part of a building, i.e. the Nazi Antarctic Expedition, the digging into the lowest level of hell and the alliance made with the resurrection, Amos 9:2 Job 26 5,6 Isa 14:9) **nor does he give heed** (in a legal sense) **to the loud clamor of their oppressing ruler.** (Satan as embodied in his son Adolf Hitler? Isa 14:9) **What is left of the mountains** (7 prior kingdoms, Rev 17:9-11) **is his grazing land. And the hind part** (the last kingdom) **he** (Satan as the Antichrist - Hitler?) **Seeks the end of every green thing.** (False Tribulation of Antichrist during final 8th empire) **Will the wild bull** (as the unicorn, perhaps the little horn of Dan 8:9,10) **from its conspicuousness consent to serve you and stay permanently in your stall? Can you confine his bindings in the grave or will he plough up the depth after you. Will you trust him because his power is great or will you relinquish your labor and goods to him? Will you establish belief in him because he will return again and gather up to take away your seed to an open place?** (A threshing floor perhaps implying a False "rapture" and 2nd coming of Antichrist)

Leap for joy screeching fowl from its harsh sounds, in flight to an extremity of land, or give feathers of flight to the kind maternal (in a religious sense) **stork** (U.S.?) **As the ostrich which leaves her eggs in the dust and forgets that the foot may crush them or that the spread out beast may trample them** (cf/w Isa 14:11 Dan 8:10) **She is unfeeling to her young ones** (abortions for desired genetic material and or abductions of an entire generation?) **Her labor is in vain without alarm, because God has caused her to forget wisdom** (in an ethical sense) **neither has he imparted to her understanding or discernment. At an appointed time she rebelled, lifting herself up as filthy to a high place. She makes folly with the horse and his rider.** (Cf/w Rev 6:2, Rev 17:3, Possible alliance with Nazis +operation Paperclip and Lusty) **Have you given the horse** (as vehicle i.e. Nazis\New Age) **strength and clothed him with confinement upon his neck?** (As a burden or task) **Can you make him afraid as the locusts**

that rapidly increase? The imposing form and appearance of his forced breathing is like a boogeyman. (his second coming) **He digs into the deep** (the abyss)**and rejoices in his power and strength. He goes forth to encounter the armed men. He mocks fear and is not broken down by it, nor does he turn back from the sword. The quiver rattles against him the polished sword and shield. He devours the earth with sudden fierceness and rage.** (Like a locust's swarm covering everything, a successful infiltration) **Neither does he believe it is the sound of the trumpet.** (Final judgment 1 Co 5:52, 1Thess 4:16, Joel 2:1) **He says amongst the warnings, "Ha Ha!" And he perceives the battle far off, the crashing thunder of the rulers and the clamor. Does the predatory bird (**Hawk**) fly by perceptive understanding to break off and disperse to the extreme land in the south?**(Antarctic can be no more than the extreme south!) **The eagle raises high above the edge of the opening** (or mouth) **so as to assist to raise a nest above.**(U.S. desire to develop a space program actually aids former enemy?) **She dwells and obstinately stays upon the ivory cliffs of the fortress and defensive stronghold.** (Dan 11:36-38) **Her young ones drink up death and bloodshed and where the failure, pollution or death are, there she is.** (Mat 24:28). **Job39.**

A symbolic prophetic fulfillment of current events or merely a commentary about animals?

Clearly, this is describing much more than nature and animals. By using a combination of the full variable meanings of these words, this paraphrase is reasonably within proper interpretive methods used. It is uncanny at how this came together.

In the first part we see the events taking place underground as the rebel spirits and their offspring are repaired and restored in the sense of a resurrection. He-goats are the fallen angels that sinned and their offspring the famous men of renown, part angelic creature and part human mentioned in the Genesis 6 account before the flood. These judged spirits mentioned by Peter and Jude are in the disembodied form of a ghost in the continual cycle of going up and down. Isaiah mentions that they would be allowed to be set loose for judgment. Job here and in 26:6 describes this process as being restored to health. We get a vague alluding here to this being a genetic accomplishment of splicing their offspring as they "lower" themselves to a lesser form to produce an offspring by forcing the "does" to birth which cannot be prevented or protected from this act. This could be the Biblical reasoning for the many accounts claimed to be "alien abductions" with the removal of sperm, eggs and fetuses. This activity is also mentioned by Daniel in 2:43 as happening in the last and final kingdom before the Lord's return. **"They shall mingle themselves with the seed of men"**. The next verse says that they will not cleave one to another. This is not meaning the lack of success, but rather the clinical process of procreation outside of marriage or a relationship and not like it was before the flood which involved a marriage and relationship.

We then see the encounter of the descendants of Cain as the wild ass and the earthly peoples that fled to the extreme south in a fortress as joined together in this effort. (The escape of the Nazis to the Antarctic) The deceased Antichrist (Adolf Hitler?) being also with them and by his understanding they "open the doorway" to loose the bands of their fellow rebels. His "snorting" or forced breathing is possibly a reference to his resurrection and second appearance, like a boogeyman. This was the actual translation! We then get the specific location of an extreme land in the south with ivory cliffs as a fortress and stronghold. This could only be the South Pole! The very place rumored to be the last bastion of a Nazi underground stronghold!

The horse and his rider is in reference to the Antichrist mentioned in;

Rev 6:2, "And I saw and behold a white horse: and he that sat on him had a bow; and a crown was given unto him: and he went forth conquering and to conquer."

The rider is the Antichrist and the horse, the vehicle by which he went forth to conquer. The horse being at first the Nazi political party and second, the philosophy of Nazism turned into a religion, the New Age movement.

We see an interaction with another group, a maternal bird, the stork who acts as an ostrich. This stork is given the feathers of flight! (Anti-gravity disk technology and or a space program?) She becomes forgetful of her heritage and her young. She becomes a "partner" with the horse and his rider thinking because she cloths and strengthens them they will do her bidding, when in fact they convert her, she becoming the woman who rides the beast mentioned in Rev 17:1-3. As this activity comes to fullness in the remote safety of this fortress they scan their prey from afar (both time and space). They believe they are completing their agenda and plan when they are actually only heading to their judgment signified by the sound of the trumpet which they deny. Exploiting every opportunity, the eagle and her young play "World Police" wherever there is failure, corruption and death, they are there to influence and exploit it with ulterior motives, being in league with the horse and his rider. This could be none other than the United States! "Her young" being the United Nations. They are a land that sits upon many waters, Rev 17:1. They are a nation once a maternal and moral nation in a religious sense of having a rightness with God. Job 39:13 says that she forgets her sense of ethics and as judgment from God Himself, removes discernment and understanding from her. Jeremiah mentions this nation sitting upon many waters as the hindmost of nations, a hammer of the world, a great voice with influence who mounts up to heaven. (Jer 50:23, 51:7, 13, 53, 55.) This is the last beast empire Daniel and John saw Dan 7:2-7, Rev 13:2. This was a nation set apart by God yet infiltrated by Satan. A nation that would be like a Dr. Jekyll and Mr. Hyde, with dual opposite roles to play. Just as her great Seal has two sides with opposing meanings and her one dollar bill that displays two different belief systems. The United States of America! Mystery Babylon the Great, The Mother of Harlots and Abominations of the Earth. (Rev 17:5)

Part Three

The Second Wave: Armageddon

Why Invade Israel?

In the second wave an actual invasion will take place that ends up in the plains of Megiddo in Israel.

Once this total rebel alliance has conditioned the masses and made an entire generation desirous of them and their global agenda, they will appear as saviors during a time of conflict. The result will be that friendly Alien/Angels (this image of the beast) will be given charge over the nations and worshipped.

> **"But in his estate shall he honor the God of forces: and a god whom his fathers knew not shall he honor with gold, and silver, and with precious stones, and pleasant things. Thus shall he do in the most**

> **strong holds with a strange (alien!) god, whom he
> shall acknowledge and increase with glory: and he
> shall cause them to rule over many, and shall divide
> the land for gain". Dan 11:37-38 (KJV)**

It is in this time that the disguised Antichrist will reveal his true
identity as Adolf Hitler much to the horror of Israel. As they reject
Hitler they also embrace their true messiah Jesus Christ. In their
national repentance they also resist the Global Agenda. Closing
their borders to the Antichrist and his military hoard initiates an
invasion but Why? What is so important about tiny little Israel
other than their faith in the one true God? This invasion may in
part be motivated by the Antichrist. Adhering to specific occult
doctrines, the Antichrist will believe that he must be in a certain
place at a certain time to "eternalize" this dimension. The specific
occult traditions when understood in light of what the Bible has
to declare makes this quite clear.

Finding the Center of the Axis Pole

From Delphi in ancient Greece to the Norse ash tree Yagdrasil
to the Sun Pole of the Sioux Indians, every culture once had a
sacred place that it believed to be the symbolic center of the
world. The supernatural was once believed to enter the world
at its center, a sacred place often marked by what was known
as a "navel stone". It was through this stone that an imaginary
vertical line or axis ran, and this axis linked the material world
with the mystical, spiritual world.

Here access might be gained to other worlds, heaven, hell and
the realms of spirits and the dead. The imaginary vertical line
that runs through the center is often referred to as the cosmic
axis. It is called this because it places the earth at the center of
the cosmos with heaven above and the underworld below. The
"sacred" center is commonly known by its Greek name omphalos,
which means "navel of the world".

To ancient peoples, locating the omphalos was essential to the
creation of civilization, culture and religion because it helped
separate the safe, human world from the dangerous world full of
natural forces. To locate and mark the center of the earth, ancient
peoples hoped to chart the natural world and even gain control
of it. Medieval European cities often contained navel stones like
the London stone, the stone of Tubingen Germany and the "blue
stane" in St. Andrews Scotland, all representing the cosmic axis
and center. In the Ancient Chinese book, *Chou-li*, the axis is

described as "a magical place where opposites come together, time and space are wiped out; the four seasons merge and the opposing principles of yin and yang come into eternal harmony". Vortex patterns depicted as swirls are often carved into the navel stones. In all of this is the image of everything having the ability to come together including time and space!

In the myth of this cosmic axis and the center of the earth, is there an encrypted knowledge of physics forbidden to fallen man? Fringe Science researchers, Bruce L. Cathie author of *The Energy Grid* and David Hatcher Childress author of *Anti-Gravity and the World Grid* are but two of many to proclaim that there is a magnetic grid like a screen covering the earth, which is a natural flow of magnetic energy. The intersections create a vortex of energy that they say can be tapped into and utilized. Some have claimed that the mystery spots and ancient mysterious ruins from around the world are locations where these vortexes exist. This screen like covering might be alluded to in the scriptures in Ezekiel 28 as what Satan was given to provide and protect God's creation. This knowledge being a part of what he traded back to mankind so he could control creation! The same screen Enoch described as the pathways of the angles, the wing's of the wind.

In the mind of the Antichrist following these occult traditions, could he understand some applied physics to eternalize this linear dimension into his own eternal state? Is there a certain date and time He must stand in this center to make this happen? Could this also be the reason the Nazis and their allies were called the AXIS POWERS? The catch phrase common to occultists is, "As above so below" which may also be Satan's battle cry and ultimate goal! More than just speculation this evidence reveals the importance of Israel and the location of Jerusalem and the temple mound. We can only begin to see this reality by going back to the scriptures to verify such a thing.

The Bible Reveals the Center of the Earth!

> **"This is Jerusalem, I have set her in the center of the nations, with countries round about her."**
>
> **Ezk 5:5**

It is quite clear that the Bible claims that the center of the earth terrestrially is in Jerusalem. In context we are not talking in any figurative sense but one of geography. An even further description and miracle helps to confirm this idea. 1Kings 11:36 states,

"......Jerusalem, the city which I have chosen me to put my name there."

How literal could this statement be? In context he is describing the lineage of David and the promised line Jesus, as Messiah would come from. But there might be more to this in a physical way also!

In the VHS tape, *Globalism, Iron Mountain and UFOs*, (Prophecy club, Topeka KS) Researcher/Pastor Norm Frantz reveals a Topographical map of Israel. On his map is an existing dot for the location of the temple mount, which is the location of the holy of holies, the central point of the entire temple in Jerusalem. He then places a transparency over the area with Hebrew writing on it. Part of this writing includes a dot as part of the letter. The entire inscription lines right up with the mountain ranges and the dot matching up with the temple location. The amazing thing is that the Hebrew writing is the name for God! This is no coincidence by any stretch of the imagination but it is a confirmation of ownership!

Not only is Jerusalem the center of the world but a name of ownership has been placed upon it! When you understand these occult doctrines and contrast them to recent scientific speculations as well as these few key scriptures from the Bible, a clear plan of the Antichrist is revealed! We have discovered the central point and location where the antichrist must be and now we possibly have the year and day right down to the minute.

The Window of Opportunity December 21, 2012

The Mayan calendar ends the current cycle at this date of 2012. Astronomically, our solar system is on the outer ridge of one of the arms, however on this date our entire solar system will be centrally located on the flat plain of our galaxy. The twelve zodiac signs will be around us. In the center of our galaxy, there is a dark rift, and within this rift, scientists recently believe the darkness is caused by the existence of a large black hole. Could this kind of equinox be a window of opportunity for some kind of applied physics that could alter our current linear state? This has all of the elements of a sci-fi thriller with ideas of space and time which might just hold more truth than fiction. Recent crop circles could also allude to this coming event. So what are crop circles? I believe they are the powers of darkness communicating their deceptions in intriguing ways appealing to mankind's sense of mystery and drama. Closely connected to the idea of UFOs and Aliens, they are making their suggestions and connections setting up mankind for this great global deception.

Right: **Theosophy symbol: Religion of the New Age, Occult Philosophy of the Nazis** Left: **Recent Crop circle, Ouroboros is wrapped around the Earth and Moon**

To increase this sense of mystery, recently a documentary about crystal skulls proclaimed the newest New Age quest for some researchers. This myth has been the main topic of the newest Indiana Jones movie and will soon become well known. The created myth has been put forth that the skulls are to be placed somewhere important like a power point vortex area on December 21, 2012 to save the world from the coming doom of Dec 21st 2012. Supposedly there has to be 13skulls but only 12 have been discovered so far. What is true and rather mysterious about these skulls, is the fact that some of these skulls have modern tooling marks. Because of this, more contemporary scientists date them as being made in the late 19th century. The chemical composition is identical to modern quartz crystals that are synthetically manufactured and used as computer chips for storing electronic data. When various spectrums of light were passed through the skull called the Michael-Hedges skull, the skull revealed intricate pathways and sections that indicated possible similar data storage may exist. If there is any element of truth to these myths, you might wonder if these skulls could contain the technology to focus or dial the power of this black hole into our earth's grid and alter it. Personally, I believe this might be yet another New Age wild goose chance that goes nowhere. In any case, all of this would certainly not indicate Alien technology but rather the completion of an occult plan designed by Satan, provided by fallen angels and desired by man. The Nazis and their occult beliefs have much to do with this as the receivers of this knowledge with the United States gleaning some of it after the War. Even in my skepticism, I am keeping a watchful eye, as this is the very way Satan would use to accomplish his desired goals.In whatever way and manner Satan does choose to try to eternalize this linear situation, He will ultimately fail

Part Four

The God of the Bible Wins!

Rev 19:11-21

"And I saw heaven opened, and behold a white horse; and he that sat upon him was called Faithful and True, and in righteousness he doth judge and make war. 12 His eyes were as a flame of fire, and on his head were many crowns; and he had a name written, that no man knew, but he himself. 13 And he was clothed with a vesture dipped in blood: and his name is called The Word of God. 14 And the armies which were in heaven followed him upon white horses, clothed in fine linen, white and clean. 15 And out of his mouth goes a sharp sword, that with it he should smite the nations: and he shall rule them with a rod of iron: and he treads the winepress of the fierceness and wrath of Almighty God. 16 And he hath on his vesture and on his thigh a name written, KING OF KINGS, AND LORD OF LORDS. 17 And I saw an angel standing in the sun; and he cried with a loud voice, saying to all the fowls that fly in the midst of heaven, Come and gather yourselves together unto the supper of the great God; 18 That ye may eat the flesh of kings, and the flesh of captains, and the flesh of mighty men, and the flesh of horses, and of them that sit on them, and the flesh of all men, both free and bond, both small and great. 19 And I saw the beast, and the kings of the earth, and their armies, gathered together to make war against him that sat on the horse, and against his army. 20And the beast was taken, and with him the false prophet that wrought miracles before him, with which he deceived them that had received the mark of the beast, and them that worshiped his image. These both were cast alive into a lake of fire burning with brimstone. 21 And the remnant were slain with the sword of him that sat upon the horse,

**which sword proceeded out of his mouth: and all
the fowls were filled with their flesh."**

(KJV).

In Job 39 it is said that the rider on the horse, (the Antichrist) hears and sees the battle from far off but does not believe that it is his own judgment. He is motivated by insanity. No matter how intelligent he is, like his father the devil he is insane. He will always come to the wrong conclusions.

Conclusion

Part One

The Alien Roundup

In conclusion about Aliens, it can really come down to semantics. Call them Aliens or call them Fallen Angels, they are all one in the same and still the bad guys. We have seen that the Bible provides a description of the various beings encountered by people all throughout history. The Bible even alludes to a heavenly point of origin that corresponds to what they claim about themselves. We have seen that although they are quite physical, they are subject to spiritual laws and warfare. We are warned of a time of abductions and a genetic tampering with humanity. We are warned that abductions are a means of providing genetically engineered "earth suits" for the disembodied spirits and all other fallen angels. They would infiltrate all through time and create a spiritual conditioning that ultimately leads to the physical takeover of our planet. We have seen that the Bible indicates that the "Aliens" are in league with a Globalist elite, a military leader understanding the occult and his vehicle, a political group turned into a religious movement. The Alien and the Flying Saucer is a large part of the end time delusion warned about. They are the signs and lying wonders. None of this is by chance or coincidence. I have not forced the Bible to declare these truths, they were there on their own merit waiting for the time when knowledge would increase and people would travel to (one dimension) and fro (into another dimension). I think that means now!

Part Two

Alien Life Outside of This Scenario?

In light of this understanding, we are in an altered parallel universe. A dimension created solely by the wrong choice of man offered by Satan. This fallen universe is a product centered on the human race. Linear time is our quarantine from the rest of the universe and/or dimensions. Part of Satan's plan is to eternalize this linear state as his own "heaven" or eternal state. That would mean that any other entity in this fallen universe would either be part of the Rebel Alliance or part of the Kingdom of God. Yes, we are that important and yes, it really is all about us at least in this quarantined condition. Knowing this, the fallen dimension would not and did not make provisions for anything else in a neutral state. It is black and white. You are on one side or the other with nothing in between.

Now in God's perfect willed dimension? Wow! That is another situation altogether.

We are given scripture that alludes to cycles or ages.

> **"There is no remembrance of former things; neither shall there be any remembrance of things that are to come with those that shall come after."**
> **Eccl 1:11(KJV)**

Even the Greek words associated to eternal life (aeon) in the New Testament are indicative of continual life in ages or cycles. This is in no way to be confused with the cycle of reincarnation. There is only one lifetime allowed in this quarantined linear life.

> **"And as it is appointed unto men once to die, but after this the judgment: So Christ was once offered to bear the sins of many; ..."**
> **Heb 9:27-28**

Exactly what is going to be, we are only given a vague picture but it is a very good one!

Shortly after I invited Christ into my life, one of the first things the Lord impressed on me was, "Jim you always dreamed of going into space, what awaits you in heaven is that and much more!"

As the Biblical promise states to be a joint heir and directing angelic affairs tells me that we are doing a whole lot more than sitting on a cloud strumming on a harp! Perhaps there are other universes? (1Co 6:3, Rom 8:17) No one knows for sure, but what does wait for us will be Beyond Science Fiction and my wildest dreams!

Chapter Nineteen
What should I do?

Part One
So what is left?

In this book I have told you a fascinating yet horrific story. It would not be fair to leave you hanging here with a vague description of heaven and not tell you how to make sure you get there. In these closing days toward the "New Age" or the End of the Age, what I share next may be the only hope you can have. I can assure you that I have not told you all of this just to sell you Jesus. I can't do that, no one can. We all have to make our own choices. In this book you have read about many mysteries explained by the Bible in ways you never thought possible and yet it is all very logical. With the same attention, read on to find out why things had to be that way and above all how you can be ready.

Why Does This Have to Happen?

The next most logical question we need to ask is Why? Why did a loving God allow such a horrible thing to happen? And why do these future events have to happen?

Not to lower God's concept of love to Man's carnal level, but so that you can relate to His eternal supreme majesty and power; Imagine if you will, that you had all the power over minds and hearts to make everyone automatically love you. The result of this would be total acceptance by everyone. In our baser desires and wants, you would have friendship, love and romance by anyone and everyone at your personal desire. A novel idea at first but in time this would begin to be empty in the sense of always knowing that it was your power over them that made everyone respond to you. How much deeper, how much richer would the relationships be if they chose you because they wanted to, or that they even were aware of a choice?

In the same respect but of a much higher level than man's carnal idea of love, God, desired to bring this love relationship with His creation further along. This higher level of love is not motivated in the sense that God is lacking anything. Rather, it is His desire for a more richly, deeper, mature relationship with His creation. His creation never knew anything but perfection. They never experienced or knew of anything less. Not being their fault, but they would be like a bunch of spoiled rich kids! This situation is not the result that they were doing anything wrong. They simply could not appreciate what they had because they had never experienced anything else!

The only way a mature relationship could be accomplished would be to give creation a choice. This choice would obviously mean the creation of something with the potential of being the opposite and in contrast of Himself. Satan was created as God's right hand man. Man then, stood in the middle, the outcome was already known and the plan made ready. Man would choose the wrong tree or path and it would then only be fair that God Himself would have to correct the error.

In doing this, when all is come to completion, man and all of creation sees by experience what anything less than God's perfection would be like. Mankind would also appreciate much deeper the relationship they have with their Creator. Because God's love for his creation is so great He insures that none of his creation will be "lost" in the whole process. This is why everyone in his or her own personal way (who was in the original plan, or the "Book of Life" as God's seed, there are two seeds) will respond to His love in their time of mortal life. All they would have to do is exercise their own free will to overcome the artificial realities of this mortal life and respond to God's prompting and Love. And they will! It is God's guarantee of faithfulness and love for his creation.(Jo10:28,29)

What is gained by all of this? Man receives a deeper appreciation of the person of God. He receives a forever awe of the willing price God himself was willing to make to have this deeper relationship. He enters into a maturity knowing and experiencing something opposite of God's perfection. Nothing is taken for granted and everything is appreciated with a depth that could not be realized in any other way. This new and deeper relationship with God is so Heaven and Earth shaking that it is necessary that a "new heaven and a new earth are created to contain it!

This creation, unlike anything before has now overcome an experience with something less than perfection. The added result is wisdom to rule. As children and part of God's personal family we are offered to be joint heirs to His throne! No angel has ever been granted this kind of offer but mankind has. All we do is accept the one provision God made in this overall plan. Accept the way that has been made for you. Like everything else in this book so far, let me back this up with the Scriptures.

> **"And I saw a new heaven and a new earth: for the first heaven and the first earth were passed away;..."**
>
> **Rev 21:1**

In the Old Heaven, all of God's creations were like children who though they were rich and well provided for, they could never appreciate it, as they had never known anything else. In the New Heaven, they are over comers. They have known the difference by experience, and by faith accepted the way of redemption. Now they experience their relationship as mature children. They know their inheritance as co-rulers joint heirs with Jesus!

> **"He that overcomes shall inherit all things; and I will be his God, and he shall be my son."**
>
> **Rev 21:7**

> **" The Spirit itself bears witness with our spirit, that we are the children of God: And if children, then heirs; heirs of God, and joint-heirs with Christ;..."**
>
> **Rom 8:16-17**

God as Creator and ruler of all, slides over to the side of this throne and offers each one of us to come and sit next to Him and help rule! This is not the scene the Scientists Priests convey to the unbelieving world of today. This is not the action of a threatened God trying to maintain power and rule over his creation. This is the act of a God that loves His creation so much that he desired to pay the entire price to achieve a higher and deeper relationship with each one by Himself!

Why you might ask, can't God just cut this short and spare the pain?

> **"The Lord is not slack concerning his promise, as some men count slackness; but is longsuffering to us-ward, not willing that any should perish, but that all should come to repentance."**
>
> **2 Pet 3:9**

Imagine a pool of clear water, so quiet and clear that it reflects the sky, shoreline and trees like a perfect mirror. Then imagine someone throwing a big rock in the middle of the pond. The rippling waves create a disturbance that must be carried out to completion until the last wave is played out before the original state is restored. The fall of Satan, mankind and this dimension is the same way. Everyone God intended to create as "His seed" must experience their own ripple in linear time in order to gain the wisdom and respond to the love relationship that pulls them out.

What about our memory of those who we knew and loved who were of the anomalous seed (covered in my next book)...the ones who reject Jesus and the only way out of this dimension? God says He will personally wipe away every tear.

> **"And God shall wipe away all tears from their eyes; and there shall be no more death, neither sorrow, nor crying, neither shall there be any more pain: for the former things are passed away...Behold, I make all things new...He that overcomes shall inherit all things; and I will be his God, and he shall be my son.**
>
> **Rev 21:4.**

How does this happen? Our understanding of all things will be complete, even as we are complete.

> **"For now we see through a glass, darkly; but then face to face: now I know in part; but then shall I know even as also I am known.**
>
> **1 Cor 13:12**

This was the plan all along! This is the answer to WHY?! This can be your strength for the times to come! Next we need to know how, exactly how do we get back to where we need to be?

We have studied the same but opposite patterns performed by the rebel alliance. God also performed a same but opposite. What happened in the Garden of Eden resulted in our human form being changed in a very physical way. We then need to know just what changed in man that needed a reverse action by God to fix. It is all about blood.

Blood In, Blood Out

It was blood that got us into a mortal existence and a different blood, that once shed would bring us back to the previous existence. Redemption would be in two phases, first spiritually and upon death with the promised a resurrection, the physical restoration. Let's understand this concept by the Scriptures.

1. Adam's statement in regards to the newly formed Eve,

> **"And Adam said, "This is now bone of my bones and flesh of my flesh."**
> **Gen2:23.**

I believe the absence of the mention of blood is very important. This was before the temptation and they had no blood as they were created like their Father. After the resurrection, Jesus describes Himself as not a spirit but as a living being flesh and bone minus blood. He is in the eternal state without blood.

2. "The life of the flesh is in the blood." Lev 17:11

Mortal life is in the blood. This mortal life was given only as a result of the wrong choice during the temptation. Blood is the only dietary law carried over into the New Testament, in the prohibition of eating it. Lev 17:10 and Acts 21:25.

3. "Flesh and Blood cannot inherit the Kingdom of God." 1Co 15:50

In God's eternal kingdom, only perfection according to His will, can exist with Him, Flesh and Blood not Included. In context, celestial and terrestrial bodies are compared. The blooded terrestrial body must die

Mortal life is produced by the addition of a blood system from a wrong choice. In 1Co 15:38-58 a distinction is made between two physical forms. There is a glory of a terrestrial body. But it was created in corruption, dishonor and weakness, it only produced death. Existing in this form, we are "natural" and inclined to behave in the natural manner. It is not our fault, as if we had any choice in the matter, all descendants afterward would simply behave and take on the nature that this linear environment dictated.

Interesting is that the Hebrew word for "blood" is **"dam"**. In this sense we are all damned to certain behavior patterns based on this linear dimension.

This was the whole point and mission of God becoming a man. The second Adam would undo what was done in the Garden in the same manner only with the elimination (or pouring out) of a blood foreign to the influence of this altered state.

Mankind Placed in Quarantine

4. Old Testament Law dictated that:

> **"It is the blood that makes atonement for the soul."**
>
>

Lev 17:11.

This is further explained in the New Testament in

> **Heb 9:22, "...without the shedding of blood is no remission."**

Jesus said in Matt 26:28:

> **"...for this is my blood of the New Testament, which is shed for many for remission of sins**

One wrong decision allowed Satan (the rebel usurper) to alter God's creation into a lesser form. God had to put mankind into a linear existence as a "holding pattern" so he would not become eternally stuck in this lesser state.

> **"Behold the man has become as one of us, to know good and evil; and now lest he put forth his hand, and take also of the tree of life, and eat, and live forever:.. Therefore the Lord God sent him forth from the garden of Eden."**
>
>

Genesis 3:22

This was the beginning of linear time, human history as we know it today. Man had to leave the eternal realm for his own protection. Separated from his intended home until a time when God would be able to restore all things.

The Uniqueness of One

"For as by one man's disobedience many were made sinners, so by the obedience of one shall many be made righteous."

Romans 5:19,

One act brought about this lesser existence and one more act brought a way back. This is what the Gospel is all about! Gospel means Good News. There is a uniqueness in the person of Christ. Only he as God, became a man, like us in every way except his blood unnatural to this dimension. This gave Him the power to overcome this world system and altered universe. Representing His own dimension He lived out a life according to His own ways (The Law). By this He was not subject to the laws of this universe which state that all have sinned and the wages are death. Rom 6:23. We were already damned.(or blooded) Rom3:23.

The fact is we didn't have to do anything. By being born into this dimension, it and everything in it is missing the mark, which is the definition for sin. Because of this we are naturally going to go the way of this universe. How fruitless it is to try and work or be good enough to go somewhere else. God says it is impossible for man. Only what one unique man did could change it. We can't earn it or work for it we just accept it as a free gift. He did it for us. It is so easy that it is offensive to many. You can't do anything but accept it. This is why He dwells with the humble and contrite of spirit.(Isa57:15) That is what it takes on our part. Submission to the one who loved us so much he had a plan of self sacrifice right from the beginning. In this context you can understand all of Christianity's narrow focus upon only one way with one person. It is not intolerance, as many have accused Christian's of being. It is the realization that only one person accomplished the sacrifice to make a way out for all of us stuck in this fallen dimension. Jesus himself made this most narrow minded statement and rightly so,

> **"I am the way, the truth, and the life: no man cometh unto the Father but by me."**
>
> **John 14:6**

He made no doubt about his uniqueness.

> **"I am the door: by me if any man enter in, he shall be saved,...He that enters not by the door into the sheepfold, but climbs up some other way, the same is a thief and a robber."**
>
> **John 10:9+p1.**

The fact of only one way by one person has nothing to do with accumulating knowledge or levels or steps to anything. In light of understanding two dimensions and the fact that we are caught in the lesser one, powerless to deliver ourselves, it is the act of Love that has made a way out for us. No "ascended master," "Avatar" prophet or "Christ conscienceless" sacrificed himself and rose from the dead to make a way of restoration. This was a free gift of grace, a sole act of God himself that accomplished this task. He made the way freely because he knew we were powerless to do anything ourselves. You cannot "learn" your way out of this dimension, You cannot "earn" your way out of it. You can only humbly submit to the free gift and offer to come back to the path, away from the tree of knowledge of good and evil, to the path that leads to the tree of life. In this sense, we are no different than Adam and Eve. We have the same choice they had to make in our own life. One tree or dimension leads to death, one leads to life. It can't get any simpler than that.

Part Two

It's your Choice

The greatest message from space is still and always has been and always will be John 3:16,

> **"For God so loved the world that He gave His only begotten son that whosoever believes in Him should not perish but has everlasting life."**

In 1974, like you, I read a book, The Late Great Planet Earth by Hal Lindsay. For the first time I had my prior beliefs challenged by the many scriptures Hal brought out about our world today. I was not fully convinced but he offered the reader a prayer of introduction and invitation to accept Jesus as Savior and Lord. I was convinced that if there was anything to His claims, I would be foolish to pass it up. I mean what was the harm of praying. The worst that could happen is I would look foolish talking to thin air, at best I could meet my creator.

"For whosoever shall call upon the name of the Lord shall be saved."
Rom 10:13 (KJV)

This free gift of grace cost everything in the sense that you unconditionally surrender your life to your creator. You take the first step and are willing for him to lead your life from that point on. God answered my prayer on a hot July day in 1974. I said Jesus "IF" and that was good enough for him to come into my heart and forever change my life. What about you. Are you willing to take the challenge to the only way out of this mess? It is a prayer away. Jesus said,

"Behold, I stand at the door, and knock: if any man hear my voice, and open the door, I will come in to him, and will sup with him, and he with me. To him that overcomes will I grant to sit with me in my throne, even as I also overcame, and am set down with my Father in his throne.
Rev 3:20-22 (KJV)

Right now in a simple prayer you can take this first step, Pray:

"Jesus, I believe you are the one who made the way for me. I ask that you forgive me of my sins and come into my heart and help me to live for you. I thank you Jesus for saving me. Amen"

"But as many as received Him, to them gave He power to become the sons of God, even to them that believe on His name:"
John 1:12 (KJV)

If you have prayed this for the first time you need to follow up by finding a local Church of fellow believers. Not every Church that claims to be "Christian" is necessarily Christian anymore. Seek out a co-worker or family member that you know has claimed to be "Born Again" or professes a relationship with Jesus. Everyone knows these people, they are the ones called "religious" or "Jesus freaks". If you draw a blank, E-mail me and I will help you find a good place to get grounded.

If you have prayed this prayer Happy Birthday! You have just passed from a certain death to eternal life as a Child of God. If you have not responded to this plea, you need to read this last section. If I have offended you I am sorry. I am obligated to share this process of hope. I would not be doing anyone, God or man justice to do anything less.

Part Three

A Balanced Response to the Things in this Book

The Enemy Among Us!

This concept has the most dangerous implications and possibilities. To think that these non-human entities would be allowed to mix in with human society and cause havoc is just unthinkable to many. Yet this is the very thing we are warned of in the Bible! It happened just before the flood and was the reason for it. It would also happen prior to the return of Christ in the last days. Again, I remind you of Jude who warned of these entities in his epistle.

Look at the description he gives, "Clouds without water, twice dead, wandering stars whom is reserved everlasting darkness" clearly defines non-human entities!

The concern I have in writing and warning about such a horrible thing is the possible actions of reactionary people who suddenly feel they have a ministry of judgments from God. That somehow they are able to detect and destroy these aliens from our life here on earth. For those having no faith in a personal God but you understand this deception, you may be compelled to become some kind of "alien" hunter. That course will lead to frustration and futility. Nowhere in the Bible will you find this irresponsible and ungodly kind of action. It is the same mentality that caused the Salem witch burnings, the Crusades and the Spanish inquisition. Upon learning this horrible truth, too many people want to react defensibly in their own understanding and within their own power. This is not part of any plan of God's! This is not the reason for understanding these horrible truths.

We are told so that we can be aware of just who and what we may be dealing with. We use this kind of knowledgeable insight on a very singular personal level with individuals. It is to help pull them out of the fires of wrong believing or at times when being prompted to back off, we obey. We can change things only on an individual basis within one heart at a time. The reality is that on a broad scale, the masses will be deceived, the conspiracy for a season will be effective. To try and change that fact will only change you into something less than your calling. You are to over come by the blood of the Lamb and the word of your testimony, and love not your life even to the end.(Rev 12:20) That my friend, is the tough one but the only standing orders you have with this information.

As I stated in the introduction I do not expect you to believe these things right away no matter how logical they may seem. At the same time I hope you do not just discredit these things as impossible. Just file them in your mind in a neutral position, and having been exposed to these ideas have a "wait and see attitude". If strange events lead up to the scenario I have presented here, you just might have a good source of scriptural reference for them.

We are to be aware of the dangerous surroundings we live in. We are not called to change it on any global scale. We are not going to change the whole world. However, individual lives can be saved as we continue to live a rather ordinary life in obedience to Christ. That means instead of digging bunkers, storing food and guns in certain "key" safe places or refusing to pay taxes, we remain rather mundane and "normal" in our lifestyles and actions.

On a personal level we should be motivated to become grounded in Christ's love, enabling us to be better parents, sons and daughters, friends and neighbors, employees and employers. We do not live in fear of who and where they are or when they are going to come. We have not been given a spirit of fear but of love power and a sound mind (2Tim1:7). Greater is He that is in you than He that is in the world (1 John 4:4). If God is going to expect any kind of radical behavior from you, it will only be radical Love. We must allow God, by His Holy Spirit to instill in us the kind of love that enables you to love those that hate you or despitefully use you. That is the only radical behavior which is Biblically sound.

Other Extreme Topics

A Hollow Earth in spite of what assumed modern scientists-priests may say, is a reality. Laughable and debatable today, tomorrow it may be a preferred Biblical understanding to help explain some aspects of the coming "Big Lie".

Time Travel as controversial as it is, is also a reality. I wrestled with this as the Lord had first revealed this to me. I read many books about the subject and could not reconcile how this technology could be given to fallen man, especially an evil one without it becoming an uncontrollable loose cannon. I also remembered the grandfather paradox which states if you went back into time and killed your grandfather, then how could you have gone back into time in the first place. The resulting theories are the complete destruction of the cosmos created by this paradox.

Another 4:00 o'clock in the mourning wake up call, The Lord reminded me how I always wondered why He would let things go so far, The mass extermination of believers being beheaded, (Rev 13:7, 20:4)

A short time power over all nations (Rev 13:8) Worshiped as a God, standing in the temple as God, (2Thess2:4) Geeze Lord it looks like they won! Bingo, that is the idea Jim, I let them think they won on purpose. Then he reminded me of a prophetic scripture in 2 Thessalonians.

> **"And for this cause God shall send them strong delusion, that they should believe a lie: that they all might be damned who believed not the truth, but had pleasure in unrighteousness."**
> **2Thess 2:11**

Funny, I never realized this before. This scripture is always quoted about the coming big end time delusion which is perpetrated by Satan. While that will happen and is true with many other scriptures to support it, this scripture is saying something different. This is a deception imposed by God to those who reject him. This includes angels as well as humans, even Satan, is what I hear the Lord tell me. That means God has caused a strong delusion to be placed on Satan and all of his followers.

The Lord continued to tell me that the first time human agents (Nazis) utilized this technology, they appeared at the very moment it looked like they one. Seeing their leader standing in the temple as victor about to throw this whole linear existence into an eternal realm they have Won!. Being in the future, they now have a blueprint of everything to do and not do that will create this scenario going all the way back to Eden! This is all a part of the Fall! They will not deviate from this one in any manner or they jeopardize the end result which they have now witnessed. In this they fulfill God's ultimate will and are only puppets to God's eternal plans!

Other ideas like the "Mark of the Beast", "Hitler as the Antichrist", the "Rapture of the Church" are not conclusive. This is unconditional Prophecy that will not be divinely revealed until we need to know and when we can no longer interfere with it.

If nothing else, I hope I have shown that it is more important to be grounded in a relationship with Christ. Therein lies true security and safety. Assumed knowledge of prophetic events alone will only produce the same results it did for the Jewish leaders 2,000 years ago. As they stood confident with their assumed knowledge, they put to death their long awaited hopes and dreams. Please don't do the same.

I have one more word to share with everybody. At four in the mourning on my birthday, July 22, 1996, I was awakened by that small still voice of the Lord. He said to write down what he was about to tell me word for word. He said at the time much of it would not make sense to me and I shouldn't presume upon it or be embarrassed either. Well, some of this sounds plagiarized from parts in the Bible. I can't justify or defend it, I can only present what I have been told. You may take this for what you want. I felt several groups were being addressed here.

Part Four

Prophecy of July 22 1996

Oh America, Oh America how I desired to gather you under my wings and protect you from this hour. For once you walked with Me; your roots were embedded deep upon a firm foundation. Your spirit was that of My Spirit and a great voice was given you declaring My glory. A golden cup filled with the new wine of the covenant did you let the nations of the earth freely drink who thirst. I led the nations to flow into you that they would taste and know that their God was good. You were a light to the nations, to teach them to walk in My ways.

But you did not learn from Israel, and made the same error. Have I not warned, not to take the spoils of war, the idols of the heathen into yourself so as to contaminate you? Yet this you have done and corrupt from within, you have slowly become what you once abhorred. The great voice now speaks lies, the bride became a whore. The chalice is filled with filth that makes the world mad.

Do you think that I am blind and see not the evil that is being done? The hidden evil that is not known? Do you think I cannot see the rage of the beast that is to prosper? Have you not read, do you not know that you reap your own doom and damnation? Am I blind and see not the tribulation that you have prepared. I am He that formed you, I am He that wrote of you and I am He that will utterly destroy you again from the face of the earth. The blood of your brother does cry from the dust. Do you think I cannot hear? Do you think I hear not the pleas of my people for your murders? Their pleas have come up to me as a testimony of their faith in the midst of this evil.

Does the creation think he can wipe away the Creator? Does the hand say I have done this great thing and need no other part? Therefore I will cut you off as an offence. As it is written for within one hour you shall be no more. The cry of my people will become the winepress of my wrath. Though you turn the moon to blood, yet have I redeemed them that no man may pluck them from me.

Oh Babylon! you mother of harlots, creator of abominations, you cannot wipe away my work or my memory. What you have purposed to do will come back on you double. I know of your works, and I know of your wrath hidden in secret places. They shall fail, you shall fail as I alone shall lead you to your own destruction, you vain and conceited whore. You sit upon and ride this beast as if you do no wrong, "it is for the good of the whole that this be done." Are you so foolish to think I see not what is in you? Dead men's bones and the stink of death. You have the soul of a beast, the spirit of a whore and the body of an abomination. Do you think you cheat death and hell? I tell you it was made for you and your kind, and there you shall dwell.

I am the Lord your God and beside me is no other. You shall not ascend unto my place; but cast down, you Will be a desolation and a mockery of yourself. This is the end of the matter: and you will not prosper forever.

Quotes and Text used from Researched Books:

1.Above Top Secret by Timothy Good Quill William Morrow 1988

pg 262,263 -- Death of Capt Mantel-

pg 391,392 -- Alleged captive dead bodies of Grey's + description

pg 409,410 -- Alleged captive dead bodies of Hybrids+ description

2.Aliens Among Us by Ruth Montgomery Fawcett Crest Books New York 1985

Pg 43 -- "Channeled" message to Thelma Terrel known as "Tuella" (her space name) about "Project World Evacuation"

pg-219 – Montgomery's own channeled message about a coming shift and evacuation.

3.Alien Impact by Michael Craft St Martin's Paperbacks 1996

pg100 – Nikola Tesla,and project Rainbow

pg 102-104 – Wilhelm Reich's "orgone research, weather and mind alteration

W pg 107 – Warring factions of Aliens with man in the middle

pg110 – Krupp/ITT connection to ex-Nazi scientists research at Montauk

pg 94,95 – Psychotronic technology

B pg 219 – lavatsky' background and relationship with "immortal masters"

pg 220 – Masters aligned against "sinister forces" dedicated to prevent the evolution of mankind.

pg 225 – Aliens warning of coming disaster and evacuation

pg250 – New age movement as combined product of GoldenDawn's Magik, OTO and Crowley's Magik and Theosophy's Asian philosophy

pg 253 – Alien and "channeled masters" names same as ancient names of demons, angels etc. (Good Angel Alien/Bad Angel aliens

pg254,255 – Enochian encryption

pg 258, – Alister Crowley's contact with "entities"

T pg 259 – imothy Leary's "alien communications"

Pg 260,261 – Jack Parson's Alien contact Babylon Working project and Death

4.Arktos: The Myth of the Pole in Science, Symbolism, and Nazi Survival by Joscelyn Goodwin Adventures unlimited Press 1996

pg 52 -- Nazi elite practiced Hebraism

pg54 -- Early Thulists globalists with expectation of coming messiah

pg 70 + 102 – Hindu prophecy of Tenth Avatar Hitler

Pg86 – Fictional Book Beasts, Men and Gods 1922 Ossendoski Agratha 2029 invasion from inner earth to surface.

pg113 – HM Howell Eden in inner earth

pg 115-117 – Koresh

pg 135 – Blavatsky's Polar description's accepted and understood by Hitler

pg 136 – Pole reversal making Pit place of prominence

Pg 147-149 – Symbolic Pole Myth

5.An Alien Harvest by Linda Moulton Howe LMH Prod. 1990-1997

pg 60 – Human mutilations

pg129,130 – John Keel's Hypnotic pawns and another group trying to alert us.(Good Alien, Bad alien scenario)

Quote from John J Dalton The cattle Mutilations, about human race is an experiment with another group trying to set us free. (Good Alien, Bad) pg 131,132

pg135,136 – Alleged Air Force official Richard Doty's declaration of US\ Alien pact

pg 149 – Alleged Govt Doc on Alien Crash recoveries with bodies

pg 150 – Greys origin- underground colony on earth

pg 151 – Greys creating Jesus

pg 152 – Greys and Nordic's conflict

pg 155 – Greys claim reincarnation for humans

pg 159-163 – Greys physical description

pg 193 Written Greys language similar to Hindu and Tibetan

pg 296 – Greys claim to creating all of earths religions-

pg297 – Abduction scenario

pg 111 – Bovine blood used for Humans, Chromosomes match

pg 4,65 – Typical cattle mutilation

6.Alien Discussions (Proceedings of the Abduction Study Conference held at Mit, Cambridge, Ma. 1992 by Andrea and David Pritchard, John E. Mack Pam Kasey, Claudia Yapp: Editors North Cambridge Press 1994

pg 69 -- "Good and Bad Aliens"

pg 72 – Warnings and prophecies

pg 73,74 – Transitions and Subterranean destinations as viewed by captives -

pg 90 – Alien types

pg 92 – Good Angel alien connection

pg235,236 – Identification with Jesus stopped abduction

pg 563 – Abductees leaning toward New Age theology after encounter

7.Barnes' Notes on the New Testament by Albert Barnes
Kregel Publications 1980

8.Behold A Pale Horse by Milton William Cooper Light Technology Pub. 1991

pg 68-70 – Secret societies general descript and philosophy -

pg77 – Adam Weishaup's quote -

pg 85 – Every CIA Director a member of CFR -

M pg 85 – J-12 all CFR -

pg 89,90 – Pope John Paul's early history -

pg 92 – Current ruling body of Illuminati -The Bilderburg Group-

pg196,197 – Crash and recovery of craft and alien bodies -

pg 212 – Alien (greys) claims of using all religions to control mankind , earth on eve of destruction -

pg 215 – Alternative plans instituted 1,2,3 -

pg 214 – Rand Corp. massive digging and tunneling

pgs 228-230 – MUFON and many UFOlogists as Govt opps. -

pg235 – Summary Aliens real or not a plot for NWO -

9.Chariots of the God's by Eric Von Daniken 1970 Bantam Books

pg – Bison with bullet hole -

pg – Conduit -

10.Dan The Pioneer of Israel by Col J.C. Gawler WH Guest London 1880

pg 6,7 – Scriptural references as clues to where Dan went

pg6 – Dan sea faring people -

pg 11-16 – Dan in Greece -

pg 17-22 – Dan in Black Sea -

pg 23-28 – Dan among Scythians -

pg 29-32 – Dan in Scandinavia, Ireland -

12.Extra-Terrestrials Among Us by George C. Andrews Llewllyn Pub 1986-1995

US service regulation JANAP-146 prohibiting Govt officials from making unauthorized statements about UFOs -

Ancient Chinese di - pg 47-49

Ancient India Vishuna Purana - pg 49-51

Babylon - pg 51.52

Ancient Grecian Incantation (to the great bear, big dipper Const) pg 52

Compared Enoch's experience to an abduction pg55

Tibetan prophecy of "new Age" - pg75

Morris K Jessup's "suicide" notes found about two ET types pg164,165

Nazis, s men and paperclip - pg 165

Dr. James E. McDonald "suicide"-pg 169-172

Gehlen\Dulles Nazi-CIA connection - pg 174

Wilhelm Reich's "death" - pg179

Cattle Mutilations typical description - pg181, 209

Human bovine compatibility - pg 231,232

Cro-Magnon + Boskop man - pg 239

Grey's description - pg 241-245

13.Extra-Terrestrial Friends and Foes by George C. Andrews Illuminet Press 1993

Experiments and towers in Nazi Germany producing same effects as UFO's on automobiles - pg 49 (From Hitler's Secret Sciences Nigel

Pennick 1987

Parsons\Ron L. Hubbard joint venture+ accident pg 116

Crowley's encounter with LAM -pg117

Linda Moulten-Howells story about Greys and Christ - 167

Greys alledged pact with US govt. - 168

Greys :harvesting of genetic material and blood 168

Greys use of religion as control device on mankind - 173

Underground complex strange experiment claims - 199-205

14.. Fingerprints of the Gods by Graham Hancock Three Rivers Press NY 1995

Piri Reis Map - pg 4-13

Tiahuanaco, Viracoas and legend of building site - pg 72

Extinct animals depicted on reliefs at Tiahuanaco - pg 85

Giza Pyramids percise construction - pg 275-2789

15.Guardians of the Grail by J. R. Church Prophecy Pub. Ok. 1989

Hitler's belief as the reincarnation of Landulph of Capra, possessor of the spirit of antichrist. - 43

German influence of Holy Roman Empire- pg 67

Myth of Morovee's bloodline (Germanic leader of the Franc's)origin as part son of Neptune (god of the ocean and underworld.) - pg 102

Nordic mythology as clue to Morovees linage - pg 102

Morovee-Danite connection to Romans - pgs 103-130

16. The Genesis Record by Henry M. Morris Baker Book House Grand Rapids Mich 1976

Serpent as shinning upright creature - pg 108,109

Comments on Gen 3 pg 120-123

Pre-flood world - pgs 142-145

time between creation and flood - pg 154

Comments on the "sons of God" - pgs 163-175

World wide flood - pgs 194-207

"Peleg" thoughts about his significance to continents - pg 260,261

Joseph's prophecy about Judah pg 653-656

17. Hitler's Cross: by Erwin W. Lutzer Moody Press 1995

Neitzsche as prophet pg 27

Nazi philosophy=New Age philosophy pg 29

Deitrich Echart as Satantic John the Baptist- pg 61

Karl Houshofer's influence in eastern occultism pg 61

Hitler as a religious figure identifying with Christ pg 62

Worshiped by- pg 63b pg83

Man as God premise of Hitler's beleifs pg 71

18. Hebrew-Greek Key Study Bible Edited by Spiros Zodhiates ThD AMG Publishers 1984, 1991

Comment on Gen 3 to "curse" - reference sec pg 1601

Cain and Abel as "Twins" comment pg 8

Comments about "Son's of God" - pg 11

Comment on word "visited" of Isa26 - reference section pg 1651

Comments on Gen 6 - pg 11

Comments on Gen 6 word saw #7200 pg 1658

Comments on Gen 6 word fair #2896 - pg1617

Comments on Gen 6 word choose #1602

19. Light Years by Gary Kinder Atlantic Monthly Press New York 1987

Billy Meier on Pleiadians agenda - pgs 184,185

Meier's explaination of propulsion drives of Pleiadians - pg186,187

Kinder's conclusions: - pg263-265

20.Man Made Ufo's 1944-1994 Renato Vesco + David Hatcher Childeress

Adventure Press 1994

Quote's from Sir Roy Feddon and Capt E. Ruppert about German aircraft pg 6 of Introduction

German Antarctic expedition pg 6 of intro

Surrender of U530 and 977 pg7 of intro

Admril Byrd"s Antarctic expedition pg 7 of intro

About Capt of U530- pg 11 of intro

Rebuttal to claims of underground Antarctic fort - pg 12,13 of intro

Nazi Scientists whereabouts at wars end pg 14 of intro

Nazi rocket development plates between pg 27,28

Foo fighters over Germany pgs 81-85

Neu-Schwabenland plates 6-10 between pgs133,134

Paperclip Gehln OSS\Cia plates 11-16 between pgs. 133,134

Viktor Schauberger Saucer developement Plates 1-14 between pgs 241,242

Marconi's "South American Bases" pg361-364

German tech combinations= saucers pg 365

U859's strange cargo of 33 tons of mercury pg 365

Arguments for last Nazi holdout in Antarctica pg 366,367

Gehlen's creation of CIA -pg 368

21.Mein Kampf by Adolf Hitler Verlag Frz 1927 Houghton Miffen Co 1971

"higher humanity" as a goal by the country with the ability to accomplish it. Pg 392

Propaganda, members and supporters Ch11 pgs 579-586

22. The Hollow Earth Enigma by Alec Maclellan 1999 Souvenir Press U.K.

Pg 32,33 - various myths of inner origins of man

pg 35 - Halley's work on Hollow Earth

pg 90 - Hitler's attitude about truth in Myths

pg 106 - Admiral Byrd's flights, 1929 movie

pg 108-110 - Admiral Byrd's "lost diary"

pg 113 - Last diary entry of Byrd's before death

23. The Lost World of Agharti The mystery of Vril Power by Alec Maclellan 1982,1996

Souvenir Press

pg 25 - integral part of Buddhist beliefs are Agharti, the subterranean World of which Buddhism is the philosophy of

pg29-33 - various myths and legends of inner realm

pg 102 - Hitler's influence by " The Coming Race"

pg 104 - Buddhist inner earth belief and influence on Hitler

pg 109 - Nazi's import Lamas to Germany, declare the knowledge of inner earth opening

pgs 118-121, 137,139, - various myths of South American "white tribes that live in caves

pg 160 - Shawnees belief of prior "white" tribe existing in Florida before they did

pg 227,228 Quote and Prophecy from "King of the World" as given to Ossendowski from Tibetan Lama

24.The Mourning of the Magicians: by Louis Pauwels And Jacques Bergier Scarborough House Pub. 1960-1991

pg 147 – Vril Society The coming race

pg 149 – Hitler's quote about seeing the NEW Man

Pg 154-157 – Hans Horbiger and doctrine of Fire and Ice

Pg172 – Hitler's quote on Globalism and elite who shall rule

pg 173 – Hitler's concept of monism

pg 177 – Hitlers complete quote about rebuilding Man

pg 180 -- "The great innovation of Nazi Germany was to mix magic with science and technology"

Pg 203 – Hitlers quote about the God-Men as an object of worship

25. Space Aliens from the Pentagon by William R. Lyne Creatopia Prod 1993,1995

pg3 of Intro. 73,87-89, 229 – Nazi Saucer Origin -

pg24,25 – Occult "Ether Physics" German transfer to America Opp. PaperClip -

pg95 – Von Braun's alleged US rocket projects prior to WWII -

pg230 – Cautions on alleged German origins claims-

26**Secret Agenda** by Linda Hunt St martins Press New York 1991

pg 1 – PaperClip ongoing and vast -

pg 2 – over 7,000 US solders used in experiments by ex Nazi scientists in US 1947-1966 -

pg 128,129 – Nazi scientists encouraged to work in US Universities as teachers -

pages 148-149 – US Lt Col William Henery Whalen arrested 7-22-66 sold atomic, missile plans to Russians, He was director of JIOA and ran PaperClip at time of arrest. Plate 12 between

pg 168,169 – SS Brigadear Gen Walter Schieber -

pg 162-163 – Karl Tauboeck leading expert on "stearilzation drugs for IG Farbin- working for Edgewood Arsinal Baltimore My on LSD pg180,181 – Maj Gen SS Kurt Bloom expert in biological warfare and US project 63 -

pg 234,239 – Nazi scientists worked on LSD projects for CIA at Edgewood MK-Ultra-

pg 264,265 PaperClips "evolution" through the decades -

27.The Bible and Flying Saucers by Barry H. Downing Berkley Books New York 1970

pg213 – Substitute "flying saucers" for the clouds of heaven -

pg 214 – Paul's experience "forced"

28.The Book of Enoch Translated by Richard Laurence LLD 1821

Artisan Sales 1980

Chapt. 18:1-7 – Quote about gravity and the pathways of the angels -

29. The Cosmic Conspiracy by Stan Deyo1978-1994 Adventures Unlimited Press

pg208 – Comment about designs of craft and earthbound style similar

30.The God's of Eden by William Bramley Avon Books New York 1990

pg 39-44 – Genesis according to Mesopotamian tablets

pg 45 – Conditions for the human "slave race" -

pg 46-52 – Comparison to Bibles version and re-interpretation -

pg 53-56 – Brotherhood of the snake (serpent as the "good guy") -

pg 73-84 – O.T. Jehovah as "alien manipulators" -

pg 95 – Nazi belief of Aryan ET origin -

pg 95 – South Americas Viracohas "white masters" huge white men from the heavens -

pg 97 – Hindu Vedas concerning Et gods -

pg 100,101 – Swastika's possible origin -

pg 377 – Hitler proclaimed "German Messiah" 9/25/25 -

Pg 382 – Nazi's as religious group -

pg384 – Himmler's vision of SS nation the envy of the world -

pg 385-387 – German corporations supporting Nazis -

pg388 – Nazi beleif in Aryan "supermen" that exist underground -

pg390 – Nazi influence after the war: CIA, Interpole, Bilderburgs -

31The New Strong's Exhaustive Concordance of the Bible

by James Strong Thomas Nelson_Pub 1990

The New Ungers Bible Dictionary by Merrill F. Unger

Moody Press 1957-1988

32. The Occult Roots of Nazism: Nicholas Goodrick-Clarke New York University Press 1985-1992

pg19-22 – Blavatsky, Theosophyical Breakdown Secret Doctrine

33. The Occult Connection: U.F.O.'s Secret Societies and Ancient Gods :by Ken Hudnall Omega Foundation 1990

pgs 24-31 – Black robbed figures influenced and assisted in revolutions throughout history -

pg 27-31 – George Washington's encounter with an "angel" and 3 part vision-

pg 196+197 – Vril Hollow earth Hitler's desire to contact

Pg 19 – Victor Schauberger

pg 139 – Contactees encounter with German speaking "aliens"

pg198+199 – Adamski/Pelly connection-

pg 201 Apendix – Adm. Byrd's "Lost Diary" -

pg 201 – Missing Scientists - Antarctic refuge-

34. The Occult Conspiracy: by Michael Howard Destiny Books 1989

pg63 – Illuminati after order of Mithraic Mysteries of Roman Empire-

pg6 – View of Church-

pg86 – Illuminati eye on US dollar-

pg 86 – Symbols as a "revived Roman Empire"

pg 87,95 – Occult symbolic influence and belief that US would play major role in "New Age"

pg109 – Bulwer Lytton's background-107 influence

pg110 – Guido Von List background OTO influence-

pgs 112,113 – Lanz Von Liebenfenls, Order of new Templers role in Nazi's and link to America-

pg 123 – Hitler's prophecy about losing WW1 -

pg124 – Sebottendorf Thule Society Background

pg 125 – Thule Society membership

pg 125 – Eckart seance and coming messiah -

pg 126 – Thulist's "Revived Holy Roman Empire"

pg 128 – Communist fears of rich succumbed to Hitler -

pg 128 – Karl Housofer background, beliefs, influence

pg 128,129 – Gurdjieff one world religion -

pg129 – Agarthi, underground kingdom writing of Secret Doctrine -

pg130 – Hindu caste system = to Alanteans -

pg131 – Hitlers quote of a new order -

pg 133 – Crowely's Nazi influence while in America

pg 135 – Crowely and Hitler

pg140 – Why the public was never told of specific occult activity of Nazi's

pg 173 – New Age in a nutshell-

pg 174 – occult revival-

pg175 -- subtle acceptance-

35.The Omega Conspiracy by I.D.E. Thomas Hearthstone Pub Ok 1986

pg 84 – Parallel between Genesis Apocryphon of "Dead Sea scrolls" and Gen 6 -

pg95,96 Sons of God in Septuagint and Alexandrian text -

pg 97 – Philo of Alexandra :Concerning the Giants" (Jewish Rabbi) -

pg97 – Quote from Antioch-Nicene Fathers on Gen 6 (Early Church) -

pg98 – Josephus quote on Gen 6 in :Antiquities of the jews" -

pg110-111 – Validity of the Book of Enoch -

pg 114 – Enoch describes fallen angels as "withered and the silence of their mouths perpetual"(description of greys?) -

pg 115, 118 – Watcher "Azazel" accused of scattering secrets of heaven over the earth. -

pg 119 – Nephilim Sentenced as disembodied spirits -

pg125-126 – Various other cultural and religious accounts of the same Gen 6 event -

pg140-142 – Jesus's decent into the earth and encounter with the spirits in the earth -

pg 152-156 – Nephilim 's return after flood and linage traces -

36.The Splendid Blond Beast: by Christopher Simpson Common Courage Press 1995

pgs 12,13. 20,21 – Background of Allan and John Foster Dulles

pg 48,49, – Connecting American/German corporate alliances

pg 64 – Roosevelt warned by ambassador Dodd of alliances

pg 81 – Corporate elite aware of extermination camps

pg 90 conditions 91 – Corporation concentration camps of Krupp, Daimler Benz, IG Farbin

pg 155 – Financial and industrial elites connection to Himmler and SS

pg196-197 – US intentions to "denazify" German Business/Finance structure

pg 197 – Key man to decide Allan Dulles

pg 199,217-227 – Dulles implementation of "directives"

37.The Sign: by Robert Van Kampen Crossway Books 1992

pg202-205 – Scripture references to Hitler as Antichrist -

" pg207 – sword" as figurative meaning during battle -

pg 209 – Deification of Hitler

pg 210,211 – Coming world catastrophe (Theosophical view)

pg211 – Hitler's dream\vison of "the new man" -

pg212 – Hitler's quote about the man-god to be worshipped (image of the beast?)

pg 212 – Hitler's last words quoted, " break up and scatter to the West" asked "For whom should we fight for now?" in a monotone voice Hitler replies "For the coming Man"

pg 476 – Image of the beast as plural -

pg473,474 – Beast empire breakdown-

pg 475 – Hitler Catholic church connection -

38.The Unseen Hand by Ralph Eperson Publius Press 1985 Tucson Ariz

139-141 – The Rothschild's five son's heads of five nations distribution of banking and quote about control -

pg 264,26 – Hitler 1/4 Jewish and possible member of Rothschild family-

39.Unholy Alliance: by Peter Levenda 1995 Avon Books

pg 15 – Blavatsky's Theosophy connection to Nazi Party -

pg 15 – occult significance of the swastika

pg 3 – Hitler a vegetarian -

pg37 – Dudly Pelly's belief of Aryans as descendants of an alien master race-

pg 40 – Theosophy's Great white brotherhood and German Volkisch beliefs of purification of earth from inferior races re-alinement of inner masters to themselves-

Pg 41. – various ideas of hidden masters from an inner earth

pg45 – Von Liebenfels statement inferior races incinerated as sacrifice to god

pg64 – Bulwer-Lytton The Coming Race-

pg 97 – Aleister Crowley 's encounter with Awiaz

pg98 – The mention of the War Lord of the fourties -

pg 147 – Hitlers quote about the take over of occult-

pg160 – Himmeler's lamented quote about Pagans and witches murdered by the church-

pg161-162 – Connection with Nazi beliefs and eastern philosophy -

pg -- Aztecs waiting for return of "White God" from Tulla

pg166 -- Rudolph Von Gorsleben's occult tradition concerning crystals-

pg230 – Parson's Ron L. Hubbard Crowely-pg315 – Hitler's quote about National Socialism's rebuilding the New man -

pg318 – Himmler's qoute to his staff about reincarnation-

pg320 – Himmler's association of Nazi's to India's caste system

pgs 168-167 – Icelandic expeditions Edda's contained secret keys to original Aryan heritage from the stars.

pgs 172-178 – Dr Schafer SS Ahnenerbe expedition to Tibet

pg 178-183 – Hans Horbiger Doctrine of Fire and Ice

40. The Young Earth by John D. Morris PhD Master Books 1994-1997

Comments on Fossilization, World wide Flood - pg 119-125

41.Understanding the New Age by Russell Chandler Zondervan Pub 1991,1993 Grand Rapids Mich.

pg 46 – Los Angeles Times quote Blavatski the "godmother of the new age movement." -

pg 94 – Indian legends of 144,00 triggering off harmonic convergence -

pg 96,97 – The Hundereth Monkey theory -

pg 191 – Theosophy as origin of "Modern New Age Movement" -

pg 187 – Adaptability of New Age movement -

pg 191 – Blavatsky, Bailey, Besant -

pg 213 – Quote in opposition to conspiratorial ideas of "New Age"-

pg 228 – Carl Jung and synchronicity -

pg 229 – J.S. Bell's experiment -

pg 230,231 – Ilya Prigogine's theory -

Vine's Expository Dictionary of Biblical Words

Copyright (C) 1985, Thomas Nelson Publishers

1. Centuries of Contact John S. Carpenter 1997 Carpenter Research Layout: Kory R. Johnson

2. UFO's and Paranormal Phenomena 1996 Produced by Juhann af Grann Dist Madacy Inc.

3. UFO Diaries Republic Pictures 1995

4. Sightings The UFO Report 1995 Paramount Pictures Prod Henry Winkler

5. UFO's A need to know 1991 Eyes Only Video

6. **From Beyond: Strange Harvests** 1988 1995 LMH Prod. Dist Simitar Ent.

7. The Alien Files: UFO Investigations 1995 Brentwood Home Video

1. Journey to the Hollow Earth by International Society for a Complete Earth 1995 Indy Home Video

2. UFO: Deception of the New World Order by Prophecy Club Topeka Kansas.

1.The Mysterious Origins of Man BC Video Produced by Bill and Carol Cote and John Chesire 1996 Most material taken from Forbidden Archeology by Michael Cremo and Richard Thompson Various Archeological anomalies.

2. Lost Cities and Ancient Technology by David Hatcher Childress Adventures Unlimited

Hindu legends, Archeological coverups, Vimna craft.

Unsolved Mysteries of World War II Madacy Group Entertainment 1998

Eye of the Storm Narrated by Stan Deyo Adventures Unlimited

UFO The Early Years: Secret of the 3rd Reich Simitar Entertainment 1996

Occult History of the 3rd Reich 1991 Video Treasures Inc.

Internet Documents1.

The evidence for Ancient Atomic Warfare extracted from chapter6 of "Technologies of the Gods: The incredible Sciences of the Ancients by Daviv Hatcher Childress Pub by Adventures Unlimited

Other book used but not directly quoted:

1. Time Warps by Dr. John Gribbin 1979 Delacorte Press/Eleanor Friede

2. Visitors from Time The secret of the UFO'S by Marc Davenport 1992,1994

3. Messengers of Deception UFO contacts and Cults by Jacques Vallee Bantam Books 1980

4. Ancient Empires of the New Age by Paul DeParrie and Mary Pride Crossway Books 1989

Although not directly quoted in my book, this book covers many post flood civilizations and their human sacrificial practices and cultural emphasis on blood. In many cases relating them back to "learned and remembered" practices from an earlier time. For doubters who have been told of the "superior" heights of these "great" civilizations this should be a must read. The authors do a good job of presenting the "Dark side" of the New Age roots.

Appendix

Debate of Gen 6

There are three main ideas about the text of Genesis 6. Because of the great controversy and the importance of understanding the proper events that follow a pattern of influence to us today, it becomes important to be familiar with all three.

What I call the "naturalist's interpretation" attempts to take away the miraculous claims of this event and rationalize events to understandable natural terms. This idea first appeared in history around the 4th century A.D within certain Hebrew Kabbala circles. The 5th century church began to accept this less embarrassing view but did not gain any broad acceptance until the end of the 19th century,(about the same time Darwin's theory and Blavatsky became popular). Unfortunately today this is a very popular and accepted view. It is losing ground because it is wrong and now important to understand it as such. I personally believe God at this time is confirming this error, because this is fast becoming a life and death situation for many.

This idea states that the "sons of God" are the righteous descendants of the line of Seth. The basis for this is in Gen 4:22 where it is said, "...then began men to call upon the name of the Lord." This text is footnoted in most Bibles as better rendered, "to call themselves by the name of the Lord." This latter is assumed to be the sons of God. Nowhere else in the Old Testament is this term used for a human being nor is it used in this text. In any case, they would be marrying the daughters of men. The words used here are female descendants of mankind. Not denoting any particular portion of mankind, just mankind in general, using the broadest generic word. It is assumed however that this refers to the descendants of Cain. The general thought here is that believers in God are marrying non-believers. Now I have to ask, What kind of God do you have? Just what is your image or understanding of a God that lacks patience or understanding to where he would wipe out an entire earth for doing something that mankind has continued to do throughout his entire history. This idea lacks the understanding and integrity of God's character as the loving patient Father. It also makes no sense or logic to the continuity to the story of mankind''s redemption. Cain's descendants were banished from off the face of the earth at this time. I believe they did play a part in this event, but certainly not as the daughters of men. This idea lacks proper etymology in word usage and assumes way too much. It also ignores other scriptures supporting a different view. There is further difficulty in the sense of the separation of sexes. Why are only the men of Seth's linage, and the daughters of Cain the ungodly ones? What about the daughters of Seth and the sons of Cain? Are they good? The text says that the whole world became contaminated, except eight people, Noah and his family. This very unsound idea only raises more questions and offers no real explanation consistent to the Bible"s overall story. It offers no real answers or help to explain the many questions we are faced with in our present situation.

The second idea is the newest "Liberal" interpretation. This one is based upon recent archeological discoveries where rulers used the title "sons of God". Upon this evidence and based on Gen 4:22 alone, an entire doctrine is developed whereby earthly rulers began to pick multiple wives for themselves breaking God"s laws of marriage. This act produced further moral decay. Again I have to ask, what kind of God do you serve? Is God going to wipe out an entire world for adultery and polygamy? This idea is as unsound as any fictional story. Based on conjecture alone, it then describes the same wrathful God destroying an entire world for doing what has been done throughout the entire normal line of human history. That concept can only give a person the idea of a wrathful, ill tempered God. That is not my God! My God was provoked by something so horrible it is unimaginable! Something so irreversible he was left with no other choice than to start over. He had to stop the perversion of the human bloodlines before this act doomed mankind into an eternal fallen state! Something drastic happened, unlike anything in normal human history, apart from anything that continued as a part of the human experience , only to be repeated at the end time of history. Satan was only eight people away from completing this linear existence into an eternal state according to his own desire and will and cutting off the human linage from ever having the Messiah born to redeem this present state! This was a very drastic problem unique from normal history, that required an equally unique and drastic solution. The total destruction of the Old World by a flood!

The last idea about this text in Gen 6 is the original belief held by the ancient religious leaders. It needs no conjecture or speculation. There are many cross referenced scriptures and using proper etymology that verify that the sons of God were in fact "fallen angels".

Job 1:6, "Now there was a day when the sons of God came to present themselves before the Lord, and Satan came also among them."

This was a scene taking place in heaven not on earth. This was not earthly men before the Lord. In Job 38:7 there is a heavenly scene as the sons of God shout for joy at creation. The sons of God are clearly heavenly beings. When the Jewish translators transferred the Scriptures from Hebrew to Greek, in the Septuagint, they rendered the term, "Angles of God" for sons of God in Gen 6. This idea was accepted as common knowledge without dispute or debate in the time of Christ who would have used the Septuagint. All period historical literature from that time period and Rabbinical comments without controversy accepted this understanding.

Too many sincere Christians have become victim to the influence of "naturalists" and "liberal" interpretation. Some great men of God, profound teachers of the Word have adhered to very unsound ideas and added to its credibility. I believe there are two reasons for a refusal to follow traditional etymology (the study of word usage, history and cultural application) concerning this text of scripture.

1. There is a fear of what the implications suggest by following proper interpretive guidelines. In the minds of too many Christians there is this never- never land separation of spirit and flesh with an unscriptural idea that the two never meet or dwell in the same dimension.

2. This unfounded idea is aided by the lack of understanding the rebellion of Satan, the fall of man and the restoration by God as an ongoing process throughout all of linear time. No Bible story is separate from other stories. All stories are interconnected and tell of one story with many different episodes, characters and events of paradise lost and regained. God is the central focus with man as the main character and Satan as the leader of a great rebellion still being played out in linear time.

Debate of "Old Earth vs Young Earth"

I will be brief but just a few points that should be addressed for all of you weaned on Evolution, Darwin and the concept of billions of years of cycles. Everything might be a whole lot simpler than the complexities man likes to create. I hope I have shown by the many fossil anomalies that we really need to reconsider much of what we so vainly assume. These anomalies in themselves should be conclusive enough. Mathematical calculations from several hundred years of measuring and observation of natural elements such as salt in the ocean, hydrogen in our air, magnetism of the earth, and erosion of the continents have all been accepted that yes we have a known formula for the rate of increase or decrease. But when we project these findings even to a point of zero which we know could never have been, all accounts go no further than 10,000 years. Most recently in the November 12, 1997 issue of Trends in Ecology and Evolution vol. 12 had an article about the most recent known formula for mitochondrial mutation. The controversy is in the fact that while the formula is accepted as true, the projection states that the first female, Eve was approximately alive only 6,500 years ago! That is exactly what the Bible time line states. Of course the article tells how controversial this claim is in light of "modern science". It then expounds with the standard rhetoric of the scientists- priests in debunking the conclusions but offering no further substantial proof.

Satan's actual fall
Lucifers fall becoming Satan

It has always been assumed that Lucifer rebelled and fell in some ancient time past before the creation of man. There are no actual scriptures to indicate this. The only vague reference would be the two words *Tohuw* and *Bohuw* used in Gen1:2. The prior rebellion was used to explain the destructive state of earth before creation or re-creation.

Understanding the idea of wrapping time from beginning to end together does not require a previous rebellion in some ancient time past. As I have said before, this idea filled an apparent gap but was based on conjecture alone. I believe the scriptures make it quite clear where, when and why Lucifer fell to become Satan.

The Anointed cherub that covers...in the Garden of Eden

The prophet Ezekiel while directing a lamentation to the King of Tyre reveals much about the original position, ministry and domain of Lucifer. We also see the flaw in his nature at his very creation and his eventual fall and end.

Ezekiel 28:13-19, "Thou hast been in Eden the garden of God; every precious stone was thy covering, the sardius, topaz, and the diamond, the beryl, the onyx, and the jasper, the sapphire, the emerald, and carbuncle, and gold: the workmanship of thy tabrets and of thy pipes was prepared in thee the day you were created. You are the anointed cherub that covers; and I have set thee so; you were upon the holy mountain of God; thou hast walked up and down in the midst of the stones of fire. You were perfect in your ways from the day that you were created, till iniquity was found in you. By the multitude of your merchandise they have filled the midst of you with violence, and you have sinned: therefore I will cast you as profane out of the mountain of God and I will destroy you, O covering cherub, from the midst of the stones of fire. Your heart was lifted up because of your beauty, you have corrupted your wisdom by reason of your brightness: I will cast you to the ground, I will lay you before kings, that they may behold thee. You have defiled your sanctuaries by the multitude of your iniquities, by the iniquity of your traffic; therefore will I bring forth a fire in the midst of you, it shall devour you, and I will bring you to ashes upon the earth in the sight of all them that behold you. All they that know you among the people shall be astonished at you: You shall be a terror, and never shall you be any more."

His resources provided

From this text, we can see that the provisions to Lucifer were "every precious stone was thy covering." In the Hebrew, *Yaqar eben mecukkah* means "that every rare and valuable stone in the sense, to build or construct, was his fence or entwining as a screen to cover and protect". In a sense, these stones are construction elements used to build. What is being built is a fence, entwined like a screen for the purpose of protection. Where was this happening? This was happening in the Garden of Eden.

Only recently, have many "fringe" scientists become aware of an electro-magnetic "grid" that covers the earth. In disk technology as well as the presence of "ghosts" and also demonic activity, all have been with the presence of certain electro-magnetic disturbances. Enoch describes seeing the path of the angles in relation to the winds of the earth. This could be the physics behind Satan as the "prince of the power of the air" Eph 2:2. This entwining fence now being used to control the earth was supposed to be for protecting the garden, (or intended creation).

His instructions and duty given

He is described as, "the anointed cherub that covers." This is a description of his position and created state. He was anointed. That is he was selected as separate, apart and above his normal position as a cherub to a special purpose. That purpose was to protect the Garden of Eden! A cherub is an order of angelic being. They are described as flanking God's throne Ps 99:1. They are an image hovering over the Ark of the Covenant. Ezk 9:3 They are also described as a vehicle of Jehovah. Ps18:10 2 Sam 22:11.

Authority given

He had complete access to God and mobility through his creation as the highest in command of angelic beings. "Thou wast upon the holy mountain of God, thou hast walked up and down in the midst of the stones of fire."(the planets?) "...the workmanship of thy tabrets and of thy pipes was prepared in thee in the day that thou was created." "...thou wast perfect in thy ways from the day that thou wast created, till iniquity was found in thee."

Personal attributes

The workmanship or ministry (as in the sense of a job or duty) of the tambourine and of thy pipes or bezel (a facet to hold a gemstone) was instilled into him at his creation. This is rather a poetic way of describing the special abilities Lucifer was endowed with. If you think of the function of a tambourine; by shaking with one hand and striking with the other, you produce a sound that creates rhythm harmonious to the surrounding accompaniment. A bezel is for the purpose of holding and securing something valuable in place. Shaking, striking and holding to produce harmony, balance and protection of God's creation was Lucifer's natural ability. (The name Lucifer means light bearer) In this sense he was the highest extension of God's grace; provider and protector. All resources were at his use, all mobility was provided, and authority was given to him to protect and to serve.

Character Flaw: Vanity and Pride

This was not good enough. Pride from a sense of self-importance caused him to usurp God's authority. The great wisdom that was his became corrupted by his own intellect. His peace of mind and soundness became defiled by his iniquity. Hatred, rage and anger welling up to a deluded state that would consume him from within. "Thine heart was lifted up because of thy beauty, thou hast corrupted thy wisdom by reason of thy brightness... thou hast defiled thy sanctuaries by thy iniquities... therefore I will bring forth a fire from the midst of thee, it shall devour thee..." This is the sin and the disturbing results of sin in Lucifer's own mind and mental condition.

How He acted upon this flaw

What was the act he committed? "By the multitude of thy merchandise they have filled the midst of thee with violence, and thou hast sinned...by the iniquity of thy traffic."

It can be understood, from this mention here that Lucifer made merchandise of God's knowledge and "traded" it for the inheritance of Adam and Eve. From that point on Lucifer, now Satan would continue to trade "secret and or forbidden knowledge" to mankind for a price. That price being the ability to manipulate and exercise power and control according to his will in their lives.

His current position as the result

I will cast thee as profane out of the mountain of God...I will cast thee to the ground, I will lay thee before kings, that they may behold thee."

"Behold" here means "to have knowledge of to understand and perceive". By making merchandise of God's knowledge and twisting it, he becomes the "god of this world."2 Cor 4:4 His initial trade was in the garden of Eden when he tricked mankind on the path away from the tree of life to the tree of the knowledge of good and evil. This gave him a linear existence to usurp creation and conform it into his own desire. He will not be successful.

His promised end

"I will destroy thee O covering cherub, from the midst of the stones of fire...I will bring thee to ashes upon the earth in the sight of all them that behold thee...All thee that know thee shall be astonished at thee: thou shalt be a terror, and never shalt thou be any more."

Jim Wilhelmsen

The "Fall" is an ongoing part of linear life

Understanding that Lucifer"s fall was not in some ancient past before the creation of man but was in fact in the garden as God's protector turned rebel, we can also grasp the fact that this fall is a continual ongoing process. Satan has fallen, is falling and will continue to fall until he is cast into the lake of fire. In linear experience the fall is ongoing because this is the fall! This makes Satan a far worse enemy. He, being deluded, actually believes he has a chance to beat God at his own game. He has a strategy and a plan and so far he is right on time...this makes him much more dangerous.

Roswell Update:

In the four years My wife and I lived in Roswell NM I had a small bookstore-museum across the street from the International UFO Museum and Research center. I enjoyed two years of effective ministry to many from all over the US and the entire world. My main focus was on presenting the Biblical perspective on UFO's and Aliens and including all subjects of the paranormal and supernatural. I had the walls on my place set up with story boards on a time line that informed visitors of the Biblical perspective with a 21st century look at the scriptures much like the content of this book. Below the story boards by corresponding topics I had books by any and all Christians dealing with the various subjects. I even included secular books that had good information and raw data that was sound. I may not have agreed with some of the premise or conclusions but the content was good enough to consider. I also had a live internet radio broadcast from the store once a week. Many lives had been challenged and changed by that little store. On my web site I have posted the various testimonies by individuals. This experience for me took many of the things in this book from theory to fact as I saw the fruit of their application to explain away the illusive lies and false representations and bring people back to a belief in the claims of the Bible and the hope that exists in a relationship with Jesus Christ. My store was less a business and more of a missionary outreach composed of the apologetics of the Christian Biblical faith.

Suddenly I had to leave Roswell and go back to Michigan. I did not know why but there was an urgency that I simply obeyed. I felt like I was abandoning my post by leaving but I knew I was supposed to do this. There were other things gong on at the time and it made this act necessary.

326

The first week back and I got a good paying job with medical benefits, something I had not had in twenty years. This was in 2007 in Detroit which was one of the hardest hit areas by the slumping economy. This was a miracle! As soon as my insurance came into effect, I went to get a general physical. I had tightness in my chest for several years and at my age I thought it wise to get a check up now that I had insurance.

I was rushed to an intensive care unit and told that I needed a five arty bypass surgery right away. I had four arteries 98% collapsed and one 90%. Had I stayed in Roswell, I would have died there of a massive heart attack.

The Lord had impressed to me that I had more to do to try and reach out to the Christians in Roswell. Most Christians do not believe anything important or real is happening with UFOs and Aliens, to most of them like others elsewhere, this was rather a laughable Jerry Springer topic or just an opportunity to make a few bucks from an unreal fad.

Before I left Roswell, the Lord gave me Zechariah 5th chapter and began to show me the importance of the Roswell Crash of 1947. There is so much to this revelation I have made a separate book about it. This scripture is not only describing the Roswell crash but more emphasis is in describing the aftermath results of the crash. Lofty sounding but I explain the entire vision of the scripture with many other cross-references to show how real and consistent this idea is within the scriptures and the recent history of Roswell itself.

Now, I am retired with all the time in the world to do this kind of work full time. The Lord has told me to begin to finish the third phase of my museum that was never realized while I was down there. This was to use my talent as an artist to create sculptures depicting the many Biblical concepts and stories in art to add another dimension to what I had. I am going back to Roswell and not alone! With the help of many others, and the proceeds from this book and others I wrote, the funding will be provided for all future ministry endeavors, including another store/museum in Roswell. Thank You for your support!

For more details see echoesofenoch.com or write me for specifics at: Awitness41@aol.com